THE DEVIL YOU DON'T KNOW

ISBN 978-0-86356-649-3

First published by Saqi, 2009
Copyright © Zuhair al-Jezairy, 2009
Translation © John West, 2009

A full CIP record for this book is available from the British Library.
A full CIP record for this book is available from the Library of Congress.

Manufactured in Lebanon

SAQI
26 Westbourne Grove, London W2 5RH
Tabet Building, Mneimneh Street, Hamra, Beirut
www.saqibooks.com

Zuhair al-Jezairy

The Devil You Don't Know
Going Back to Iraq

Translated from the Arabic by
John West

SAQI

Contents

Going Home

A War Observed

I follow the war on TV like an addict, alarmed by the sheer quantity of weapons. Battleships like iron islands, groaning with the weight of soldiers and rockets aimed at Iraq. Aircraft carriers lull, stationary in the waters of the Gulf, while planes rise from their decks, heading for a country that specialises in waiting for destruction and death.

What could be calmer than these waters, yet what more frightening than their cargo?

Entire platoons of soldiers in full kit board the planes. A correspondent asks one of the paratroopers at the foot of plane's stairway what they trained for.

His answer: 'to kill and destroy'.

I follow the war from my armchair in London. I get alarmed when the military analyst says: 'Never in military history has there been such a build-up of arms against one place'.

The screen holds me like an addict, the scenes merge with my shaky memory. Is this the country I come from? It's the preoccupation of the world. But not because of its role as the cradle of civilisation, or as the seat of the Abbasid Empire; no, everyone is counting the seconds until it explodes.

My daughter keeps turning it off, or switching channels.

'Why do you torture yourself watching things you can't change?' she asks.

'This is the only thing I *can* do: watch and agonise ...'

I want to go up to picture on the screen, break its cold glass, and touch the flesh and bones behind it. But I get exhausted by my powerlessness. I join my hands behind my head, stare at a point on the ceiling and try to stop grinding my teeth. What is it between me, and this distant, burning country? Here I am in my house in Greenford, my books ignored but neatly stacked on the shelves behind me, my computer and keyboard lying in front of me, awaiting my touch. I continue to ignore it. What is the use of everything I have read and written if our destiny is to be this martial madness?

I look out of the front window onto Millet Road. Christine the housewife passes, pushing a pram containing her two boys, while her two daughters follow behind. She says hello to her neighbour, who looks like the greyhound trotting along in front of him. Our own neighbour Athul, who started to lose her hair after her husband died, had asked me as I passed her house earlier: 'What is going on in your country?'

'Sheer madness,' I replied.

'Do you have family over there?'

'All my family are there. I am the branch cut from the tree.'

I hate this compassion. It is a brief compassion, hoping to be done with it in a few conventional words of sympathy:

> *We hope the war will be over soon.*
> *Our hearts are with you.*
> *May God be with you.*

I look up at the leaden sky, endlessly drizzling on the lush greenery and the roofs. Behind this colourless, shapeless cloud lies a sun forever veiled from us. We see its light, but we do not see it.

I am now in a country where, after ten years, I know what is going to happen. My life is secure; so are my family and house. Even my music system is secure. I get crates of wine delivered to the door and soon the onions I planted in the garden will be ready to dig up. I have enough paper and thoughts to write for the rest of my life. Why do I torture myself with things I can't change?

My wife Ronak is like me. She cannot tear herself away from the television, her nerves taut.

She shouts as I sit down: 'What are they waiting for? Why did they go all that way? Will more people die? Why don't they bomb the palace, not bridges that the people use?'

She screams at me as though I were responsible for the misconduct of the war. I scream back at her that like her I am incapable of changing the course of the war.

And then it is *she* who calms *me* down.

'Forgive me, please,' she says. 'There's no one to shout at except you. I can't help shouting at what I'm seeing.'

I try to sleep, to dream again as I did the day before of wet, white geese tickling my stomach. But neither the safety of my current life nor the prospect of sleep calms me. Anxiety gnaws at me. Maybe something new has happened. Surely something has occurred in the last few minutes?

I return to the TV and to the same scenes: ghostly planes bomb nighttime Baghdad. I see the dark sky and the glare of explosions. I try to make out the location of the minaret where the call to prayer was just cut short, as its crescent vanishes in the glare.

The destruction has fired my memories. Real life Baghdad has vanished, replaced by the places in my mind, present now among the fires and the rubble. Off the edge of the screen, I search for the entrance to Rashid Street, where I would come back at the end of a night, drunk and drawn by the smell of *hommous* wafting from a food vendor's stand. A rooster stood on the roof, its feathers soaked, dizzy from the breath of the revellers and the smoke but still standing. Where has that rooster gone to escape the explosions?

I turn a little more, looking for the back entrance to the same building. I used to sneak through that door with Wedad to make love in the photographer's studio. There were enlarged photographs everywhere. Portraits of writers and artists, old Palestinians, a thin Eritrean warrior, peasants from the villages of southern Iraq, village women carrying buckets of water who stopped to stare at us shamelessly, men with turbans on their way to the mosque, children who had stopped playing, frozen by the camera's lens. All of them looked at us in the dim light creeping through the studio partition. We would make them avert their eyes by our panting, and throw ourselves down on the bed. Where have they all gone, those witnesses who saw us naked in that room?

I look around, in the glare of the explosions on TV, for the albums scattered by the bomb that hit Chakmakji's stores: Hudairy Abu Aziz and *The Rose Sellers*, Nazim al-Ghazzali and *All the Gifts You Like for the Feast, Golden Bracelets, Rubies,* and *The Priceless Bracelet and the Expensive Scent*, Saleema Basha and her *Lover Addicted to Travel*, Masoud al Ammar Teli and '*She Carried the Water with Both Her Hands to Nasiriyya*, Yousuf Umar and the Al Orfa maqaam *Every Day I Have Rivers of Tears on the Garden of Her Cheeks, like Clouds Pouring Rain*, Frank Sinatra and *Strangers in the Night*, Nat King Cole and *The Wanderer* and his *Unrequited Love*. Where did all these gods go when the earth trembled, and the records were blown up?

I mark all the air raids on the mental map I brought into exile. After all this time, it is now imaginary, no longer accurate enough to measure. That bomb fell near my family's house ... The worst kinds of images seize me during the news: children scream in terror as the bombs fall, the build-up of fear inside the shelters, the dust that shakes down from the ceilings when the earth rattles like judgment day, the fevered chanting of prayers by mothers as they cradle their children's heads in their laps.

High in the sky, with the smoke of the fires hanging, I angrily follow the progress of the pilot crouched in his cockpit, suspended over our cities. He sees it through the forward window, with no human contact, just the targets for his bombs. After his mission, the pilot takes off his visor and says, to camera and the correspondent waiting for him on the airstrip: 'Bull's eye. I saw it light up beneath me like a Christmas tree'.

The B-52 takes ten hours from British airports to reach Baghdad.

I measure that time precisely. When will it reach my family? It has crossed the channel and reached France. The ladies of the night are still plying their trade in Pigalle, youngsters still queue in front of the nightclubs. I think of the pilot crossing on his long night journey, entering Italian airspace, where the night has just begun in Rome's Piazza Navona and the tramps sleep rough on the streets, having forgotten their names after their latest heroin fix.

None of these countries attract the pilot. He must unleash his cargo elsewhere. Onwards south into the Balkans crossing mountains – only recently healed from war – capped with snow. The men in the cafes won't even raise their eyes to look at these planes from hell. Did the pilot once carry out the same mission here? The pilot looks at his wristwatch as he crosses the slow, calm Mediterranean where the cruise ships light up the black waters like stars in a night sky. Only a few hours to go. He is close to target now, towns where the lights of the minarets twinkle, and the congregations are deep in their prayers.

The pilot passes over all these cities to reach our city, besieged by fear, where the mothers have shrunk into the narrowest corners, their arms wrapped around their pale children, and the fathers scuttle across the streets between one raid and the next, their heads bent so low they look nailed to their shoulders.

The pilot passes by all the other towns and mountain ranges to drop tonnes of bombs on his target, a city, a large city full of millions of people. And then he'll return to his wife and children.

It is a war without heroes or combats, a conflict which will be settled by men in the air who see their targets but not their victims.

A War Which Did Not Happen

I flee from the conflicted thoughts which eat at me and join other Iraqis gathering in London like frightened birds.

We are divided ideologically into those who support the war, and those who oppose it. I am divided in myself: against anyone who supports the war (and ready to argue it out almost to the point of blows – how can any person of culture support a war which is destroying his country and killing his people?). And yet I am against those who oppose the war (they want to prolong the dictatorship, whether they admit it or not). Each time, I fight and argue with myself.

Every Saturday, I walk with thousands of protestors in the streets of London to condemn the war. The gatherings lend me importance. I am from the country upon whose behalf all these people – parliamentarians, leaders of political parties and trade unions, famous writers, Jewish, Christian and Muslim men of the cloth – demonstrate. I understand their fear of a one-superpower-world and the imposition of solutions by force. But, at the same time, I am angry because no one condemns that vile coward who led us from war to war while gathering medals on his chest and stars on his shoulders.

Exhausted from my outer-and-inner-conflict, I come back to the TV, seeking pictures, although they only increase my suffering and sense of inadequacy.

I have actually lived through many wars: as a civilian, journalist and occasionally a combatant. The war of the Palestinian guerrillas with the Israeli army in the Jordan Valley in the summer of '69; Black September; the war of the Palestinian factions with the Jordanian army in '70; the Middle East war of October '73; seven years of the Lebanese civil war from 1975–82; war in the Sahara Desert between the Moroccan army and the Polisario movement from 1980–83; two-and-a-half years in the mountains of Iraqi Kurdistan with the Kurdish Peshmerga guerrillas fighting against the Iraqi government. I know war and have lived it with my senses, my emotions, my intellect.

In the thick of war, the body devotes itself to fighting and survival, leaving no room for the mind to wallow in hesitation and despair. Those previous wars were all around me, demanding all my senses. I must listen to the sound of the shells, so I can figure out their origin and direction, and react accordingly. Nothing protects us in war except the walls. And yet these walls are our enemy, because the bombs target them – they become our hiding place and our tomb.

I would come out of the shelter after the end of a bombardment to see the situation, smell the fiery destruction, and decide what to do next – a decision my family and I made with our whole beings. I used to live wars with the fibres of my body, which transformed my fear into action.

But this war is more emotionally painful because I observe it, yet do not live it. The war is in front of me, but between us lies this little, grey screen. The TV has drawn me so close I can almost touch the war; I can almost smell the ruddy dust that cloaks the American soldiers as they creep towards my country. I know that smoke. I've almost choked to death on it.

The many correspondents (and their presence at the front line) have made the fighting seem close. And then there are the graphics. On Abu Dhabi TV a middle-aged man, well dressed, sits in the studio with a laptop, to show us the progress of the war in all its depth and breadth. He shows us the front line of the invaders, the numerical distribution of the forces, battalions and divisions. He almost seems to direct the war inside the studio, using small symbols instead of iron tanks and flesh and blood men, little arrows instead of trails of blood. War there seems like a thought experiment. And yet it is a real war.

During the battle of Umm Qasr, I followed the fighting in live coverage from three camera angles. American and British soldiers take cover behind a dirt barrier, firing their automatic machine guns. Then they leave their positions to adopt other ones further forward. On the left of the screen, in the distance, others closer to the target attempt to encircle it and are answered by a hail of bullets. In the distance, we see helicopters and fighter planes strafe a row of houses. The correspondent narrates these moments to us.

We are seeing what the actual combatant cannot see and yet what the TV offers us is hypothetical. This world that we can see with all its tanks digging into the ground, and its soldiers weighed down by their ammunition – it is unreal despite the fact that we are living it in its entirety. The strangest of all is that we see more here, and more widely, than those who are crouching in their billets there. But we do not see it in *3D*. We do not touch its flesh, or smell the bombs. Our rooms do not shake with impact of the explosions. Death, like the image itself, is a mental construct, not real.

I am torn between the idea and the sensation. Mentally, I am *there* in the middle of the war with my nerves and fears. But physically, I am *here* in this room in the house on Millet Road, West London, rooted to the sofa. Through the window behind the TV is the maple tree, born like me in exile, it leaves will soon be ripe for syrup. I am sitting *here* but the event which sucks me in is *there*. I am consumed, just sitting here doing nothing. This increases my feeling of powerlessness, because I am in a war and not doing anything.

After talking on the phone to my sister Dhikra and brother Sabeeh in Baghdad, their voices weak and intermittent, the line is cut. Last we had heard they were all alive and gathered in the family house: 'We're all here. So far the bombing has not come close. The windows in the house are rattling but the explosions are far off.'

'They're only striking specific targets,' Dhikra said.

'But many of those targets are in residential zones,' I said.

She mumbled, struggling to reply.

We know they know other things they don't want to tell us. As far as they are concerned we are on another planet, unable to help them. So they content themselves with reassuring us, bracing themselves for their fate in the middle of an inferno.

'We're all still alive. Don't worry about us,' they say.

My family who have lived through all of Iraq's wars are worried for us worrying for them over here in this cold city. The voices of our family had given us a feeling of being part of it. We have family there and we share something in common with the people under threat, moving from place to place. And then Baghdad plunged into deep darkness in front of us on the TV just as the phone was cut. In the silence and the darkness, my family had slipped away into the unknown recesses of the war and we left them to their fates. We left them, and were ourselves left with just the country, the whole country, as an abstract.

American forces have surrounded Baghdad from all sides and the regime's screeching spokesman declares to the journalists: 'We have a surprise for them.' We imagine the worst. The Tyrant would not shrink from the adage 'upon me and upon my enemies, O Lord'.

We are all apprehensive. What is this surprise? Sometimes we guess, but are afraid to say, even to ourselves. I remember how our voices rose as the ill-omened announcer declared 'he will turn Baghdad into Halabja'. 'No,' we shouted.

Fall of a Monument

I grit my teeth and tense every muscle in my body to help the man, naked waist up, who is striking with his heavy hammer at the base of the statue, to topple the Tyrant from his throne of concrete. The crowd around him are pulling on the rope. Some of them have climbed the statue to deface his head. The statue still remains upright, greeting the masses, unaware of those digging away at its base.

He is like that in real life too. Wars eat up his country, his forces are smashed, his economy collapses, the whole country is taken hostage and inspections teams are sent even into his many bedrooms. Yet he lingers, unmoved, haughty with 'the spirit of victory', waving his hand airily to greet the masses under the pedestal while they shout 'Our blood for you, Saddam, our lives for you, Saddam' with all the violence of a curse. That is how he always was. He sees what he wants to see, and hears from his entourage what he wants to hear. And they learned in the school of Fear not to say anything else to him.

Gathered around the TV, we all shouted in unison when the monument started to lean a little.

Use of image has been central to the powerbase of all the tyrants who have ruled us. Pictures are distributed, spread by the security forces. If there is danger, the real flesh and blood man hides, becomes a prisoner in his palace. The palace itself becomes a symbol. The people do not actually see him when he leaves it. They see his fleeting motorcade in the flash of an eye, or maybe they see his outline; or the outline of a double behind the reinforced window of his car. The man's existence becomes an idea. These heavy wall paintings and huge statues, at the entrances of streets and in the squares, are his embodiment. The spread of these images are the symbolic extent of his authority.

Gradually, billboard portraits are replaced by wall paintings on concrete and statues made of iron. The deepening solidity of materials signifies the embedding of his image across time, confronting the powerless hatred of the people. The cringing, isolated masses can never topple their dictators by themselves. The coup leaders do that. The masses have to make do with bringing down the billboards or the statues.

Our last dictator built his authority with images that spread to every place and every object. Streets, squares, entries to towns and institutions, in all official rooms, on the cover of school books and exercise books, on wrist watches, dinner plates, pens, paper and coin currency. In short, he wanted to hammer his image into the subconscious of every citizen like a nail. When insurgents tore up his posters in 1991 he switched them for statues of concrete and iron, struggling to transcend time, visualising eternity.

This man of paper and iron has stolen half my life and all my hopes. I have spent more than 1,300 pages of foolscap on him during a quarter century of exile. I have come to know him through thinking about him so much. What tired me most when I wrote my novel *Terrifying and Terrified* was how much I hated him. I had hoped to find at least childish delight in him when he saw his own image on TV, tearful sadness as he shot those closest to him, disgust at the flattery of those who surrounded him. I wanted to find a real moment just before he takes the decision to annihilate an entire village with its people.

I only met this man, who has fashioned my life and that of my family and children, once, in March 1979, in the summer resort of Salahuddin, in Kurdistan. I was with a press pack covering the celebrations of the Kurdish New Year (*Now-Rooz*). I did not copy down his words like the others as we listened to him, for the very simple reason that the newspaper which I worked for had just been closed, on his orders. I stared at him despite myself. I was shocked by the yellow of his face, the kind of pallor you see in a dead man, or someone close to dying.

Throughout the press conference, he talked about the TV cameras that had covered his recent trip to the marshes in the south. Talking of course in his capacity as a director and actor, irritated by the fact the cameras had failed to capture those moments which were most expressive of those simple people's affection for him. He talked as though he had the camera trained on them himself, as he shook hands with them and kissed their children. He spoke sarcastically of the marshes which would shake the boat and the camera.

Throughout his discourse I stared into his face, that childish smile. Where was the man who just days before had decreed the death of twenty-one soldiers convicted of setting up a communist cell inside the army? He was startled when our eyes met. I was the only one looking at him. The others gazed at his words as they wrote them down in their notebooks.

Apart from that meeting, I followed him through the image, in the newspapers and on TV. I didn't just look at the images, I tried to discern what was behind them, what the camera concealed, especially with someone like him who was practised in both acting and orchestrating scenes. He loved the camera right up until the last moment of his life. For him it was a tool to remove an unwelcome reality and replace it with a make-believe one.

In my work as a TV producer, I would linger over footage with shots of him, slowing down or freezing the frame. The way he leans forward as he enters a conference room, and how he circles the table to greet his ministers. I watch the body language of his entourage, how tense they are, and then how they relax when he lightens the atmosphere with a joke. I'm amazed at their movements, how they resemble a troupe of actors tasked with presenting the mask of eternal devotion.

I would watch him as he mounted a stage to speak, his hand raised in salutation. He did not see the audience as individuals but as an undifferentiated mass, a horizon. As I cut pictures I would always ask myself, is that him or is it one of his doubles? Am I seeing what is in the picture, or am I imposing my own assumptions on it?

The man obsessed us as he rose from number two to number one. We talked about him in a trembling whisper as long as we were under his rule. When we escaped his grasp and went to live in Beirut, my first place of exile, I wanted to free myself by writing about him.

We saw his agents in Beirut, their fingers on their silencers. Many people warned me against writing about him – 'His arm is long' they would say – but I could not stop. It was a feud between me and him, personal and to the end. I used to write about him to know, or picture, his innermost secrets.

In my imagination, he also knew me. In my dreams, I saw him turning the pages, shaking his head, half angry, half bewildered – 'How did that bastard find me out?'

An American tank came to the assistance of the crowd, dragging the statue. Its legs were ripped from its feet, which stayed rooted to the pedestal. The torso leant forward as though hailing the ground beneath it. I willed the crowd on as they broke the base of the Monument. In the end, the iron broke and the crowd rushed on the statue with all the pent-up anger of thirty years of oppression and blood. At the same time, we all leaped up from our chairs and embraced each other. The bastard has gone.

When I go to the newsroom of the *al-Arabiya* TV channel, the question is waiting for me: 'Where is the army we were relying on to defeat the Americans?'

In the cafeteria, my colleague watches American tanks crossing the bridges of Baghdad and slaps his hands together in frustration. He had the same question just posed to me by my Pakistani cab driver: 'Where are the weapons Saddam promised us, that we put all our hopes in?'

'How can the Iraqi army collapse so easily?'

They ask these questions twice or three times, choosing not to learn from experience as there is a whole landscape littered with incidents of this kind. The questioners stay with the same delusions that defeats should have shattered. The kings of defeat stay on their thrones, in government, and in the fantasies of the people. Illusion, in fact, becomes a necessity, the recompense for weakness and loss.

There are always demagogues who can turn defeats into victories. What concerns them is the 'spirit of victory', not material victory. Defiance alone is enough for them, regardless of its stupidity or the losses it entails. For them, huge loss is intrinsic to the Arab world. What interests them is the sanctification of martyrdom regardless of what it achieves. These intellectuals can explain away everything with conspiracy theories that strip defeats of all internal precursors or causes, and project them onto an external agent that plotted and prepared for it. We must just enter defeat as our allotted Destiny.

Everyone in the Arab world wanted our army and people to fight until the last bullet, the last soldier, and the last drop of blood – except us Iraqis. For the rabble rousers, our people are predestined for martyrdom. We must conform to their preconceptions and desires, and if their expectations are frustrated they turn it into a question of betrayal. Whether it is treachery by the opposition, or those close to Saddam, what matters for them is that their naive hopes are not undermined by the reality that our army and our people are tired of Saddam's wars. Wars that took them back to ground zero. They are tired of all the blood.

Every place I go to, they welcome me as a son of this heroic people that has stood fast through three wars and a lethal sanctions regime. The word I hate the most is this 'steadfast'. No one except Iraqi mothers seems to understand it is a word written with blood and hunger. During the last war we used to beg that our soldiers would surrender before the decisive conflict. We wanted them to save their lives. We did not want a homeland built on skulls and blood. Let the rock be broken! Lower the flag! The rock, the cloth, and all the other symbols. The main thing is that the human being should remain alive, able to build new symbols which are more pragmatic, and a country which is less bloody.

On the Road to Baghdad

I drive myself crazy pacing up and down in this hotel in Dubai. I don't know how to get into Iraq although the borders are open.

Many went in with the American tanks. I had decided at once that I would not use this path, either as an embedded journalist, or as an invader. I remembered the German writers Thomas Mann and Bertold Brecht who accompanied the victorious Allied troops into Germany against the Nazis. But it is not a precedent which appeals. I imagined coming in, protected by tanks, while bomb throwers watched us from narrow alleyways and palm tree groves. At that moment we would become bloody power and they would be the resistance.

I had been shaped by the Left of the 60s, the spirit of Vietnam

War protests, the revolution of Che Guevara. That spirit of resistance which has owned the greater part of my life has forged its own rules inside me. This image contradicted my own of returning in true victory. I was looking for another way in, either as a non-embedded journalist or as an ordinary person.

I call a friend in Kuwait who told me to send a copy of my passport and to wait.

'How long will I have to wait?' I asked.

'One or two weeks,' he replied.

The same time it would take to enter via Damascus. Wasn't there a shorter route?

The wait tortured me as I had to hang around in the hotel. Russian hookers looking for rich clients accosted me: 'Come here, baby'. In the coffee shop, Gulfis sat in their white *dishdasha*s playing dominoes or smoking the *nargila*, no care or haste. They are in their own stable country. They can predict what will happen a decade from now. In a little while, at 1.30 PM to be precise, their children will come home from school. Then they will have to get moving and leave the cafe for their homes to eat a meal which their wives, scrupulous timekeepers, have prepared. And I will be left lounging on my own in the hotel.

Hotel staff politely take their leave, watching me fret.

'Anything I can do for you?' a few ask. I feel like replying: 'Yes. I want Iraq'. It seems all ways in are either with the tanks, or take time.

'Why don't you ask the British embassy?' my friend asks.

'In my capacity as ...?'

'In your capacity as a British citizen,' he replies.

I had forgotten this small detail when Iraq had opened the borders. My Iraqi identity had taken over.

At the British embassy in Dubai the official in charge of enquiries did not understand the ramifications of my situation, so referred me to the consul. The consul did not understand my question: 'How can I get into Iraq?'

'Why are you asking us, exactly?' he asked.

'First, because I am a British citizen. Second, because you are occupying my country,' I replied.

The consul went back to his computer to look for an answer. He handed me a print-out which said the British authorities advised all subjects of the United Kingdom to leave Iraq and not to visit it, since war had broken out.

Normally an Iraqi faces problems when he tries to leave his country. My problem was getting in.

Late one night, the opening came. The TV channel *al-Arabiyya* was sending a crew to Iraq and they wanted to film me. The crew would travel at dawn tomorrow. It seemed there was no one except me ready to undertake such a trip at short notice. I started packing my suitcase for dawn. I conceal my nervousness at the lack of certainty in the arrangements and imitate my wife. She is packing her cases like a woman who knows how to leave. There is no free space in the suitcase because we always have to squeeze our belongings into the smallest possible space. We do it all ourselves as we set out for a new exile.

I pack my suitcase, anticipating failure. I am not prepared for this impossible journey, and I am going in at the wrong time and in the wrong way. But anyway, I brush my fears and dark mood aside and get on with it as if someone else had ordered me to do it.

Short, vivid dreams perturb the few hours I sleep after taking two capsules. I dreamed our car had stopped at a border checkpoint which was abandoned. From inside the car we look around for someone to search us. The foreboding absence of anyone scares us. I see all my identity papers scattered across a street in Baghdad and can't pick them up. Then I feel the bed I am on slipping into a sandstorm. I awake, not knowing how many minutes I've been asleep. The hotel concierge rings me. The car is waiting. I shut my suitcases and stumble down. Where are you going, I asked myself?

We set out for Iraq from Amman in the night. I didn't ask about the last illuminated towns we passed through before the border. Between me and Iraq was this desert, stretching to the edge of the horizon. For me, the desert represents the polar opposite of the sea. The sea connects its edges. The desert divides.

I had left Iraq in 1979 across this desert with a forged passport, in a hurry to reach exile which at that point was a refuge from the police hunting me down.

We Iraqis are not used to travelling as much as our neighbours who border the sea. Lebanese expatriates outnumber those who have stayed. They are found in the furthest country in Latin America or Africa, even in the unknown interior. Sometimes you might think Lebanon is not so much a country for its children as a staging post for their future exile. Our Mediterranean neighbours, near to the sea, have learned how to look at other countries as potential new homes.

But for us, travel was an impossible dream. I remember when I was young I met a painter, Monem al-Azeem, who carried on his back a suitcase full of tin cans, wearing standard military issue boots. He had come to say goodbye to us at the Institute of Fine Arts.

'Where are you going?' I asked.

'To another continent,' he replied, confidently.

We left the bar jealous at his boldness in breaking the established custom of family, tribe and city. Two days later we found him again, in the same corner of the same bar, waiting for the gang.

'Failed again,' he sighed.

Monem justified his fear of travel by saying: travel is simply a state of mind. You can travel while staying here.

Our poet Badr Shaker al-Siyaab went to Kuwait for medical

treatment. Kuwait lies within sight of his home town of Basra and yet he stood at the edge of the narrow gulf and shouted: 'I shout at the Gulf. Gulf! Gulf! Giver of pearls, giver of death.'

Our lives and habits are rooted in customs from our home villages and towns. We can be surrealist, but we are Lamian or Jabbourian or Qaysi. Existentialist, yes, but it is Nasiriyah or Kirkouk which binds us together. The ancestral homelands we abandoned to come to Baghdad, the chaotic sprawling capital, stay embedded within us. And those solid customs give us emotional security. We return to our people when life gets hard.

In the generation before mine, many aristocrats left the country to study at the government's or their own family's expense. We looked at them with envy, and sensed ourselves to be poseurs. We were always talking about Soho and getting lost in it, or the cafes of Paris, or the bars where Hemingway brought his funny moving feast. We would talk of them as though we were there. But in fact here we were in the same cafe, just as every day, the same bar, with the same gang of friends.

And then later, the forced movement of exile imposed a strange ambiguity on our lives. We are both *here*, in this new place, and *there* in that place which keeps our dear ones, as we had made our families. The constant movement between places of exile filled our lives with turbulence, just as politics, culture and women had done before it. We did not have one place of exile, but many.

In every new place, I would make a home, a library, put up pictures, get to know the neighbours, make new friends and say: this is a second homeland. Then I would leave it for a new home and begin again. The bed, the library, the pictures on the walls, the new connections and a second homeland to the second homeland. Every aspect of the new exile would efface the one before it in my mind and memories.

But now I was saying to myself hopefully: exile has finished, and the homeland has begun.

I am in a rush to get there and the desert expanses tire me beyond all belief. No trees or mountains, or any break in the eye-line. One sand dune folds into the next. The darkness of night has fallen, and the car, with its lights, seems like a boat in the mist. Everything around me, including my fellow passengers who have fallen asleep from boredom, makes me turn inwards, towards myself. My impressions are fleeting and scattered. They cannot stabilise into articulate thought. I left Iraq for exile on 19 July 1979 crossing this desert and now I am returning to it across the same desert. How will I face what is to come? Am I really going back to this impossible country?

I fantasise that on a hill in that dark night, there is a fox following me with his yellow eyes. I am afraid that if I turn to him, he will discover my inmost secrets.

I could not believe we were approaching the border. Night was delivering me to the Unknown. There was no visible sign of what we were passing into. When the first road sign appeared – Rweished-Baghdad – my heart pumped with fear, not joy. And the yellow eyes of the fox were still following me.

Fear gripped me the more real it all became.

There was a crowd of returning Iraqis milling at the Jordanian border post, suitcases on the top of their cars. I joined them in the melee. We tried to encourage each other to feel we had made the right decision; that we were ahead of the game.

A young woman jammed beside her sister in the back of the car asked me where I had been in exile. If you were Iraqi there, it was obvious you had been in exile; the only question was where and for how long. When I told her I had come from London, she called over her frightened mother to join us: 'Come and see, mama. This gentleman has left London to return!'

Amman was exile next door. Life there didn't encourage staying. I had seen the long shadow of Iraqis in the squares and streets of Amman. Men selling cigarettes one by one, porters, lines of journeymen waiting to be picked by passing contractors for a single day's work. Then there were the artists selling their canvases for a meal, or writers waiting for their fees while they plunged into debt. You would never think they came from an oil-rich country.

Their deep sense of the injustice of their situation prevented them from feeling any gratitude to their host country. One of these was a lawyer, who stood up to deliver a speech in the middle of the border post. Letting rip for the first time after so much self-censorship, he swore at the border officials.

'Saddam, whom you loved so much, has gone and won't come back. We'll be dealing with you shortly.'

Amazingly, the police came round the counter to calm him down and apologise.

The returnees kept quizzing each other, to assure themselves that this decision they had made to come back was right. I heard a woman hassling her husband: 'Ask this gentleman.' She meant me. My sympathies were with the husband, who had locked up his house and cut all ties of return to exile, to come home and live the pangs of labour and rebirth of his country. I freely engaged with all the people around me, and felt sure I was in the right place as I took my place in the queue.

The Borders, the Borders

The first thing to welcome me at the border, in the early dawn, was Saddam Hussein in his *uqqal* and *keffiya*. He smiled a welcome at me despite the bullets shot through his mouth and eye.

I wondered about the man who had shot at the poster, if he was really shooting his own personal history of fear. Images are always guarded by a projection of power, whether that force is physically present, or just in the mind. Zero hour in the 1991 intifada had been the first shot on a poster of Saddam in Basra. Zero hour for the return of his authority had been when his image had re-entered Iraqi towns on the front of the tanks.

Standing beneath the wall painting of the Great Smiling Victor was an American soldier in full army issue. How had that soldier, in all his incredible kit, arrived at that place? It reminded me of Picasso's *Massacre in Korea*. Men wearing Roman-style breastplates and carrying futuristic machine guns fired as they advanced.

Everything in that picture was out of time and place and logic. Just like this American soldier standing in front of the queue of returning Iraqis. He hurried over to stop us from filming. When I told him it was me they were filming he threatened to destroy the tape if we shot footage of any of his soldiers. Another soldier came over and said hello in Arabic. He asked if I was a VIP. I said my importance was in the fact that I was returning to my country.

'Welcome home,' he said in English, with all the confidence of the man who owned the house.

Everything here was beyond my imagination. I was overwhelmed, giddy and light headed. Saddam was above me, smiling, greeting me with a half-raised arm. An American soldier was checking my papers, and I was entering my country on a foreign passport. Nothing felt real or made sense.

As they went through my papers, that old feeling of fear at border posts surged through me. Neither the open borders of Europe, nor the fact I was carrying a British passport, possibly one of the oldest and most distinguished in the world, could efface the feeling that, in essence, I stood accused, and carried the virus of doubt and fear inside me.

Fear had often impelled me to lie to border police, even when I did not need to. I would always imagine how the policeman would look up to compare me to my picture, then leave his cubicle with my passport, then come back with another officer to summon me for interrogation.

Some twenty-four years before, I had passed through this border post with a forged Jordanian passport in the name of Nazem Kamal, a trader in spare parts for cars. The man at the border post had been looking for a fugitive called Zuhair al-Jezairy. I had got my life back that time when he returned my passport, and motioned me forward to join the others.

Because of the number of times I have travelled with false or stolen passports from other countries, I developed a sense that my passports and I were two different people. It would confuse me, the task of borrowing this other person's identity and playing it. I would always breathe a deep sigh of relief to hear the muffled, wooden sound of a visa being stamped on the passport – 'I've escaped' – and I could flee the immigration barrier, back into life.

I know these sand dunes tinged with black. I know the colour of this salty soil, covered with blackened earth. This is Iraqi soil. I always have pangs when I pass through the places I have lived in, a combination of melancholic longing and lost love for the time that has been scattered across these places. In every place, there are both memories and a sense of disappointment that I have left no trace in these places I have left behind. And that whole process is the legacy of leaving Iraq, my first place. The place I am now heading for in the early dawn.

Every now and then, the cameraman would point to the side of the road, where there would be a tank upturned on its tracks on the ground, its tower ripped off by a bomb, human remains lying around. A little further off-road, sometimes hung on desert scrub, were the burned remains of soldiers who had fled the inferno inside the tank. The amount of destroyed weaponry rose as we got further into Iraq. Stripped and exposed now, these weapons had lost their power. They seemed like the skeletons of extinct dinosaurs.

I wondered what had happened to the poor fellows who had been inside them. This was the weaponry the dictator had spent so much money on. Money that could have transformed this desert: cultivated booming towns that would have raised its young men, these soldiers lurking among the dunes, into engineers and musicians – builders of civilisation.

On one of the hills, I saw the little blackened bouquet left by the aerial bombardment. At the top of it, sandbags and soldiers' helmets and boots had been scattered. I compared what I was seeing now with the scenes I had seen on TV. Death here seemed so anti-climatic Fragmenting steel ripped apart human bodies, their dreams and fears just a trivial detail.

Underneath a bridge which had been crushed by a missile from the air, I saw a pile of armoured vehicles and tanks which the bombardment had melted. Their iron flanks had folded in on each other, and the soldiers manning them broken apart like matchsticks by the bombing, their boots scattered around in the sand. Grey dusty wolves stopped eating the bodies when we passed closer, gazing into our cars for a while. Then they carried on chewing. My imagination flew from the killing scene we were passing through to the American pilot, and the Iraqi mother.

The pilot had released his bombs with the press of a button, laughing confidently when he told his command that the strike had been 100 percent 'spot on'. His business was with machines, not with thinking about the people who were ripped apart at the moment of impact. Military science had taught him that war was war, and victory required killing.

Meanwhile, in some wretched village in the middle of Iraq, there is a mother of the soldier now ravaged by jackals. She had not received the body of her son and so carried on pacing about, fretting, just as my mother would. She imagined the fate of her son whom she had borne for nine months, whom she had watched grow until he became a man, a candidate victim for a piece of burning steel.

The driver told us to hide our money. It was getting more dangerous as we approached the towns. Towns and townsfolk had once offered a feeling of security after the dangers of this road, which had tired even Ali ibn Abi Taleb in the seventh century, making him write 'Oh how tiring the path, how few the provisions, how long the journey'. But no longer. People are now what we fear the most in a country where a holy law of the jungle rules. Modern highwaymen, in their fast cars, could surge out from behind these hills and hold us up. The worst time and place to die: only an hour from Baghdad on the verge of fulfilling a life-long dream.

Before we got to Ramadi, the driver had been filling us with fear with his stories 'from only the other day' of killing and looting. It was promising ground for attackers, nestled in between houses, palm groves and the river.

'Just my bad luck, at this moment the back tire blew,' he said. 'Maybe the brigands spread nails in the dirt to make it happen. One of their cars stopped right by me and I asked for help. "Yes, we *do* need to help you," said one of them, as he pointed his revolver at my head. He told me to get out of the car. Then he fired at the ground between my feet. "Get the passengers out."'

Meanwhile, as he says this, I look at the wide eyes of the driver and ask myself – what's to stop there being an arrangement between the driver and the highwaymen?

We watched the road until the end of the journey, trying to spot where they would come out from these hills, willing our car on to the speed of a bird in flight. My fear distracted me from seeing what would have told me, finally, that we are in Iraq. The rich, black mud and the river, and the banks of palm trees ... as the great eleventh-century poet Abu Ala al-Ma'arri put it: 'We have drunk the sweetest water of the Tigris, and visited the palm, noblest of trees.'

What is it about the beauty of the palm tree that binds it so closely to the Iraqi spirit? Once when I went to Granada, in southern Spain, there was a row of palm trees and it surprised me, as though I had seen Iraq itself, and the question had sprung into my head: what are they doing *here*? Because Iraq has a monopoly on the palm tree and it had no business being anywhere else.

Amer Badr Hassoun and I once made a film about our children, Iraqis who had left the country when still young. We asked them: 'What do you remember about Iraq?' Their answer was nearly unanimous: 'Granny, and palm trees leaning over the surface of the water.'

So the question again: what is the secret that ties the palm tree to the Iraqi spirit?

The palm tree is the most symmetric tree. It doesn't have branches which break the harmony of its straight trunk. Nor does the palm tree offer its beauty all at once to a man, just because he has approached it. As with the traveller who sees it from the desert, horizontally, the yield is gradual. Winning the fruit itself requires a journey upwards, beginning from small mounds of earth next to the tree, continuing on up the trunk to get to the bliss above.

The form of the palm tree is part desert flower, part parasol projecting a circle of shade from the sun. But the secret of the palm tree, the reason it is held sacred, is because of the way it looms in the desert, locale of death and thirst, promising life, signalling an oasis and water.

What makes the palm tree close to the Iraqi spirit is its capacity to endure: the ability to dominate trees more chaotic in form, less tall, less able to endure the challenges of survival in this region. The palm tree has endured through centuries, wars, and years of drought.

While we were in the palm groves, we were forced off the road to make way for an American convoy heading to Baghdad before us. The display of force was imposing, and created a spontaneous counter-action. At that moment when they passed us, we forgot that we were the locals and they were intruders. They looked at us, we looked at them, and we each asked: why are *you* going to Baghdad?

The soldier hunched behind the machine gun was so close. But I could make him out behind his protective armour and helmet. His eyes were hidden behind dark glasses. It seemed like he was actually built into the Hummer the roof of which he poked out of. When our gazes met, he smiled at me like someone welcoming an unexpected guest. He was going to Baghdad before us and the road in front was even, and open.

Baghdad, only 10 miles away now, has always been open to its conquerors. That is why the Mongol commander Hulaku wrote a letter of reproach to al-Mustansir in the thirteenth century: 'Baghdad's gates were not closed to the emirs. Why are they now?'

Iraqis always wait for the new invaders, as in C. P. Cafavy's poem *Waiting for the Barbarians*. They gather around the *suq* to wait. The merchants put out their best cloths expecting the invaders to choose the most beautiful of them. The guardians of the city prepare welcoming speeches and learn them by heart, singling out the best characteristics of the barbarian, and imploring his mercy. The poets dust off the elegiacs of praise they gave to the last invaders and adapt them to suit the new ones. The governors choose the best golden swords out of the museum, forged by their ancestors, to offer them to the new invaders, bowing their heads in submission, ready for the sword to strike.

The Iraqis get bored with their new invaders after a time. The invaders also tire of how unwilling the Iraqis are to put up with oppression. Oppression, after all, is a necessary part of ruling. The defender cannot hang around to read the Qur'an, to distinguish the righteous from the unjust. So oppression becomes everyone's allotted fate, indiscriminately.

Oppression begets rebelliousness, and is fed by it in turn. Over the course of time, oppression accumulates for the Iraqis and turns into a sort of self-hating scorn for putting up with oppression and acceptance of torment. The Iraqi begins by agonising over the oppression of the present. But this soon turns to indifference when the oppression continues, and then to open anger. It is an anger which is long, bleak and sometimes melodramatic. It is provoked by new cycles of oppression by the invader because monotony in the forms of oppression would create habituation among his subjects, and perhaps rebellion. A fluid, thickening period begins which has the colour of blood and the bitter taste of hatred. After a time, patience is exhausted and a sense of inadequacy and hatred reinforced. Life seems impossible now without some new invaders to sweep the old ones away. But always the Iraqis are disappointed with the new invaders as they deal out death, rape and pillage to them.

In 1258 Hulaku took only seven days to kill 800,000 people. In the end, corpses were piled up in little mountains in the alleyways of Baghdad, trampled under the hooves of the Mongol cavalry. It rained heavily, to wash the blood away. Instead, many more that were hiding in wells and cisterns drowned.

The second Mongol invasion began with torture, pillage and annihilation of the cities under Timurlane. Just as Hulaku had, Timurlane revolved the cycle, appearing to Baghdadis as their saviour from Caliph Ahmed.

And now here she was, Baghdad on the morning of 24 April 2003, after everything she had been through. As old as time. The city did not seem like a city, more like a monument to a history of destruction. The first thing that struck me was her colour. She was colourless, as if covered by dust from her graves. The destruction in her reflected both her history and her present. On my right was Abu Ghraib prison, now empty of its inmates. Saddam's son, Qusai, had freed criminals with heavy sentences a few days before the end of the regime, and liquidated the political prisoners. I forgot Baghdad looming out of the horizon for a moment, my eye fixed on the prison. In the light of day, it looked ordinary. Impossible to imagine what torments had been hidden behind those walls.

Successive rulers did not just inherit the building, which dates back to the monarchy, but also their knowledge of torture, which they renewed with all their imaginations could proffer. Later, I was to be surprised by how easily the 'civilised' mind could revert to barbarism, when pictures were published of atrocities committed by American soldiers there on the prisoners. This is a prison which fashions its jailers as much as its prisoners.

The night many years before I had listened to one of its former inmates recount his experiences, as the Mediterranean lapped the shores beneath our Beirut flat, I could not sleep. I felt physically oppressed as I imagined myself jammed between two other bodies, unable to turn over onto my back, listening to the long screams of a woman, the grinding of the iron bolt as the door opened, and the footsteps of the guards as they came to take a prisoner away for torture or execution.

After the prison, new roads built during my time away began to criss-cross. While in exile, I had had a dream which recurred about once a month. I had returned to Baghdad in the middle of the night, and found myself with my suitcase in the middle of a maze of new roads that had been built while I was away. By my side was the case that contained all my smuggled papers. Day would begin shortly, and with it I would be exposed to the street informers. This is a homeland which we always remember with fear, sown in our hearts by the terrorising Power. A homeland of informers, our stake in it is fear, as the famous poet Saadi Youssef described: 'My homeland is the policeman, with the soil of Iraq, as old as time, in his fist.'

Scenes of devastation confronted me wherever I looked. The air force command headquarters were rubble, nothing left of it except an aeroplane-statue at the entrance. Mansour Central Market had been pounded from above, the goods inside it, which drew the customers, crushed. The frame of Baghdad Exhibition Centre, where I had seen television for the first time, was smashed in. Fighters hiding inside it had burned to death in a visitation from hell. Saddam Communications Tower, which the maximum leader had always wanted so much – how hard it is to build, how easy to destroy.

The zoo was as empty as a sweep of desert. There were more piles of burned ordnances under the trees, which had once shaded the lunchtime trysts of lovers. The lions had eaten the donkeys when the wardens fled and their food supply was cut off. The monkeys had fled their cages, terrified by the bombing. Where had that hyena gone, the one who had scared me as he prowled back and forth in his cage, lowering his head to the ground, while I imagined the bars of his cage widening to allow him out?

But worst of all was Rasheed Street. I could not help myself, and struck my head with my hand when I learned from the driver that these piles of rubbish that stray dogs were scavenging were ... Rasheed Street. This was the street which in exile I had vied with all my friends to name every shop of, beginning from Liberation Square. I cursed the street. I cursed the people walking in it, hurrying to avoid unwanted attention. The driver stepped on the accelerator, speeding away. Was some mishap about to strike?

Our convoy of four cars pulled into the parking lot of the

Sheraton Hotel. The end of these overwhelming scenes, this continual astonishment as we passed through the streets, the questions seeking certainty ('Is this Mansour?', 'Alawy al-Hilwa?', 'the Ahrar Bridge?').

Home

Looking for Home

We're driving around, the driver and me, guided by a map drawn by a relative in Dubai, looking for my old house. We establish the gate of Mustansiriya University as the point of departure, then I try to summon into memory from a quarter century back which way to go. At that time, there was nothing standing between our house and the university but a few scattered houses. But now it's fully built up with houses and markets, and so we got lost, the driver and I. Digging into the far off past, I can see landmarks telling me we're in the right area – a row of shops on a street nearby, that empty lot that was supposed to be developed into a school. I stand with my back to the university and can picture the empty space there used to be, the guard hut and the garden with two palm trees in it.

Then I reprimand myself: 'Stop living in the past, you old fool; it's the present you're looking for.'

We went to the district mayor and asked him for the house of the late Mr Ali al-Jezairy.

'What, Abu Zuhair, *the father of Zuhair*?' he asked, using the traditional patronym. I was so happy my name was still attached to my father's. I had always imagined he would have abandoned it, fled the burden of a son who was in the opposition and in exile. Was that his own doing, or was it just thrust upon him? The mayor sent a lad to show us the house as he knew that exiles would return, wandering around lost. As we turned into the street, I was taken aback by the staring eyes, and shouting.

'It's him! Zuhair!'

My family. We were speechless as we stood hugging. Then a long scream. How much cries of joy and pain resemble each other in Iraq, those high-pitched ululations of women. Who was it shouting? I looked out through my own veil of tears to see the neighbours, who had come into the street and onto the roofs at the sound of the screaming. A plump woman out on a terrace wiped the tears from her eyes.

Just before I stepped through the gate, there was another woman, shrouded in black, wide-eyed. She disappeared suddenly, before I could ask about her. I entered the compound in a daze, under a flurry of hands on my back. I look at the faces, amazed at what time has done. The little girls we left behind have become mothers, the young women grandmothers who presented their progeny one by one, after the first breathless exchanges.

'This is Yasser, Sabeeh's son, and this is his daughter.'

'This is Ban, Ahlam's daughter, and that's her daughter.'

'Guess whose child this is?'

I was overwhelmed by so many branches and people, and asked for a little time to take it in. They looked at me and said to each other: 'He's so like Baba.' Up until then I had postponed the question of my mother and father. I had stayed in the garden to avoid the fact that they were no longer here.

But our neighbour, Umm Hassan, wept: 'Your mother waited for this day for twenty-five years.' She did not go on, leaving me the space to imagine that perhaps they were still here, peacefully sleeping in their beds.

I looked at the palm tree, telling my friends that this was the tree my father had planted just before I left for exile. The tree bore witness to the painful length of time we had been apart.

I entered the house slowly and uncertainly. Time had left its mark everywhere. The walls had cracks in them and turned yellow. Damp had crept across the white ceilings. Old things were piled up here and there as though the occupants were getting ready to leave. As I went round the rooms, images began to flood back to me, for it is the house which preserves our past and frames it.

On the walls were pictures of the departed. My grandfather Abdel-Karim with King Faisal II and Noori Saeed visiting the shrine of Imam Ali at Najaf. So often had my father told the story of this photo, taken in 1945, that I still remembered it. The king had come to persuade the religious scholars, including my grandfather, to play a role in calming the rioting which had begun in Najaf and which, day by day, was spreading across Iraq. Next to it the picture of my father's cousin Sheikh Ahmed who died in exile in suspicious circumstances. My father in his fifties, in the middle of the school yard, looking at my brother Tha'ir, who was killed in the war with Iran.

Ikram: I had last seen her when she left London to go home to die. The doctors had failed to cure her of cancer and she left us knowing she had only weeks left to live. The dead hung on the walls; the living on the shelves. But I was not among them. Fear of the regime had made my family deny me utterly.

As it grew dark, the guests dispersed to avoid the night. But while they filed out, the lady in black stayed, the lady I had seen through the window, enveloped and wide-eyed, with a beauty shrouded by sadness and defeat. She presented herself.

'I am one of the leftovers of the regime,' she said.

'We're all its leftovers, or maybe I should say its rubble,' I replied.

She put me right when I politely inquired more about her, stating clearly that she was the second wife of a head of secret police now held by the Americans. A distant cousin, she had begged to be taken in by my family and they had accepted without hesitation.

My Father's Dishdasha, My Mother's Bed

My sister Dhikra gave me my father's old *dishdasha* to wear and my mother's old bed to sleep in. My parents' single beds had remained just where they were. They spent the last ten years of their lives together in this room, watching time go by, breathing in synch, and looking at the same spot on the ceiling – the same thought coming to them at the same time.

I knew this because I had cross-examined my sister Ahlam when I saw her in Cairo for the first time in twenty years. I had sat her down on the bed in the hotel room and said: 'Now, Ahlam, I don't want generalities. Give me details, facts. Talk me through a day of their last years, and then a year.'

How hard life became for my parents after their children started dying, Tha'ir killed by a piece of shrapnel in the war with Iran, just twenty years old, my sister Ikram, who died of cancer in her thirties, the victim of enriched uranium which the air carried from the battlefields. And life became harder again when they became hostages to fate, waiting for hand outs from others and selling what they owned. My mother was the more sensitive, and virtually stopped talking, using tiny gestures instead. And now I was in their place, wearing my father's *dishdasha* and sleeping in my mother's bed. I thought about them. To be honest, I thought about each of them in me. My father was water and my mother fire and they met in my body and made their peace there.

Ali Hadi al-Jezairy was born an orphan. His father had died from tuberculosis a few months before he was born and his mother died a couple of years later. Perhaps she caught tuberculosis from kissing him. His brother died a few years later, leaving him with no family except a sister, Zohouri.

He lived as an orphan, cut off and isolated. But it marked him not with tragedy, but with the taste of freedom. Nobody told him to wear a skullcap. He was the odd one out among his cousins because he wore Western dress and went to a state school rather than the *madrasa*. On Fridays he would go to the sports club, not the mosque. He went further, becoming a music teacher, playing the *aoud*. He staged Najaf's first theatrical performances.

My father was won to secular culture by reading books, and *Helal* magazine. And I picked up this secular way of thinking from him and from my mother's brothers, finally vaunting my atheism in adolescence. In contrast to my mother, who filled the house with arguments and worry, my father would spread mirth and laughter, defending the worst things we did. My elder sister and I would watch Mirza Jameel Alley from behind the curtains to see my father coming at the end of the evening, tall, well-dressed, throwing his shadow before him. We would know from his gait how much *arak* he had drunk. When we heard the key in the lock, we would rush to bed and close our eyes, pretending to be asleep, only to open them when he kissed us.

Each month there was one day of panic, when my father went into the desert to hunt gazelles. Then the pride as the little boys of the alley ran to us saying: 'Your father's coming back with six gazelles!'

I don't remember ever seeing my father angry. Ironic certainly, flushed in his cups, semi-conscious, eating in slow motion.

As a child, my father spent time with his uncles who were farmers in the village of Sahla and learned farming from them, arable and pastoral. My strongest image of him is bent over, pruning the trees in the garden, and his voice ringing out as he sang the Rust *maqam*, and watered the leaves of the orange and lemon trees.

As a child, I hated the garden for how it took my father away from us. But later, when I acquired a garden in London, I found I had taken on his habits unthinkingly. The computer was set up facing the garden. The writer would begin writing, mastering the sight of the trees and the flowers budding and the drops of water on the leaves. He would leave the real world to enter the world of imagination. But when thoughts or words dried up, my father the peasant would surge up out of me and I would go out into the garden to turn the earth over, or do some weeding, clip the rose bushes or water the lawn with the hose. I would do this ignorant of the right time to plough, prune or plant seed, just from the need to replace intellectual with manual labour. And when I got tired and stood up straight, I would remember how my father stood exactly the same, and, like him, sing the Rust *maqam* under my breath.

As well as the garden itself, my father kept a lot of animals, flying, swimming and crawling, from the fish in the pond to the love birds and nightingales and chickens in cages, to rabbits and gazelles. We got to recognise when he was coming by the surge of animal din. They knew he was coming by the sound of the key in the lock to the enclosure. The chicken would flap in its cage, the other birds would chirp and flutter their wings, and the goat would strain on its leash as it tried to reach him.

He would religiously feed all the animals before sitting down to eat himself. My mother was mortally jealous, complaining that they were dirty and had fleas and that his clothes stank of them. But it seemed to me, now wearing his *dishdasha*, that it smelled more of the grass than of the animals. Even at the end of his days, my father would still go up the palm tree to gather the dates, and go out onto the terrace to feed the nightingale, which liked to fly out of its cage and sit on his shoulder.

My father relished happiness and fled problems, leaving cares to my mother, who was consumed by them. I am a mixture of fire and water. I learned from my father and from my life in London to ration anger. The water flows in my spirit. But sometimes – when reasonable words fail – the fire of my mother rages.

My relatives gather round, fascinated to see how my parents are reproduced in me. I have my father's profile, his hair and his hands. As I sat there eating, my nieces exclaimed: 'You're just like Baba when he was eating.'

I also picked up some of his bad points, the habit of leaving household chores to my wife, always out and away from the house.

The wind blows between the *dishdasha* and my skin. I feel it touching us together, me and my father.

On the bed, I feel my mother's place, the bumps and undulations she has left in it from turning over in bed. I look to see if she left me a grey hair on the pillow. I sleep on my back, looking at the same spot on the ceiling that she did. I want to reach that morbid sensitivity that she looked at the world with, always expecting the worst. She had extraordinary powers of repression, love as well as hatred. She taught herself in the house of her father, who married five women in all and had fifteen sons and daughters by them. All of them lived in the same house and spied on each other.

Sometimes I could see her recoiling in her chair, her features recoiling, from the pressure inside that ate her up. My mother's emotions were caught up in love and the opposite, extreme harshness. These two extremes mingled in her, confusingly. With me she was more harshness than love. Contrary to my father, I cannot remember my mother except with worry on her face, struggling with the tensions inside her. Even in moments of joy she would be struck with bad presentiments, expecting something terrible to happen.

But my sisters rebutted my image of her. They said that towards the end of her life she changed completely. The anxiety drained out of her. She was at peace, a model of calm.

Caught in the rhythm of her dark moods, I wake up in the middle of the night dreading something. The black of night and the obscurity of the room deepen this feeling. I am sweating and can feel my heart beating loudly. I feel like I will die right now from these fears. Yet daylight and the normal daily routine will scatter them.

I don't remember my mother ever being affectionate to my father. Hers was a love which showed itself through loss. When he went to hunt gazelles in the desert she would wander round the house, desperately afraid for him. But as soon as he got back, she would use the worst and most trivial kind of language to him: 'If only you hadn't come back and had been buried there. Then you'd be sorry!'

She would never miss the chance to spoil my father's pleasure when he would prepare a *mezza* for drinks in the evening. My father paid no attention to her. In fact he considered it a part of family conduct, a family which was all talk and busied itself not with joy but with worries, worries that they were good at creating and then keeping alive.

If Ali Sheikh Hadi was born an orphan, free and unfettered, Amira Abdel Latif was born into a house where five wives and fifteen children lived cheek-by-jowl, squabbling over the slightest thing. Turns in the bathroom, which person gets which clothes, even which wife's turn it was to be with the husband in the evening. My grandfather watched all this rivalry from behind the curtains, laughing. He knew its result would always be in his favour. All his children were marked with the anxiety that beset the house.

Communism was spreading through Baghdad, my uncles signed on, and my sister was influenced by that.

My mother's most serene hours were when she was at the sewing machine. She could work miracles with that machine, reworking old clothes to hide our poverty. When they made us wear trousers at school, my mother adjusted my father's old trousers to fit me. She would make dresses for my sisters from old clothes, and each time one of them grew out of one, she would adjust it for the next one down. Behind that machine, her face was clear and pure, free from worry. She would only raise her head to say to one of us: 'Come here and let me measure you.'

Her real joy was embroidery. Every household thing we owned had an embroidered cover, with gardens and tile work depicted on them and strange flying creatures that were half-eagle and half *Buraq*, the legendary horse that the Prophet Muhammad travelled to heaven on. Moments of calm and stillness were rare in my mother's life. She nagged my father. When he came home after a drinking bout, she would reproach him for hanging out with the rich at the expense of his honour. When he was tipsy, she would mock him as foolish. He in his turn would make fun of her, turning to us: 'Look at her face. Can you see *Ashoora*, the feast of mourning?'

My parents never stopped having children in spite of our limited income and poverty. In this alone was my father religious, he would just sow his seed and leave it to the Lord. He never asked how we would cope. My mother was so fertile that as children we thought she gave birth every six months. We became used to coming down from our bedrooms and hearing the hoarse shout of a woman: 'Ali! Ali! Ali! Ali! Ali!' And then the cry of a child, and we knew that we had just become one more.

One day my brother Sabeeh and I came down to find a strange creature in the courtyard, in a saucepan under the sun looking something like a cooked rabbit. We wanted to touch it but a crowd of women were right there in our courtyard and they shouted: 'haram, (forbidden)'.

My mother had a miscarriage in her fifth month.

Sabeeh and I carried it into the kitchen, making our own funeral procession, urging everyone to get out of our way as we chanted: 'there is no god but God. There is no god but God'.

One of my aunts ran behind me, shouting from fear of God's anger. What we were carrying was not an animal, but a brother who had died before he was born.

So we proliferated but my father's income didn't. But when he would come drunk to our bedroom to say goodnight he would smile because we seemed to him like a whole row of peas in a pod. It was him who gave us pet names and nicknames, leaving to my mother the job of coping with the small amount of money we had, a subject of perpetual quarrelling.

Despite our poverty, everything in the house was done Najaf-style. All our beautiful best things were locked away in cupboards to keep them safe. We would steal the keys, or if we couldn't, we'd loosen the screws on the back panel of the cupboard and open it up to steal an orange, or a couple of pieces of *baklava*. Then put the dozens of screws back in. My mother would utter invocations against the Devil, amazed at how the *jinn*, her children in fact, could pass through the locks.

The thing my mother most dreaded was that our poverty became obvious to others. She would borrow luxury items like a fan or porcelain dishes from neighbours if we had guests. On such occasions, we manoeuvred between reality and appearances. Nevertheless, the truth would out from the mouths of us children, and then she would cuff us after the guests had left.

During the war with Iran my mother became like some heroine

out of a tragic novel – the Iraqi mother in the thick of it. She had two boys on the front with Iran, and a son and a daughter in the Lebanese civil war. She followed the news of the two wars with alarm. Amira Abdel-Latif al-Jezairy launched a bed strike, deciding to sleep on the hard floor as her son slept in the trenches. The small radio was her constant companion and connection to her sons. She listened to every news broadcast in turn, the last one being Radio Cairo. Her animal instincts would sniff out what was behind the news. She followed the ebb and flow of battles on a map, like a general in an operations room.

Like them, she memorised the features of the terrain and the direction of the fighting. She knew where Deezful was, where the Iranian planes were strafing, just as she knew where the locus of fighting and the supply lines were in Lebanon, where the Christian militia's mortars were falling and where the car bomb was. But there was one big difference. Unlike the generals in the operations room, she lived the war on her nerves. The battles did not interest her, nor who won and who lost, or which army advanced and which retreated. She didn't know the armies and their units, but she knew the dead, their names and faces. The centre of her map was her son stuck in a mud trench. The news, in fact, was nothing but a prompt for her imagination, adding detail to the depth of the picture she had, the picture of her son in the middle of a war. She slept with half an eye open, ears alert to the traffic in the street. Her heart would beat fast whenever a car slowed down: what if he had come back? What if others had brought him back – dead?

The closest person to my mother and the one who resembles her most is my sister Dhikra. She has the same disposition to follow bad news, the same deep feeling of others' disasters, and the dramatic nature to share their tragedies with them, to always be disappointed. The same nervousness that always flares up over the slightest thing.

The way she relates to her husband when he drinks is exactly what happened between my mother and father. Dhikra has the same knack of divining others' secrets, and of taking extreme positions of either love or hate.

My mother never went to school or learned from the mullah. But she learned how to read and write by sitting with her brothers as they read by lamplight. Unlike my uncles, my mother never believed for a minute that communism could win. But she identified with it because of her brothers who were arrested or on the run. She would always say to them: 'There are two lost causes. Palestine and communism.'

She sympathised with the movement out of that Shia identification with the underdog, and added to it the dramatic flair of the loser who wins by losing. How much she resembled the sacrificing mother, always mixed up in the tragedy of others. She passed on this trait to her sons and daughters. Normal life would divide us. It was always tragedy that would re-unite us.

Sleeping in her bed, I felt the wood of the support struts like her bones. I stretch my legs and arms out to the edge of the bed looking for her. It feels like my breathing becomes one with hers, slowing down and speeding up. When I went to sleep I dreamed she came to the side of the bed and stood silently. She wanted to say something and I almost knew what it was. I would move over in the bed to make room for her but she always stayed standing, shivering from the cold.

When my father read my name Zuhair al-Jezairy on my first published book, he was silent for a little while, trying to swallow his sense of disappointment. Then he reproached me: 'Why did you not use your patronym, Ali, as well?' I protested that there had not been enough space. But that left me with a sense of guilt later on because I had not answered him seriously. My mother was angrier and colder, because I had dedicated my first novel to my wife, 'to Suad, honouring our shared experience'. Not to the woman who had borne me for nine months, then breastfed me for two years, then worried for me all the time I was in danger.

The last time I saw my mother and father had been over twenty years before, in Beirut in 1981, after my brother Tha'ir had been killed in the war with Iran. I was shocked. Darkness had crept over them, the new colour of Iraq. Disaster beyond imagination had struck. First I met my father. He lent on my shoulder and sobbed: 'Your brother Tha'ir has gone.'

We had been apart two short years but my mother had aged more than ten. She had become my shrivelled old grandmother. She clutched at me with fingers like claws and smelled on me the smell of Tha'ir, whom she had lost to Saddam's *Qadissiya*.

We tried hard to lighten a little of the pain that bore down on her. But this stubborn woman did not want to forget. The image of her dead son was with her night and day. His face would tower over her, as bright and solid as anything. We took her to beautiful Shemlan, onto steep, narrow mountain tracks and gardens squeezed between the rocks. We took her out on family evenings. We took her to markets teeming with all kinds of goods. But she would reproach herself for any joy which distracted her for a second, and bring him into the picture: 'He could have been here. He would have liked that girl; this shirt would have suited him ...'

Any pleasure would simply remind her of the fact that Tha'ir was not with us and that any happiness, however slight, was impossible without him. Guilt tore her apart any time she felt a moment of pleasure. We introduced her to grieving Palestinian mothers who had lost two or more sons in the hope that their talking about their own tragedies would put her own in proportion. But all comparison suffocated her. Her son was different from the sons of others, because he was her son.

From time to time she would just drift off. We'd say: 'We're here' and she'd jump, wrenched back from the world of darkness she had made for herself. At other times she would grimace because the pain stung her heart like lemon juice stings a cut on the hand, and she would get up and leave us. I would get up to follow her but my sisters would say: 'Let her wallow in sadness. It's how she reaches peace.'

Sitting alone, she would mumble to herself in a strangled voice like a dirge, rocking backwards and forwards, seeking her only remedy, tears. She would sit singing sad folk songs to herself. She would only find peace when the clouds of her sadness broke and she wept out what had been building inside her for hours.

Guilt drove her sadness. She could not accept the truth that Tha'ir had gone and that guilt would not bring him back. She would remember all the chances there had been to save him and blame us for having squandered all of them. We all bore the guilt of the fact that he had stayed in a mud trench and that that mortar shell had crossed no man's land and the mine fields and a warren of other trenches and a crowd of fellow soldiers flattened against the walls of their trenches to find him, he whom she had borne for nine months, and nursed for two years and looked after him his whole nineteen years, the favoured son after Sabeeh and I left. And now a piece of metal flying across no man's land looking for human flesh to penetrate had ended all that. She thought we had all betrayed him, wasted our chances to rescue him by hesitating and postponing and forgetting it in favour of other smaller concerns. She does not see us, the living. Her eyes are on the absent, on him more than us. Among all the chairs is his chair which he fills, looking at us with a question just on the top of his tongue: 'And if ...' My mother aimed this deadly reproach at all of us. 'Why didn't you do anything to save him? Why?'

In her guilt she would see him in front of her, silent, tight-lipped, his head bowed in despair, or a strange sad smile on his lips: 'I was killed. Why didn't you do anything to rescue me?'

But he himself had done nothing when others urged him to flee, saying, 'It would only add to the misery of my family.' Only now had my mother discovered that Tha'ir had concealed the fact he was on the front line from her. He was living on a line of blood, under daily bombardment, counting each new day as a bonus from God.

My father had officially received the body, and then fainted on the casket. His son had come home with the other corpses returned to the district from the industrial fridges.

'It's Tha'ir,' he said. 'He looked like he was just asleep; the quick nap of a soldier who has come back exhausted and then bathed.' That's what my father said with a painful sigh.

My mother said she had heard, while asleep, the sound of the car as it turned over in front of the gate to the house and had said, while still asleep: 'It's the freezer'. Like thousands of Iraqi mothers, she feared the freezer trucks which circulated through the streets at night, looking for the houses to deliver the corpses of young men killed in the war.

The tragedy had sapped my father's strength. But it showed more on my mother. Life became hard for both of them after their children started dying.

Baghdad Is Burning

The roof in the West is cancelled space; at best a feature outside the house. The roof in Iraq is part of the house. There, the sloping, slippery surface makes you slide down and hit the ground. Here, the roof is a place to stand between the earth and the sky and you can stand looking up at the sky secure in your footing. Looking out from a roof is also different from windows, because with a window you see only a static, measured frame of your surrounding environment. On a roof you can turn as you wish and look all around.

By day, the roof reminds me of the palm tree of our neighbours. You can steal a look at the secrets of your neighbours, even the more distant ones. It's a hangout for adolescents. It was from the roof that I saw the female form for the first time, watching a neighbour in her dressing gown as she put out her washing, well aware of the probing eyes that pierced her body. It was from the roof that I saw another teenager 'practising the secret art' as we say of masturbation, his eyes closed, under a burning sun. And in a storage room on one of the roofs, I saw two women making love. During adolescence, the roof was my only private place. And yet I could spy on the neighbours' girls.

In winter, we would go up to the roof to have the sun warm our bones, eating lettuce in sugared vinegar, and beetroot. But the best thing was sleeping on the roof at night.

All my life in exile, I missed sleeping on the roof. It gives me a double feeling, on the one hand, of being part of the great Universe, and on the other, of being part of the neighbourhood, taking part in an age-old custom, shaded by the neighbour's palm tree.

My family warned me against sleeping on the roof, a practice they had abandoned some time ago. They warned me about being hit by stray falling bullets, and the thieves and killers who creep around on the roofs of Baghdad. Nevertheless, I took my bedding and went up there. My nieces came up with me and we all lay down in a row, like when I was a child. We didn't take an electric light with us, because we wanted to see by the light of the stars. They were full of questions, which I answered with my eyes fixed on a sky, the like of which I had never seen before. How many times I had wished when I was in exile that I could sleep like this, with the sky as my ceiling, just as it had been for my Bedouin grandfather. The stars seemed so close you could reach out and touch them; the moon as bright as porcelain. I could almost make out its features, its volcanic craters.

Lying there, I put my arms by my side, and look up into the sky. I feel shot like a rocket into the Infinite sky. Suddenly I feel grateful to the Earth for holding me up, preventing me falling into the Infinite Void down and behind me.

From the roof of our house, I saw Baghdad burning in the early morning, whirling flocks of birds set against columns of smoke in the distance. My nephew Yasser pointed out which places were burning.

'That building with the flames billowing out of the windows is the Ministry of Youth. That's the Finance Ministry, together with stacks of dinars stored there. That's the fourth time this week it's on fire. Over there, that's the Olympic Committee Centre, where Uday Hussein built an ornate garden and surrounded it with high walls, fencing it off from the hell of Iraq on the other side.'

'And this column of black smoke is from the Central Bank, which has been plundered until there's nothing left.'

Wherever I looked there were clouds of smoke. And behind the fires were the stories and rumours. Some said it was the Israeli Mossad. Others swore they had seen Kuwaitis either burning the buildings themselves, or paying young street urchins to do it for them. As for the Americans, there were plenty of people who had 'seen' them burning buildings in order to get contracts to rebuild them. And some attributed the fires to officials who had pillaged their departments and then committed arson to cover their tracks. Others said it was Saddam loyalists, carrying out one of the Leader's last orders: let them inherit destruction!

It is the nature of Magian peoples like ours to like fire. It reminds us of our distant ancestors. Fires break out whenever a regime falls and the pyromaniac people gains the upper hand. That is why a flame has always been the symbol of the freedom of the people. Wherever I look the clouds of black smoke indicate that something of substance is being burned.

It was as if Baghdad had gone back centuries in time, to the sacking of the city by Timurlane. As Abbas Azzawi said in his book *Iraq Between Two Occupations*:

> Fire repeatedly broke out inside the walls and dwellings of Baghdad, from the middle of the month of Haram in the Islamic calendar to the end of the following month Safar. There were constant fire alerts, day and night, and the people became more and more afraid. Aladdin, the chief of the court, ordered that cisterns be placed in the streets and filled with water, and that people should stand ready on their roofs to douse the fires. The reason for all these fires was unknown. People would just see them as they broke out inside their houses. One poor man sleeping on one of the bridges only woke up when the fire was at his throat. Watching for fire and saving their houses became the people's main concern. They had no interest in anything but watching for where it would break out next, and stopping it.

The fires today were the same, the perpetrators still unknown. Whoever they were, they had planted black smoke trees across the horizon of the city. The same story of burning and drowning was repeating itself in Baghdad. Nobody has ever won this city without burning it before entering in triumph. Nobody has ever lost it without burning it before he leaves in defeat.

Electricity

For fifteen years of my life in London, electricity did not occupy more than an hour's thought in total. The bill preoccupied me more than electricity itself. I learned to think of it as a basic fact of life, like wind and water. Press the button, without any effort, and the blades start spinning on the automatic razor, or the lawn mower, the reading lamp comes on, or the juicer, or the vacuum cleaner or the washing machine, or of course the lights. You press the button without looking because you are certain electricity will automatically power all these appliances.

In Baghdad, all this changed. Electricity became the concern I geared my life around. I would time where and when I slept by the hours electricity was available, and therefore fans and air conditioning. It controlled my reading and writing. My moods, even. I became conditioned to be happy when it came back after a long power cut. Light would fill the house, banishing the looming shadows in the garden and on the street. Our world became one of precise objects again. We could take comfort in a more normal course of life; see each other's faces, smile.

Coolness came with electricity, fans and air conditioners and refrigeration in the heat of Baghdad. Saddam had known before the Americans how to use electricity. He would bestow it as a gift to the people on his birthday, and then punish them collectively by depriving them of it for a period, say, until school exam time. Then he would grant it again in dribs and drabs. He distracted them from more public concerns.

The Americans took over the keys to the power stations and played with people's moods in the same way. It is just not possible that all this time could pass without finding a solution to the electricity problem. Our new rulers, who have their own generators, did not know the hardship of ordinary people when a power cut came with the temperature over 40 degrees centigrade. Anxiety rises in the home as people are stuck there killing time through the middle of the day, and newborn babies cry from the heat of an oven.

We quickly get used to the power when it comes, and imagine it will stay forever. At night, our gaze lingers on the lights. We get high on them. Then the power cut attacks us like a nightmare, cutting our pleasure. For fifteen years, the problem in Iraq has been getting worse. And yet my nephew Ali is still surprised. He praises or curses Bremer depending on whether the power has just gone on or off.

Having developed a dependency on electricity, we have not got used to adjusting to the darkness.

When I went up into the mountains in Kurdistan in 1982, it took some time before my eyes adjusted to the perpetual darkness of the mountains, but the darkness gradually became a strength. We started to sense things by intuition before seeing them with our eyes. Our feet felt their way to the next steps on steep mountain paths, sensing where danger lay. One day electricity penetrated our mountain caves. Its rays stung our eyes with their sharpness, just as a blind man might feel opening his eyes after successful surgery.

But in the city, electric light has become both our vision and our intuition. There is no obscurity in things when the light has uncovered them, lending them both solidity and shadow. But as soon as the lights go out, our nearest and dearest become unknown wraiths. We have to keep talking, to make our voices a thread to bind us together, replacing the light. When the lights go out we are plunged into darkness, and the fears begin.

There is an Iraqi joke about a tree in Paradise with golden leaves. A leaf falls from the tree every time one of God's faithful has committed blasphemy. One day all the leaves fell off in unison. Our Lord asked why, and the angels replied: 'The power has gone off in Iraq.'

James Baker, George Bush Sr's Secretary of State, has taken us back to before the Stone Age, as he promised during the first Gulf War, by striking what was left of the electricity grid. We have gone back to the appliances of our ancestors, oil lamps and candles, and hand-held fans, and cisterns for water. In the markets, we can hardly hear each other when hundreds of generators are going at the same time, and Baghdad seems like a village: the shops are lit, but the streets are dark.

Electricity divides us. There are the private rich, who have small generators of their own. And those in power with access to huge, silent generators. And then the rest of us, who wait for the miserable amount doled out by the government.

Another joke goes that the Iraqis are the first of God's people to enter Paradise because they most often repeat the prayer 'God bless the Prophet Muhammad and his House', whenever the electricity comes back on. Electricity provides the rhythm of our life. We plan our sleep and waking by it and everything we do, from washing clothes, to watching TV, to reading and writing. At night, when the generators are turned off, I don't know what to do. I climb onto the roof of the house, lie back, put my hands behind my head and watch the stars, trying to make out their orbits. They wink at me and sleep finally comes, till the first rays of dawn.

It is by electricity that Iraqis measure not just the mercy of God, but how a government is performing. It is tangible whereas all the rest – democracy, freedom of expression, pluralism – are just words. The electric current is more significant than all political currents put together.

Kidnap Alley

No one in the twenty houses of our street knows who the martyr Qahtan is that the street is named after. When I ask about him and how he died, they answer me: 'You're asking a question that has no answer. Every street in Baghdad has the name of a martyr.'

The people have lived here since the 60s without any great changes. Young men became middle aged, and retired, with children who grew up and married and were plunged into war. The young women know each other's secrets, and are torn between a marriage imposed by their families and a love that will be disappointed. When one of them is married, all her friends on the street take part in the party, as though they lived in one house. There are no secrets on the *Street of the Kidnapped*.

'This property has been returned to its owner.'

This sign has been placed on the door opposite us. The house had been owned by someone who fled at the start of the 1980s; then the leader bestowed it as a gift on a woman, whom the neighbours whispered worked in the chemical weapons programme. No doubt she had delivered more destructive weapons to the leader than her colleagues working on the death experiments. After the regime of annihilation the exile returned and reclaimed his house. Another exile reclaimed her second house and the lady of destruction was suddenly left homeless.

On those rare occasions when Abu Mai, our neighbour to the right, would come out of his house, to water the flowers in the garden, he would reassure me: 'This anarchy will soon pass, and afterward the logic of politics will triumph.' He tried to allay my fears about the rise of religious extremism: 'Don't be afraid of the turbans. Their time will be short. They will become acquainted with money when they get into office, and the perks of the job. They'll become more godless than us.'

'All these militias will disintegrate when the investment floods in, and there are jobs to be had,' he said.

He was anxious for his life, and the life of his family, but thought these bad days would soon pass: 'Two years, perhaps less, and all this will just be memories.'

He closed his pharmacy on Sheikh Omar Street after it became prey to thieves and criminals. He warned us about leaving the gate to the front garden open, and warned me specifically about the men who stopped their car in front of our gate and looked in at us menacingly: 'You are a well-known journalist who has come back from abroad. For sure you are being watched.'

It occurred to me that he was also concerned for himself, since he was also called Zuhair.

After one brother was killed in a car bomb, and another was kidnapped, Abu Mai joined the ranks of the pessimists.

'This country is turning to the bad, to destruction,' he said.

In total secrecy he gathered his family gold and mementoes, his title deeds of ownership, family photo albums and correspondence, He had a lump in his throat as he cast a last look round the house, locked up, and handed us the keys. He could barely get the words out.

'I never left this country through all the wars and the sanctions. But I must save my family. I will come back at the first opportunity.' He left for Cairo with his family and with that the second house on our street was vacated.

Our neighbour on the other side was a senior officer. The rumour in the neighbourhood was that he had been in 'the bunker' – one of the inner circle who sat in the operations room underground with Saddam and planned the war with Iran. Towards the end the war slipped out of the grasp of those who had started it. It was no longer an extension of politics; it was no longer even a war in the classic sense of the term. The men in 'the bunker' no longer decided plans to advance or retreat because the war had taken on its own dynamic. It was driven by the logic of revenge and violence breeding violence. Its fuel: humans, killers and killed. During those years our neighbour the general's job description changed. In the last years of the war soldiers would come to his house carrying boxes with TVs in them, and generators, and air conditioners, bribes so that he would grant them leave, or transfer them from the front line to the rear lines.

Now our neighbour, like all the generals, was stuck at home after Bremer had dissolved the army in a stupid decision. He became friendly to the neighbours after he had terrified them, thumping the ground with his stick as he walked down the street. He adapted perfectly to his new situation, doffing his general's uniform for a *dishdasha*, pruning the trees in his garden. From this house would come ceaseless ranting and raving. 'It's the mad old woman,' someone in the family would invariably say.

Dhikra assured me. It was thought that the old woman was nearly 110 years old and had seen both the birth of the state of Iraq and its destruction. Her family had locked her up in the bathroom.

This old woman saw the present as mere illusion. Her mind was taken up with a past where different eras mixed and mingled. She would rail at people who had been dead for decades. It seemed the dead came out of their graves and spoke to her.

The rest of the household neglected her completely, as if she did not belong to them but to a world which had passed. She in her turn saw them as enemies from the past. She would imagine that they wanted to hang her, and would cry continually for help from her children, who had already died in the wars.

Across from us was the house of Umm Hassan, who fasted all year round despite her high blood pressure. She was the closest to us and to everyone. Everything about her spoke of her kindness. She never complained, not even about her husband's second and younger wife. In fact, she supported her in her problems with their husband Abu Hassan, whom I would see sometimes looking pretty frail, tending the seedlings in his front garden, conserving his weak heart with slow movements.

Umm Hassan would visit us at least once a day and would always ask the same question: 'When will things get better, God willing, and we can live in peace?'

If you get to the end of the street and turn right, you come to Abu Saad's shop. It still bears his name although he has died. It was here that the old men of the street used to gather every evening to play backgammon, exchange the latest political gossip, and tell the latest dirty jokes. My father used to chair these sessions. He was the arbiter of any disputes or debates.

Everyone used to come at five. But it was an appointment that needed no formal notification. They discussed everything in these daily sessions except death. Death lurked shrouded in grey, sitting side by side with them as they played backgammon, these old men, waiting to pounce on one of them. They all knew he was there and they all avoided him. But when one of the old men was late, all the others would get worried and start wondering. They all had the illnesses of old age which had no cure. Any absence meant a great deal and sounded the alarm bell for the rest. The conversation and games would go on, but taut and nervous. Suddenly one of them would ask the question they were all avoiding: 'Where is Abu Hind? Did he tell you he wasn't coming?'

As I passed by the shop for the first time on my return, I noticed an old man sitting outside on a chair, looking at me through bottle-thick glasses. He watched me with amazement. As I passed him, I heard a strangled voice calling me as though from the grave. This man, his breath troubled, stretched his hand out to me, leaning on his stick to support his legs, 'Oh mercy, Lord'. He told me it was not yet time, as though Abu Zuhair had returned from the grave and was walking down the same street with those lazy steps. Abu Hind was the last elder from the district left alive. He remained sitting in the same place in front of the shop, but always feeling sad. He had stayed alive when all his friends had left. He crumpled from the emotion. I held him up as he touched my hands and face and addressed me as though I were him, my father: 'Why did you leave me by myself?'

Everyone on the street, old or young, knows everyone else like the back of their hand. They know each other's stories, they have lived together. But these days the street was filled with strange, new stories. Stories of children kidnapped on their way to school. The first child to be abducted was ten years old. He and his little brother were going to school. The little one had got away by a hair's breadth, so they took the older one. The whole neighbourhood repeated the details of the 'secret' negotiations between his father, who owned a sweet shop, and the kidnappers.

I met the child a few days after his return. He told me he had spent part of the time on a farm with a family that had children his age. What could those fathers have said to their own children about him while he sat there crying from morning till night? Later there were more abductions, of adults too, including a pharmacist who was taken just as he was closing his shop. He managed to call his family by mobile from the boot of the car he was taken away in.

These stories of kidnappings and gangs who had taken over the streets filled our houses with fear and a worry that the old secret police – very practised at kidnapping and knowing where people lived and their secrets – were behind the kidnappings.

Not far from our house was an empty home with three pieces of graffiti on it. The first said: 'This house is for rent'. The second said: 'The owner of this house is wanted in a tribal dispute'. Above both of these was a third one in black script, saying: 'He has passed to the Mercy of God'. No more than ten days passed from the appearance of the first writing to the last one.

The young men of the district set up their own defence cordon to block the killers and thieves and kidnappers. They closed the streets off with the trunks of palm trees and organised night patrols. It made them feel proud and noble to be guarding the district against the outlaws.

Looking for Baghdad

With the Soldier

Despite the proliferation of killers and kidnappers, my brother Sabeeh and I decided to start a tour of all the places in Baghdad that had stuck in my memory in exile. Our sister Dhikra stayed up all night praying for us, afraid for us, the only two men left in the family. The next morning, she insisted that we leave the house passing under a Qur'an which she held over our heads.

When we got into Sabeeh's Brazilian car, he put his hand under the seat, feeling for the Kalashnikov that was stored there. He opened the glove compartment, took out some bullets and loaded them, smiling at me: 'Better safe than sorry.' I looked at him side on as he drove and wondered what the connection was between us, how could we have led such different lives?

My brother Sabeeh, my driver on this tour and a natural soldier, was born in 1949. Those born in this year always face incredulity when they declare their birth date: *'And you're still alive?'* They are famous for being the war generation, of whom only rare samples have survived. His wife told me that for twelve years she had not seen him except when he returned home from the front, dirty and gaunt. When he got home he would sleep for an entire day, or two, without anyone disturbing him. He does not like to talk about what he has seen and takes no pride in it. For him, they are lost years.

The habits of the battlefield are still with him. He sleeps like the dead even under bombardment. When others are worried about the bombing he chides them: 'What's the matter with you? You've gone mad! It's only a few bombs in the distance. Where's the tea?'

Once I phoned him, worried because a car bomb had gone off in the place where I knew him to be. He laughed and snorted down the phone, mocking my fears: 'No way! I was over 100 metres away!'

He moves like a soldier through the house and always eats his meals quickly as if the whistle is just about to go. He goes to the bathroom in the morning with the towel draped over his shoulder. He is hard of hearing because he was in the artillery. He laughs when everyone else does but did not hear the joke. He sleeps when there's a debate because he cannot follow it.

At one time in the 1980s he served in a location very close to where I was fighting on the other side, with the Kurdish Peshmerga. He bombed our positions repeatedly, although maybe he deflected the charges a little from their precise targets. Every time at Bushtashan we heard the army was advancing I imagined meeting him as an enemy. What would I do? Would we shoot at each other, or would we embrace as brothers who had not seen each other for many long years?

And now he was driving me around Baghdad, unafraid of anything after all the things he had seen.

'Listen, Zuhair! After all I've seen and lived through I won't die that easily. It needs a bigger war than the ones I've lived through,' he said.

Sabeeh resembles our father a lot in the way he shrinks from any responsibilities or problems. He just wants to get through the day peacefully, like the soldier who knows he might die tomorrow.

His way of making light of everything springs from a false assurance, based on life as a series of random events. He parks the car in front of a burning building and says: 'Let's wait and see what's left for them to steal.'

We hear a burst of bullets inside the building. He turns to me and jokes: 'They're killing each other now inside the fire because of the loot. It's the dregs of the dregs.'

We didn't have to wait long. A group of young men, their faces blackened by the smoke, emerged. They shot wild and loose, clearing a path to their pick-up truck with their refrigerators and office tables, all that was left after the pillage of the first hours. Their eyes are stark wide open, watching for if another gang is waiting at the door to steal from them what they stole with the sweat of their brow and the blood of their rivals. In this world of looting, the prize goes to he who opens fire last. Just when the original looters think they have won and put down their weapons in a moment of quiet satisfaction.

Sabeeh stopped at Maidan Square looking for the hotel 'Rest House of the North'. We went around the square a couple of times. I spurn all these concrete buildings which were built while I was away. I'm looking for the cheap pension that looked out over the square where I stayed for my first year at university.

'I'm sure it's somewhere around here,' I say.

Sabeeh laughs. 'For sure it was here – in the time of the Ottomans.'

I remember the room I shared with a student from Mosul, who always had under his bed a saucepan full of *kebba,* or meatballs, from Mosul. He would breakfast, lunch and dine on it. Every time he'd get out the saucepan and offer some to me. This lasted for more than a year. In the end, I was cured of my hatred for *kebba* from Mosul, remembering the saucepan under the bed.

At night I would go up to sleep on the roof, edged with low iron railings. Beneath me was the square with its drunks, swaying as they peered towards where the bus would come from to take them home. Old whores would solicit passers-by, singing the famous song that goes 'My pussy has become a bird. Shoot it down, hunters!'

On the mattress beside me there would be a man and I could see his cigarette butt glowing in the dark, but not his face. He would clear his throat and start to speak. The anonymity and peace of the night would open up the path to secrets. The other guy would speak as if he was talking to himself, in whispers so as not to wake the others. Once it was a soldier who had just returned from the battlefield in the north where he had been forced against his will to take part in the torching of a village and terrorising women and children. He lived under great stress, expecting death at the hands of foes he did not hate. Or it was a farmer who had come to Baghdad to follow up a business over some land, and was facing the arrogance of government officials, and humiliation. One time it was a cautious man who listened more than he spoke, a man I later included in my novel *On the Edge of the Day of Judgment* – a communist on the run from persecution in his home town seeking refuge in Baghdad, hoping to disappear at this hotel using false papers.

Waking late in the morning, I would search among the other guests for the man who had talked to me all night long but whose face was unknown to me. I would frequent the grocer's shop beside the hotel which I hated. Every time I asked him if I could use the phone which was in the front of the shop he would shake his head without even looking at me, turning to his next customer. For a long time his denial of me hurt me, and also my own weak hatred of him.

I did not find the hotel, the guests, or the shopkeeper to ask him if he remembered me.

In Search of Woman

For days I searched for the beauty of Iraqi women that I had known in the 1970s. Women are wrapped in *hejab* in all its forms. There is the *Devil's hejab* – a mere token, it reveals more than it covers. And then there is the *Wahhabi hejab,* which projects the woman as a lumpen black object, walking behind a man with an unkempt beard and wild moustache.

The way a man looks at a woman has changed since my day.

Influenced by Egyptian cinema, and actors like Hassan Youssef and Ahmed Ramzy, the cream of the young men at the universities followed beautiful women around, striving to be elegant, gracious and witty. Flirtation was premised on mutual standing, as colleagues at work, or in class.

Men worked on their chat-up lines to win over women. The harsh Iraqi dialect was out of fashion as the language of courtship. They would use the softer Egyptian equivalent to say that all-important 'I love you', or even English.

Now, instead of seeking the friendship of women with wit, men look on women with a mixture of repression and anger. They want to frighten a woman rather than win her admiration. It is a regard of authority which seeks to impose rather than to talk. You rarely hear the word 'my love' or even 'dear' from a husband to a wife.

Once I challenged one of our relatives: 'I'll give you $50 if you say "darling" to your wife.'

He didn't do it. In fact, he blushed from embarrassment and wanted to change the subject, to hide his weakness.

Forms of discourse between a man and a woman are now based on curt imperatives, sometimes only single words 'tea', 'lunch' and 'prayer carpet'. Often a man does not look at his wife when he addresses her.

A woman once said to me openly: 'Any man can win me with one word of affection. We have not heard sweet talk for years.'

The love stories which we knew have disappeared, replaced by relations of power and surrender. A man is no longer a lover, just a home owner and a father of children. After the flower of youth was killed in the wars, an able-bodied man, any man, has become a rare commodity. Boring? Boorish? Adulterous? It doesn't matter. What matters is if he can breed, and support a household.

Women no longer take an interest in beauty. Feminine beauty is secondary now, as life itself has little value. Women became heads of family during the wars and the conscription of men, and it is common now to see a woman take on the most arduous household tasks, struggling down the street under the weight of a heavy gas canister, digging over the garden, or stretched out underneath a car, repairing it. Sometimes she will carry the Kalashnikov to defend the house against robbers who try to take advantage of the man's absence.

I scan the faces of women in the lingerie markets, searching for that beauty that does not reveal itself all at once. Beauty closed to the onlooker at first glance, afraid of looks that steal its secrets. The eyes avert, the head drops, the body recoils. I look for that special kind of Iraqi beauty which increases its obscure, magical grip on you as you move closer – fresh faces preoccupied by love, young bodies ripening.

But all I find are anxious faces, beaten down by coercion and deprivation, slackened and furrowed. Grimy skin, the roughness of which a quick dash of make-up cannot conceal. And set in these grim faces are eyes that always widened and intense, as though in a state of perpetual alarm.

I asked Yassir, who is an expert in women: 'Where are all the pretty women?'

'Hidden away at home,' he said.

I did not believe him until I went to the apartment of a friend, tucked away on the fourth floor. It was tiny and stifling with the heat. The mother attacked her son because her daughter, who was in the prime of her youth, was a house prisoner. She had not left in a month.

The son retorted to the girl's complaint: 'If you leave the house, I will cut your head off and throw it to the dogs'.

I was astonished at the harshness of the language the brother was using on his sister. But he replied dismissively: 'If she goes out alone, they will abduct, rape, and kill her. If she goes out with me, they will kill me, then abduct, rape and kill her'.

In the end, I got to see Iraqi beauty for the first time when two friends invited me to celebrate their return home from Germany. They brought along three ladies of the night for entertainment. They entered the apartment wearing a loose *hejab*. But as soon as the door had closed, they took off the long, black *abeyas*, revealing bodies as willowy and well-formed as reeds. The three of them began whispering sweet nothings in our ears and spread out between us. I got the one in the middle, who put her hand on my leg and asked me to light her cigarette. Roya filled my senses and her perfume made me dizzy. I asked her what brand it was, and she came closer still, overpowering me.

'Guess,' she said.

'Chanel?' I asked – the only brand I knew.

'Spot on,' she replied.

She made me dizzy, this brunette. But I was determined not to go into the other room with her, as my friend had so quickly. So I resorted to my skill as a journalist, engaging her in question and answer. I found out she was a graduate of the faculty of Economics and Management.

My friend came back to tell me something amazing and unsettling about the other girl.

'Can you imagine that this beautiful girl is illiterate? She can't read or write!' he said.

Her father had gone missing in the war with Iran. Her mother, who was still young, waited for a long time, her bed cold. But in the end, she had married an Egyptian and gone to live with him in Cairo. But before she left she had married off her adolescent daughter to the first man asking for her hand. He used her as a tart for his business.

The girl paid no attention to us, although she could see from the way we were looking at her that we were talking about her. She was absorbed in an Oriental dance, leaning back a little, rooted to the floor, swaying her full breasts, rotating her pelvis as though it was separate from her body. She was rejoicing in the youth and beauty of her body which carried her through such a harsh and exhausting life.

I asked some women where they went when they wanted to get out of the house.

'We don't go anywhere,' one said. 'We are planted here in the house like those palm trees. Cooking is our only pleasure. And of course TV.'

'What do you watch?' I asked.

'What we cannot have in real life. Love songs, and romantic soap operas,' she replied.

There is an informal form of solidarity between women, confronting this harsh man's world together. Neighbours sit together and share their secrets spontaneously. This solidarity became clear to me at the first session of the National Assembly.

Every man who got a chance to grab the microphone and speak looked on himself as a political and leadership project. He used the biggest words possible: 'national unity', 'democracy', 'we are all Iraqi' and 'the blood of the martyrs'. Whereas the women, who had shouldered the responsibility for civilian life when the men had gone off to war, used the most practical words: 'nurseries', 'salaries', 'widows', 'education'.

Women were the first victims when the war with Iran became a battle of wills, each side seeking to impose maximum damage on the other. Iraqi women came under pressure to breed, to bring four more mouths. Then, when the war ended, women came under suspicion for the children born in the time their husbands were at the front. A man returning from the war would spend only six months in prison for murdering his wife in an 'honour killing' even if he could not prove his suspicions. Women also had to return to the home so men could take all available jobs.

At the start of the 1990s, Saddam was over fifty years old. The wars he had lost brought him closer to old age before his time, in spite of his dyed hair. Like every authoritarian ruler, he began to commemorate his Lord by building more mosques. He hurried to appropriate religion for himself rather than leave it in the hands of his opponents. The 'believing leader, may God preserve him', began to pray before and after reading security reports, and issuing death sentences. Death began to weigh him down. He started to seek forgiveness for it, even as he wallowed in blood. He wanted to take the country with him, to either heaven or hell. He built more mosques, forbad alcohol in bars and clubs. Prayer became obligatory for all those secular Ba'athists.

With the new wave of fundamentalism, all the advances in personal status law were retracted. All the laws which had advanced women's rights in marriage, divorce, child custody and inheritance, were annulled.

His son Uday, who had been known for his riotous parties and abduction of women, began to rival his father after the assassination attempt in December 1996 which left him impotent. He sought to take revenge on women, whom he could no longer rape. He sent his thugs to behead women suspected of adultery, with one stroke of a sword, and leave their heads on their doorsteps.

After the father and his son, women also became the easy victims of the militias and armed groups. The young men who thronged the ranks of the militias were forbidden from having any romantic connections with women, and developed a sort of spite towards all women. They threw their weight around, banning women's hairdressers and clothes shops. They prevented women from going to schools and universities and the workplace. This constituency of men wanted to banish women to the house and humiliate them, using the pretext of religion.

With the exception of a minority who have resisted, women have yielded to the prevailing force in what was an unequal struggle where they found society at large standing shoulder to shoulder with fundamentalism against them. I went looking for women I had known socially in college days, and was surprised that they had returned to the veil of their mothers. One of them had always insisted on coming with us to the Beiruti cafe, where she would shake hands with the old men who hung out there and play backgammon with us. When I went to her house I found her and her daughter veiled.

'What happened?' I asked. 'When did you change and take up the veil?'

'My daughter embarrassed me into it. She wore the veil before I did,' she said, with a bitter smile.

We got out photo albums from the 70s to look at. There was one of a group of us, young men and women, dressed in the latest fashions, arms over the shoulder on the university campus, smiling into the camera with light-hearted defiance. The woman smiled sadly at that far-off time while her daughter was uncomfortable to see her mother like that, shoulder to shoulder with a man she did not know, wearing a skirt that reached above the knees and was open at the side.

'You're kidding, mama. You used to go out dressed like that?'

The boy, who was no more than thirteen years old, snatched the album away from us, ashamed at the 'nakedness' of his mother.

And the woman, who was surprised by her own past and the reactions of her children, said to me: 'Believe me. I haven't seen these photos in over fifteen years.'

A former classmate from university, whom we had dubbed the 'Brigitte Bardot' of the class, came to see me at the newspaper in a black *hejab*, with her grown-up son. I asked her at what point she had decided to put on the veil.

'I don't know. It feels like I've always worn it now,' she said.

A talented artist paints the most vivid romantic scenes at home. The women in her pictures are feminine, sexy. But the painter wears the veil, unlike the women in her pictures.

'When did you start wearing the veil?'

'In Ramadan 1993. I thought it would just be for Ramadan, but I became addicted to it,' she said. When I asked why, she replied simply: 'It's easier like this'.

In the street, at work, or in any public place, the unveiled woman finds herself besieged at the slightest excuse by eyes gawping at her in reproach. She hears the most demeaning insults and often finds threatening messages follow her if she does not wear 'the dress of Holy Law'.

The spectacle of a woman dressed in black from head to toe, walking behind a bearded man, is a total denial of her status as a human being. She becomes just a moving object, without form or features. Repression transmutes into hatred and contempt. Worst of all is this psychology of veneration for women according to religious beliefs, which in fact turns into their abject servitude.

They are Looting History

In the square below the hotel was an informal market. Here there is an archive of old music stolen from the national broadcaster, reel to reel of the songs of Daakhil Hassan going back to the 50s. At one stall I saw a heart monitor and asked the stall-keeper jokingly: 'How much will you sell this blender for?'

He did not correct me because in fact he did not know what he was selling. Another stall was selling cigars which had 'Uday Saddam Hussain' stamped on them. There were generals' uniforms, which they had abandoned on the battlefield in the moment of defeat with stars on the shoulders. Night-vision goggles, gold-covered revolvers, they were all on sale here, as well as the medals that Saddam Hussein drowned his generals in, 'the Medal of Heroism', 'the Medal of the Homeland', 'the Medal of Qadissiya'. I bought a handful of them for five dollars and gave them to friends who had not been in any war. Nothing was sacred, nothing held value, because either it came from an old time or had been the product of much labour. Everything was sold for the price of the raw materials in it.

I saw some great old field glasses in this market and bought them as a present for Sabeeh. He put them to one side saying: 'I don't want to see them. I've used them to launch over one thousand artillery shells'.

In this same market I tried on a military jacket. I had no idea which general had worn it and where he had gone. I was just checking the length of the sleeves on my hand when someone walking by that I didn't know, tapped me on the hand: 'Aren't you tired of that colour? We spent all our youth in it'. And he went off again without even waiting for a reply.

The double-decker buses are part of Baghdad's folklore. We're so attached to them from all the hours we have waited for them to go to work or come home, to go out in the evening or come back at the end of the night. I discovered a piece of old Baghdad in London when I got on the old Routemaster buses which came into Iraq during the British mandate.

As kids, we used to fight over who gets the seat at the front on the upper deck. When you sat there you felt almost like you were flying you were so high, especially when going over bridges. And yet you were safely connected to the ground. When the state collapsed the drivers stole their own buses, driving them to private garages. The public bus authority had collapsed too – free markets – and low life who couldn't drive them stole their seats and wheels and they were left sometimes lying sideways on the ground, like a great wounded beast.

I saw some looters in the barracks next to this market destroying with hammer and axe the place that we had hoped to turn one day into a cultural centre. There were three men with hard faces that reminded me of the picture *Dying Bush*, by Jawad Salim. They worked in rotation with three big axes to dig up the ground around the palace which had been built during Sulaiman Basha's time as governor of Baghdad, in 1802. It was different from the Ottoman palaces, which generally privileged stateliness over beauty. History had touched every stone of this building. These were the tiles that Hassan Basha had walked over as he contemplated his victory against the Sufis, surrounded by his Circassian Mameluks, trained to total obedience, wearing their distinctive dress. These walls also saw the Ottomans reclaim Baghdad from the Mameluks when Rida al-Aadh, the governor of Aleppo, entered the city which was suffering both from plagues and flooding.

The hammer blows will not escape the attention of the old governors of the city and their guards, who perfected the art of treachery. And the pashas with their long waxed moustaches, their Iraqi lackeys in their shadows, afraid of the occupiers. The ledger keepers and what they stole from the state in their little account books, the notaries who did not so much master reading and writing as arrogance and the taking of bribes, the Sanjak rulers and officers with their swords at their sides. All of them exchanged the turban for the tarboosh which sat strangely on their shaved heads. They surrendered to the changes that swept across the uniforms and changed their uniforms.

In this place, where looters symbolically destroy the state with their hammers, Midhat Pasha, that pioneering reformer, laid the foundations of the modern state with the system of governorates. Here was also where printing started, and the first newspaper in Iraq, *al-Zoora*.

When we saw looters destroying all this history with their hammers and axes, we shouted out, and it seemed to us that all the men of history associated with that place shouted with us: Muhammad Namuq Pasha, Abdel-Baqi al-Amari, Mansour Bek Saadoun, Yassin Hashimi, Fahmi al-Mudarris, Rassafi, Sir Percy Cox and Sheikh Dari. Everyone who knew the place and had left their mark there shouted: 'What are you doing? You're destroying the house of your forefathers!'

One of the men put down his axe and, embarrassed, pointed to his mouth in the sign of hunger. When we got close we peeked into the ditch they had dug, and realised what was going on. They were not seeking to dishonour their ancestors, or destroy history. All of that was just the by-product of what they were really after, which was to take up the cabling from underneath the building to sell it to a scrap merchant. Apparently, Iranian merchants would buy it.

So everything could be plundered. For example, the Ottoman canons just by the iron gate in front of the defence ministry, which had intrigued us as children. Or even the gate itself, through which every coup maker has entered to change Iraqi history. The old clock of the barracks, which recorded the history of all our occupations, the statue of Prime Minister Abdel Mohsein al-Saadoun, the cast pointing to his own chest, foretelling or retelling his suicide: 'I have killed myself.' Precious books and manuscripts in the national library: everything was plundered, and with it the history of a nation.

The Museum

An American tank is still standing in front of the two statues at the front entrance of the museum. But after all that has happened, what is it guarding?

How did the tank find its place beside the two statues, which each embodied the strength of the bull, with the grace of the horse, and the wisdom of men? How were the tank and the statues folded into the same scene, with all its contradictions? The bull paid no attention to the tank, the horse did not flee, and the eyes of the man remained fixed on the horizon, above the tank, transcending time and space.

The thieves had entered the museum under the nose of the tank and the statues. Major and minor gods like Analil and Anoki had fled, leaving Kodia stuck there, her hands tied behind her back, looking at her robbers like a terrified child: 'What will you do to me?'

Mami, the pregnant mother of the gods, puts her stillborn child on the open street. The abductors will not allow her even a few seconds pause to give birth. For a few moments the fighting between

Ninorta and the great bird Anzoo stops, as the thieves cut the glass pane over their heads. The high priest with his long straggly beard looks around intensely, wary of impending disaster. The landlady in the bar, who ferments wine and brews beer, closed her legs together when the rapists entered the Sumerian room.

I saw the looting on TV before I entered Iraq. They gathered up all the statues of the old gods and goddesses of ancient Sumeria and left them by the main gate, ecstatic over looting something they could not value, laughing in front of the camera, within sight of the American soldiers. We shouted at them: 'Why are you plundering your ancestors?' We asked ourselves what kind of people these were.

I know this museum piece by piece. There was a time I used to come here every week and stand in front of each exhibit, thinking I could look at the statues of all the gods with X-ray vision, that I would discover myself in their eyes. I learned the secret behind why our people and history are so tense in this museum. The musculature of the Assyrian gods is tense, every muscle as arched as a bow drawn at its tightest; the opposite of those statues of the Egyptian gods who walk with slow, relaxed steps. From this museum I also learned that Gilgamesh, who had ruled the Sumerians in 2650 BC, was the real ancestor of the Iraqi people because he sought the Impossible. He was not satisfied with his position as half king, half god. He left his mighty kingdom to search for the beast Khambaba in the forests. Just like us and our rulers, Gilgamesh sought the impossible, even at the cost of destroying his kingdom. I loved this *3D-book* of our history, and lived among its clay pages. It was in one of the corners of the museum, behind a big statue, that I looked around to check the guards weren't watching and stole my first kiss from a woman.

The two winged bulls are standing just as they were in front of the museum, with the US tank beside them. But what is there left for them to guard? There is no temple, no Uruk or Alyana, no Ibso or Arido, no Nafar or Icor.

We are a people now without history, a people bombed into the present. We have no existence now outside this time and space. The younger generations know no history except the Ba'ath party, no leader or father figure except Saddam. Just when the educated were absent, riff-raff represent us, show our face to the world, riff-raff cut off from their houses and tribes, living on the streets.

Sabeeh saw the looting up close with his own eyes. He was standing in his underwear and with a fan in his hand it was so hot, when he saw some young men of the neighbourhood that he knew steal air conditioners from a state warehouse in front of his building in the poor part of Zeyouna district. Nevertheless, he warned his children not to take advantage of his absence to steal an electric fan: 'This heat is better than the fires of Hell,' he said.

He saw the plundering of all state depots and cars, and the money boxes from the banks. He watched it all with cold fury, and laid all these disasters at Saddam's door. 'He's the one who made an entire generation of looters. He allowed his family to loot the best palace and treasures in Baghdad, and then left the rest to the riff-raff.'

In all wars, booty had been the reward of soldiers who attack first and can get to it before their colleagues. When the Iraqi army entered al-Mahmarra, the inhabitants of this ethnically Arab region of Iran were so shocked by the rapaciousness of their liberators, that they preferred to escape to their Iranian 'occupiers' rather than withstand an army of looters.

During the Kuwait war, the state itself organised the looting of what Saddam had termed 'the nineteenth governorate'. Every minister and head of department went to plunder the corresponding office in Kuwait, including cultural institutions like newspapers and cinemas and theatres. Not forgetting, of course, all the luxury cars that the president's relatives acquired. Looting became part of the culture of war. One of the regime's worst crimes was the campaign against the Kurds called Anfal, or '*the Spoils*', because killing and looting were explicitly put together.

A whole generation had grown up in the streets with no support or education from the state. Then spent half its youth fighting for a homeland in which they possessed neither houses nor land. During the sanctions, it lived with famine and humiliation and death and watched how the big men of state built palaces and smoked fat cigars without any embarrassment or concern for their subjects. The state which had brought this generation down became their enemy. That is how they could loot and set fire to it with no pang of conscience.

An Apartment on Tree Street

The trees had disappeared from Tree Street and it had become a car park. I arrived there with a TV crew to visit the last house I had lived in before exile, in Bitawin district. The driver who waited for us underneath the Jabro Hamandi building told us not to be too long because this was the most dangerous district. I didn't know what the danger was and I didn't want to know. My old house was here; it was an area I knew every last corner of. This was where Jabro used to sit every day, with his square frame, in front of the entrance to his building. He would watch the comings and goings with sparkling blue eyes, always boasting: 'This is my building! I built it with ...' and then he would stop and not finish his sentence because he built it by people's shit. Jabro had been a plumber who worked on the drains. He started out in life cleaning toilets.

When Dhikra had first visited us in this apartment, she had stood perplexed for a moment, trying to recall where she had seen this smart-looking man sitting in front of the building. Later she remembered that he had cleaned our drains in Waziriyya. Later on, Jabro had managed to buy a fleet of cars which cleaned the rubbish from the streets. And with them: the Jabro Hamandi building.

Jabro could hardly believe that what he owned was this smart residential building. He used to sit in front of it like it was a shop. He didn't understand the privacy of his tenants either. He'd bang on the door and enter their apartments with his teams of workmen without waiting for permission, unconcerned by whether they were asleep.

A woman challenged us on the stairs, asking us what we wanted. When I told her I had lived in the building twenty-five years before she told me that she was Jabro's daughter, who had died twelve years before. The building had deteriorated after that because the whole neighbourhood had changed character. All the Christians in the building had left apart from one, a paralysed drunk who I remembered as a young man.

The man who lived in the apartment where we used to live hesitated before opening the door. Even then, he only opened it a crack while he listened to us explain the reason for our visit. He was only persuaded by our Christian cameraman. It was as if I had just closed my eyes for a second as I entered, and opened them again to smell the *fusuliya* again, which my ex-wife Suad was cooking in the kitchen. I half expected Suad herself to be there standing by the window, smiling, waiting for my comment: 'What, *fusuliya*, today?' I could see Nassir on his bike by the door with the stabiliser wheels, trying to get to me. On the left was our bedroom, with its white furniture and the bed still bearing the imprint of two bodies which had only just left it. I could hear Barbara Streisand singing *'I am a woman in love ...'* with her big ranging voice. Where we had a picture of women sellers in the market that Ismail Fattah had painted, a picture of Christ now stood. The young master of the house told me about some artist or painter who had lived in the apartment before his father took it over, who had left a lot of books behind.

'You're looking at him,' I said.

There was no trace left of the bookshelves. Not even the blown-up poster of the Picasso painting *The Fall of Guernica* which I'd wanted to use in a protest against the fascism of my own country. Everything had passed into a black night after one day, in the middle of 1979; the secret police had come to ask questions after someone had confessed that the apartment was a hideout for communist meetings.

I stopped on the tiny balcony where we had passed so many evenings. From here I had looked out onto an alien world, full of stories which I never wrote. An unusual slice of Iraqi society lived in Bitawin, a mixture of poor Christians and Kurds who had left their villages in the north because of the fighting and poverty and come to Baghdad which they imagined to be full of jobs and adventure. The Christians would start their lives as waiting staff in bars and hotels, the Kurds as shoeshine boys and porters. In every apartment which surrounded ours there would be at least five families: one, sometimes two families per room, separated only by a curtain. The street in fact was the only breathing space for families living like this, and so secrets spread easily onto the street, and from there to the neighbours. We would hear arguments and fights in Assyrian, Chaldean and Arabic, morning, noon and night.

People used to fight about the most trivial things – someone else had used their soap, or hung clothes on their clothes peg, or because someone had made a pass at their teenage daughter. Lives would simply rub up against each other in this narrow space. I would hear the shouting and the swearing and try to distil a story out of it. Esho, the concierge, who'd had his rib cage shattered in a plane crash in the north, was my spy in the neighbourhood. He would tell me after the event of the reasons for the fight. But most of the stories stayed simply as half-heard and half-formed – no characters, no beginning or end.

The people here were all from other places, with no clans to support them. They knew the argument would come up again. So they imposed red lines on themselves, and did not approach each other, shouting from a distance, more to relieve themselves than anything else.

The women here worked without reprieve. They were housemaids in other people's houses, or cleaners, or servants to their little brothers and children. Hard physical work absorbed the tension of their bodies but these women were always tense mentally. What particularly concerned me, in this human ant hill, were the teenage girls. They had absolutely no space for independence, or secrets. Eyes followed their slightest movements. Every night they would see, or hear, their fathers making love to their mothers, or the neighbours. They were out of control and without protection. Their manners were crude and harsh, always angry. They would get married at fifteen and pregnant two or three months after that and by the time they were twenty they would have four children.

Drunkards would sometimes pass below the building coming home late at night, shouting and singing and arguing in the open space just by the building. I will never forget two soldiers who were due to return to their units in the north the next day. They got drunk together in the middle of the public garden. They pushed each other, then kissed and made up, then got into a real fight where blood flowed, and finally fell asleep stretched out side by side on the grass.

I looked out from this veranda every morning to watch Nassir, my son, get on the bus to take him to school. Mays was born here. Later she would take the pen from my hand and doodle on the paper. This is where writing became a serious profession for me, rather than just something to indulge in when the mood took me. I learned to listen to music as an activity in its own right rather than to accompany reading or writing or conversation. This is also where I lived a love story that is still with me. She gave me the appetite and yearning of a teenager. But then my sense of guilt increased my love for my wife Suad, and gave it edge, when danger started to gather around our apartment, suspended here high in the sky. We would find each other at night, as if we were just about to die, when the torturers who were watching us broke into the flat. Every kiss seemed like the last.

I was just repossessing all these memories when the driver came up to the apartment to warn us: 'We have to leave quickly. Things have turned bad down below.'

The square was filled with shouting and warning shots. A group of policemen in civilian clothes had broken up a gang of car thieves. We found gang members lying on the grass, their hands tied behind their backs. The Kurds, who bought the stolen cars and gave them false number plates to smuggle them away to the north, were looking on from the balconies of a nearby hotel. One of them came up to me: 'You're a journalist, yes?'

I nodded.

'Those same policemen will be back in a little while ... to sell the same cars they've just confiscated.'

Abu Nawas Corniche

I would always stop on Republic Bridge at the same point. Below me, the Tigris flowed, peaceful, ever present, as since the beginning of time. Before me: Abu Nawas corniche, embodiment of Baghdad's ties to the river.

Baghdad and life in the city were built around the Tigris. The river divided it into the districts of Karkh on the western, and Rasafa on the eastern banks, linked by a series of bridges. The old alleyways of the city, with their leaning houses and windows, led down to the river, and comfortable houses had lined its banks. The people of Baghdad found relief by the river when the summer heat risked driving them mad, and a sense of the continuity and fertility of life.

I stand at this point on the bridge and see the same scene that I left twenty-five years before: the river and the barges. I smell the same smell, of mud and fish. There is a sense of movement, but without any particular vibrancy or eventfulness. It is the same as a quarter of a century before, the same scene that my father and grandfather saw before me, and Abu Jafar Mansoor, when he chose this spot in the eighth century to found his dreamed of city of Baghdad, with its Karkh and Rasafa.

This was the spot where, as a young man, I would stop to shrug off the irritations of the TV magazine where I worked, leaning over the bridge, trying to absorb the deep flow of the water. It was my dividing line between the cares of the workplace, where I could not have any private thoughts, and my gang of friends and life at my local cafe, where many strands of thought both combined and conflicted, enriching my spirit.

The river could reach inside me, calling me to its gentle rhythm, muffled sounds and the wavering reflections of the city. Preoccupied by some thought, I would look up and the life on Abu Nawas Street would strike me in the face. All those bars that had witnessed our debates, our fierce resolutions which we never carried out! We would get more and more animated as the alcohol kicked in and it would be time for confessions, fights and suicidal talk.

Something about the interplay of iron and mud and water at this point on the bridge engaged me. It's a place which attracts stories.

Three of Ghaib Tuma Farman's novels are set in this place, among them one of the finest descriptions of Baghdad in *The Pains of Sayyid Marouf*. It was also the main location of Barhan al-Khatib's *A Flat on Abu Nawas Street*. Abdel Rahman al-Rabe'i used this place, as did Fawzi Karim in his book *Return to Cardenia*. In my own novel *Terrifying and Terrified* this is the exact point where the narrator regains his true personality from the world of lies he has been living. The character Qassem Finjan contemplates suicide but is brought back by the lights on Abu Nawas corniche.

As I looked out along the street from the bridge I tried to see as it is now, block out the memories of the past. But I could not help grieving at the ruins I saw. The questions welled up out of a deafening silence: 'Where are the cafes? Where are the bars?'

There were only empty remains. A mangy stray dog trotted along, sniffing the water down by the river, looking for sustenance. Two young lads were messing around in the water on the shallow bank, near the place where al-Jawahiri had once liked to bathe 'between the water and the mud'. On the mud bank were five more lads, watching and smoking. I could hear their loud voices, fragmented as they carried across the water. Other boys were on the paved street drawing water from the river effortlessly in large buckets, for their car-washing business. They were uninterested in the river behind them, their attention on the road and the passing cars.

Not far off, two Hummer cars stood guarding the entrance to the Meridien Hotel. In one of them I see an American soldier, a kind of action-man hero on the wild street, slowly turning his head to watch the action. For a moment, I think he's fixed his gaze on me, suspicious at how long I have been standing idle.

My nephew asked me: 'Uncle, was this street really full of cafes, lovers and families?'

This street had been the people's path to relate to the river. Before it was built, there had been many streets down by the river, but they had been places of work, defining Baghdadis' connection to the Tigris as one of base utility. They would cross it on barges, draw its water to drink from, wash their clothes and livestock in it. But Abu Nawas Street had reshaped the relationship, defining it not as one of utility, or practical self-interest, but more one of reflection. People would now sit beside by the river for long periods of time, looking at it, in some kind of dialogue with it. The river also changed social ties as the cafes alongside it became family places, not just the preserve of men. The river became a kind of lung by which the city breathed – a boon for the eye and the spirit.

Saddam severed this relationship in the mid-80s, cutting people off from the river. The street became somewhere to transit quickly and with great caution, not a place to picnic and relax. The Great Leader did not want Baghdadis to share the river with him so he fenced it off with barbed wire and sowed fear along its banks in the form of guards who stood at intervals, watching the passers-by aggressively. Pedestrians who once strolled down this street on summer evenings, now traversed it quickly, not even looking at the river, afraid that the guards would suspect them if they loitered.

On the bank of the river, drab, monotonous houses had gone up instead of the old Baghdadi houses that had been our bars and wine houses. Republican Guards lived in these houses, and with that the river became their prize. The rest of the city was cut off from it. It became an unknown place, like all the other closed-off regions of the city. I descended the steps from the deserted bridge, which had bits of rubbish blown over it, to walk a little along the riverbank. There was a fine dust raised by the wind from lands which no one now cultivated, and ships sunk in the river. On the other bank were palaces, which had been blown up along with the rest of the holdings of the ruling family on both sides of the river.

On the same spot where, in 1975, I had once waited with a distraught mother for the body of her drowned son to float to the surface, I saw one young man washing a filly. This seemed to be all that was left of Uday Hussein's famous stables. I didn't ask him how the horse could have become so thin in so few days. If I had, perhaps he would have answered me as others did: 'She refuses to eat grass because her master accustomed her to pistachios.'

At the entrance to the Meridien I saw a sight I won't soon forget. Five boys, little more than ten years old, maybe the ones I had seen before from the bridge, were splayed face down on the ground, their hands bound behind their backs. Three American soldiers were standing by their heads. The boys were begging and crying while the soldiers walked round them, their guns pointing down at them.

'What are you doing?' I shouted at the soldiers angrily.

'We are interrogating them,' one of them replied.

'Children?' I asked.

I left them there, vowing to bring back journalists and cameramen.

I returned with a TV crew. The boys were nowhere to be found but the soldiers were there at their post, ready for our questions. When a journalist asked, one of the soldiers said: 'Yes, we arrested them because we saw them hiding behind our vehicle. But then we realised they were not saboteurs. They are addicted to smelling petrol.' They kept giving me dirty looks as they talked.

Since the first days of my return, there was a seedy little cafe in a small street that connected Abu Nawas Street and Saadoun Street that had caught my eye. Its windows were covered by heavy black curtains. Drugs were sold in this cafe to criminals and murderers to calm themselves before their next crime. As well as the drugs, there were two young women who astonished me by the mix of fresh beauty and harshness in their faces the first time I saw them. Later, as I walked past I would find one of them sitting on the pavement opposite the cafe, chain smoking and watching the passers-by with both curiosity and hostility. I knew that the other one would be up on the roof, lying underneath a man she did not know. Almost certainly they had grown up on the streets and been entrapped by the proprietor of the cafe, who rented them out along with a mattress to addicts after they had watched porn videos inside the cafe. The addict would go upstairs to the roof carrying the mattress himself. The girl, drugged out, would lie down on it, barely aware of the punter or anything going on around her. If she was not sufficiently responsive, you could see her come down later on bruised and injured.

Every time I passed on my way somewhere, I saw new scars and wounds on the girls. I was amazed at how time sped up for them. The hard men and the drugs put years on them, wiping their dark beauty away and replacing it with a deadly pallor.

Rasheed Street

The shock of seeing Rasheed Street as it is now stayed with me for a long time, even after I had driven down it ten times. Everything beautiful and authentic on this street had been lost. It had been turned into a kind of graveyard without witnesses to its history.

After that first shock I had put off walking down the street like you would avoid bad news. It was months before I got up the courage to walk down it.

Rasheed Street is not just a street. It is a monument to the modern history of Iraq. All major events had started or passed through here. The first Ottoman piece of artillery. The first British armoured car. The Ottoman governor's first horse-drawn carriage. The first motor car to enter Iraq, astonishing the people, making them ask: 'How can it move without horses to pull it?' The first *effendis* had sat at the cafes here to read the newspapers which stole the light away from the mullahs. This is the place where new words and phrases were formed and took their place in the Iraqi dialect: homeland, colonialism, cinema, cigarette and cafe. This is where men first wore trousers instead of the *dishdasha*. This is where the first demonstrations and public disturbances would begin in any stage of unrest, where the first attempt to assassinate Abdel Karim Qassem took place. All things started or passed through here.

If the street had its own history, I had my own history with it. I began to frequent it from early adolescence with my friend Sabai Saadeq Watwat, with whom I afterwards lost all contact. We wore our trousers tight, turned the collars of our shirts up like James Dean, and put cigarettes, which we had bought singly, in the corners of our mouths. We'd go to the Roxy and Rex cinemas and eye up the girls. This was where I got to know the cinema and developed an interest in film.

When I got into the world of culture and books I would stroll down the street clutching books by Sartre, Camus and Colin Wilson with my friend Umran al-Qaysi. Umran always had to run from one side of the street to the other to dodge his many creditors. He showed me Cafe Brazil and pointed out through the window the famous writers Abdel Malik Noori, Fuad al-Takarli and Nezar Saleem, who had started to make their names from the second half of the 40s. They were the first modernists in Iraqi culture. There was a yawning gap between their generation and ours, children of the 60s as we were. We couldn't gather the courage to meet them and sit with them in a cafe like this, way above the level of us street punks.

We would go into the English books and LPs section of Urzady Bek, Baghdad's first department store, to find the assistant watching us closely. Clearly our grunginess marked us as not being the typical customer. And that assistant was right because we went into that shop either to look or to steal. And to watch the famous writer Jabra Ibrahim Jabra, who was a regular there. He would always ask after what was new and leave with a clutch of books and records under his arm.

Later, I hung out on the street every day with Ibrahim Zayyer and Hussain Hasan. We managed to run up debts all along the street with cafe and restaurant owners, including Jebbar Abu al-Sharbat. We would go up a rickety staircase to the upper floor of one of the old buildings on the street of which the upper floor had been transformed into a treasure house of second-hand English books. We found here the novels of Hemingway, Eliot's poems, the sexual adventures of Francoise Sagan. I found among these piles of books one which has always stayed with me – Gaetan Picon's anthology of modern French literature.

In the 70s I started frequenting the street again, this time in the company of Ghaleb Halsa. Ghaleb loved the al-Murabba neighbourhood, which with the influx of Egyptian migrant workers had been transformed into a popular neighbourhood of Cairo, with its carts selling *fool* and *ta'amiyeh,* the cries of the street sellers, and the *jellabas*. Ghaled wanted to imagine that he had never left Cairo, never been cut off from it by moving to a new place of exile. He did not leave the hotel he was staying in until he had sated himself with its atmosphere, and even after that he would come back to soak in its sights and sounds. This neighbourhood was later the backdrop for the first chapter of his novel *Three Faces of Baghdad*. In this book, everything appears ghostly to the narrator, floating and flickering, only taking on solid form when its analogy Cairo appears, Ataba, and al-Azhar and Hussein districts. The narrator needs a great force of effort to remember that he is in Baghdad, and it is not easy because Cairo completely absorbs him.

I still remember the last time I saw the street before my long exile in the middle of 1979. I had spent six months hiding out in an apartment in a modern part of Baghdad, and had just emerged into the open. A man dropped me there in the middle of the street. I stood there, lost and frightened, turning to look for a taxi to take me home to see my young children Naseer and Mays. Something had happened to the street while I was away but I could not work out what until a passer-by said: 'It looks like the brother has been abroad. They made the street one-way about a month ago'.

At that time, Rasheed Street's varied shops, and its vital energy made me forget about its role in history. I experienced the street, its evolution and the changes of its shops, every day. No need to memorise them. The street and me, we went forward together in history, we didn't need to look back.

But I did not break with the street in my many exiles. I would challenge my friends to go down the street, shop by shop. I believe I could remember every single shop from all the time I had misspent there in my youth.

But in exile I left the present and wandered into the history of the street. In many long sessions with the old Baghdadi communist Zaki Kheiri, I followed its evolution from Avenue C under the British to Rasheed Street. He knew every single cafe and who sat where. I read up on it as a solid piece of modern Iraqi history. How it was the first street allowing modern traffic circulation. How it broke up the pattern of the narrow alleyways and markets that led down to the river from Rasafa, and gathered in every section of society, Muslims, Christians and Jews. How its cafes became the haunts of the newly educated middle classes who embodied the new nationalist feeling just as they shaped the Baghdadi dialect, and even formed the character of modern Baghdad.

From the vantage point of the French windows looking out onto our garden in London, I followed the street through the eyes of that great master of the stage, the actor and director Khalil Shawqi. He would roll his eyes from side to side as he recalled in full detail the various stages of a single building on the street and what happened to its people. It was he who drew my attention to the way the cafes, bars and restaurants had gradually shifted from the main square to the Eastern Gate. In Khalil Shawqi's estimation, the street's Golden Age was at the end of the 30s and beginning of the 40s.

My fear for the street found form in a recurring nightmare while I was in exile.

In the dream, there is a patch of the street which I cannot get to for some reason. So secretly I have to enter a house which looks like a fort. There is a man who knows me there who will show me an opening in the wall of the fort, which looks like my grandfather's house in Najaf. I slip through this gap and scurry down some half-collapsed alleyways to get to the rest of the street.

When I returned to Baghdad, I knew what this hidden part of the street was. I got lost in my first days of returning before realising that some upstart bridge had been built in my absence, the Sank Bridge. To me, it seemed as though the street itself was now lost after this brutal incision. It could no longer reclaim its traditional and historic length. By cutting it off from the Mosul Road, it was cut off from its own past and its own people. And there were no witnesses left to tell the full story.

When I came back to the street now, my wariness cut through any joy I might feel. I tried to retrace the steps of that young loafing man who had walked the length of these pavements with a light step, taking in every shop, stopping at every cafe. I was aggrieved that nobody had told me about what had happened to the street while I was away. It felt like someone had squatted in my house and changed everything in it without asking me. Some time later, I met a young man who had no idea of the significance of the street.

'Why are you wasting your time on that rubbish?' he asked. 'I come from Baghdad, I'm thirty years old and I haven't walked down that street more than five times!'

The street no longer meant anything to the younger generations. They had grown up with Mansoor Street and Rubai'i Street. During our absence, the street had gone into a long decline. My friend Hussein Ajeel dated this humiliation to the start of the 90s. The cultural and historic value of the street had collapsed along with Iraq's middle class, which had given it its touch of modernity. The stalls and stands of the marginal classes crowded out the space on the pavements, and the big department stores left for the suburbs.

Months after I first arrived I ventured to walk down the street for the first time, after I had often rushed nervously along it by car, that first time with the words ringing in my ear: 'Something terrible is about to happen!'

Access to pedestrians was still blocked from its middle to the Sank Bridge after the Central Bank was ransacked in the commercial district. Nevertheless, some shops had cautiously opened their doors again, and some kind of life, albeit infused with danger, had returned to the stretch between the square and Martyrs' Bridge. Greengrocers had taken advantage of the blocking off and had installed their carts and turned part of it into a street market. Some of the shops from Sheikh Omar Street selling car parts and machinery had also installed themselves.

The Christian presence, which had lent the street an air of modernity, had also gone. No more Irshak Photo Studios or Cafe Brazil. No Restaurant Masees, or shops selling English tobacco. No more Armenians selling cakes and pastrami. The street had lost that cosmopolitan mix of religions and ethnicities which grouped together all of Iraq. It had become a place of strangers, where nobody knew anyone anymore.

I walked down the street afraid to look up. The old buildings which had given the street its distinct character and authenticity were dilapidated, and the upper floors now just warehouses for goods, devoid of any life. Which of these upper floors had the last of the Ottoman classes gathered to spread rumours against the British as they first entered Iraq? In which cafe had Hussein Rihal sat on his return from Germany by way of India, transmitting Iraq's first socialist thought at the start of the '20s? Where had Jameel Sidqi al-Zahawi waited for Rabindranath Tagore, fantasising that the Indian writer and philosopher had come to pick the summit of knowledge from his Baghdadi peer? Tagore had never come and Zahawi was left to his dreams.

Before I get to the end of the street, I look around to find the back door to the same building where I had made love with my girlfriend just as the Ba'ath were celebrating their first crop of corpses back in the late 60s. The bodies hung just a few metres away at Tahrir Square. The sight in my mind's eye of those putrid, swaying bodies disturbed me whenever I wanted to touch her body.

I turn into Khayyam Street where I had drunk my first glass of beer, and where I heard on the radio the news that had shaken my entire generation: that the charismatic Egyptian president Gamal Adel Nasser had resigned to take responsibility for the Arab defeat in the 1967 war.

It was as though I was wandering in the street seeking not a place but a lost time. Had Ghaeb Tuma Furman predicted this in his novel *Pangs of Labour*? Its hero, returning home from exile just like us, looks for his old house only to find that a new street has wiped it off the face of the map. Really, though, he is looking for his own past in the country that he left.

Iraq Breathes Again

Blood under the Monument

Liberation Square was a focal point for the old regimes and the symbolic place where the monument to freedom stood. Now it is the centre for thieves and killers and those who deal in drugs and fake Viagra from small stalls around the monument. It is they who now rule this place, and have established an authority which is without rule of law. The power vacuum has created a kind of self-centredness. It is those steeped in freedom without constraint that shape this new world and are shaped in turn by it.

Here, where everyone mixes with everyone and nobody knows anyone, the greatest crimes are committed. Cars should negotiate the square quickly and with great care, for no one will come to your rescue if something happens, or ask about you if you are killed.

Underneath the monument, where a mother is depicted mourning her martyred son, we saw the corpses of two young men, barefoot, thrown on some cardboard boxes, covered by other cardboard boxes. They were killed just minutes before we got here. The masked killers did not flee. They simply put their revolvers away and melted into the crowd. Maybe they are here among us, looking at their victims. Blood is still trickling from the impact wounds of the bullets, onto the flagstones of the pavement.

The crowd is debating the reason for the killings. Some attribute it to a blood feud. Other say they were criminals who killed each other when they fell out over the booty. Nobody lifts a finger to move the bodies. The flap of the cardboard box is lifted to look at their faces, then put back again. But nobody recognises them, here in this place where nobody knows anyone else. The bodies stay out under the fierce, bright sun. Everyone, including us, is waiting for someone in authority to come. But nobody does.

A young man about the same age as the two who were killed is selling hand grenades nearby, shouting at the top of his voice: 'Take your revenge. Only 3,000 dinars.'

Not far from him, a middle-aged man sits at another cardboard box selling his wares: Iraqi passports. He swears blind that they are real, not forged, stolen from the state. The would-be purchaser has only to give his photo, and fill in his full name and date and place of birth. The seller takes a stamp out of his coat pocket, assuring the crowd of onlookers that it is a genuine state seal. Then he stamps the passport.

'Safe travels,' he says.

He completes the transaction just as he is, sitting on the ground in the open air, shortcutting the long efforts of standing in queues, in front of a series of fractious bureaucrats, and tortuous procedures in government departments. He also cancels that traditional, accompanying fear for Iraqis: the official answer to an application 'You are forbidden from travel'.

As I watched this chaos, I was certain of one big mistake. We should not have begun with democracy. Before that, we should have built a state with teeth. Everyone afflicted by the chaos and the crime has said the same thing: we Iraqis have never known democracy. We should not have been presented with it in one go. It is counter-productive. The plundering of state resources and then the private colonisation of state posts, the haphazard building everywhere, even in public parks, the killing and looting, all of this is not, as Rumsfeld says, an expression of freedom. It is flight from it. People practise this kind of freedom-with-chaos as a kind of relief from the long self-repression the regime imposed.

The Iraqi experience shows us democracy cannot grow in a bad security environment. What good is freedom of expression, and the right to vote, if you don't have the freedom to go to the market, or freedom of movement, or the freedom to send your children to school without being afraid that they will be kidnapped or killed just because of the ID card they carry? Democracy is a culture as much as it is the function of particular institutions. It needs time to take root as a social value.

Secret Histories

With the fall of the monument and its secret world, Iraqis rediscovered a human peculiarity they had forgotten – telling real stories.

Storytelling is part of what makes us human. Work alone does not distinguish man from the animals. The donkey, after all, has greater capacity for work than the human and by work this diligent animal can adjust to the world of perpetual slavery that the human race has placed him in. What distinguishes us is thought, our unique characteristic. But thought does not forge itself. To achieve, it needs another characteristic: discourse with others, or telling stories that have meaning.

So many stories welled up all at once. Of what happened in the wars and their tragedies, of all the victims of a regime which prevented any mourning at the time, or even decent burial.

When people tell their stories over and over they normally

develop an instinct for how to narrate. They know how to find an opening in the general conversational flow, and once in it they know where they are starting from and where they will finish and can fill the gap in-between with rich, studied turns of phrase.

But the Iraqis have had no experience of this art of narration, not even in whispers. Their natural creative selves are skewed by clashing sentences and false instincts. And I, the listener, am confused. One story meshes with another and the parentheses become entire new stories.

In the family kitchen, amid the clamour of saucepans and the smells of onions frying, my uncle Abdul Amir is telling the story of the time when his son Samer was arrested for being an activist in the Da'wa Party. But suddenly a new story has leaped out from the middle of the first story and truncated it. My brain hurts. I stop him in the middle of the second story with a commanding voice: 'Stop! Stop! Let's go back to the first story.'

We had just reached the point where they had opened fire on Samer as he tried to run away. We went into the garden to escape the din of the kitchen. I wanted to hear a calm voice, and a story that was joined up.

But my uncle had forgotten which story he started telling. All his different stories are vying with each other, seeking like trapped smoke to billow out. His sentences trip over each other from excess of feeling, and his voice keeps rising until it is no longer intelligible. He keeps repeating the phrases 'Well, the main thing is ...' and 'So, what happened was ...', but he has lost what the main thing was, or the whole chain of events and the point of the story. Because each sentence begets a sub-clause, which starts and does not end, but nests another story, which nests another.

There are no listeners here. Everyone wants to speak, everyone has his own story seeking its own audience. I am the perfect listener as I have not lived through any of it. Everyone fights for a piece of me to tell me the worst things they have lived. My two nieces Noor and Sara fight over who gets to tell me stories.

'You've been talking for half an hour. It's my turn!' says one.

'Just let me finish!' the other replies.

Stories of the last war are fresh in people's minds. They told me about the missile launchers concealed in-between houses and in the schools, and the planes which would whine before the bombs fell. They took me to the little cranny where they had hidden during the bombardments. Noor said that her teeth had chattered, and that glasses had shaken on the table, just as they did when the anti-aircraft artillery started up. Just at the moment of explosion she would look in the mirror, and be alarmed by everyone's sweating faces, and their bodies which had shrunk to occupy the least possible amount of space. 'I was so afraid I almost died' became a cliché.

Hamza, not yet four, interrupts with things that bear no relation to reality. The US plane, he thinks, has landed on a branch of a tree in the garden and is shooting at the window, which will be shattered. His mother always rolls up the yellow carpet, he says, and puts down a red one when US planes bomb their garden – 'Zzzzz ... kboom'. War has poisoned our children's minds. It's what they dream of, talk of, play with.

Did the Iraqis invent their stories, or simply uncover them?

The stories existed before they were told. They existed in the secret world that surrounded people, and bound them to each other in a relation of doubt. Only the power is in the know. The people are not, or they are but cannot say. The power knows people's stories. Its real and imagined informers are everywhere. In offices, cafes, mosques and markets, even inside the home. The informer is present wherever two people have lived a story together. Barzan al-Tikriti,

Saddam's half-brother, once boasted 'We hear what the husband whispers to his wife in bed'.

The point of this stifling network of informers was not just a monopoly on knowledge for power. It was also to sow doubt and fear between people, to make it hard to trust your brother or neighbour. Because you would never know if some trifling word you said would be recorded and handed over to the security apparatus.

Creative imagination during this dark period of history was folded in on itself. In fact it split, generating stories and myths of the world of tyranny that surrounded it, this world that you could sense but not see, a world of secret prisons and torture chambers and mass graves.

If all these stories did exist before, where were they hidden? These stories are like smoke seeking a window. They have to be told one day, they have to find a listener, or they will explode. In what painful corner of the Iraqi mind were these stories locked up?

The hidden world which engulfed people and choked them was not only on the outside. It was on the inside too, since they could not relate what they knew even inside their own homes. Storytelling creates a human bond and is also the result of human bonds, but the presence of the informer, even if imagined, poisons the social fabric.

The stories dry up and people become split into two separate selves. There is a real self, buried and decaying, behind another superficial self which talks without meaning what it says, because the creative mind that buries its real stories in the inner world of secrets at the same time fabricates other stories which negate its real ones. Meaningless stories which are designed to show the suspect listener a different personality, other than what he believes. A false, trivial personality, not to be feared, preoccupied only by the everyday problems of the market, those cheating traders, and daily household chores. This artificial self always finds ways to tell narratives with no loose language that could arouse suspicion. With everything he says, the talker wants to show that he is as the Leader wants him, he gives without questioning or complaining. He praises his master as though this nightmare were a gift.

I listen to a conversation between my sister Ilham and her cleaner Um Mohamed in the front garden.

'What's wrong with Mr President that they have to talk about him in this bad way? Didn't he hand out supply cards to us?' asked Um Mohamed.

'That wasn't his money. You are the citizen of an oil-rich country,' replied Ilham.

'Even so, he used to hand out milk himself to children in the schools,' said the cleaner.

'Look at yourself, Um Mohamed,' said Ilham. 'Your husband was crippled in the war and your son, as you say yourself, has served in all the wars. And despite that, you are a cleaner in other people's houses, and don't have a house of your own. And your daughter is a cleaner instead of going to school.'

'It's true that he could have known our real situation earlier. But those around him hid the truth from him,' said Um Mohamed.

I look up from reading al-Jawhari's histories, basking in a winter sun which has warmed my bones, and ready myself to enter the discussion. I'm looking for a simple and direct phrase with which I can touch the mind or heart of this woman – 'Look at your hands'. But then I reflect that time is the only sure way this hypocrisy will be swept away. A day will come when this woman and others like her realise the price they have paid for their pride, and from this realisation could come embarrassment. Embarrassment is where real humanity begins.

In the end, she backed off her defence of Saddam and pleaded ignorance.

'What do I know? I've never seen him. He's never come to our kitchen and opened the fridge door. Even if he came there isn't a fridge to find. We've never seen a penny from him. But everyone was praising him to the skies, including all the intellectuals who read books like sir here,' – she pointed to me – 'and write the newspapers.'

Another time, the director of a government department of irrigation related the problems he had when he went to a conference of experts.

'Official orders came down to us that we should open our address with some words from the president which supported what we wanted to say,' said the official. 'I spent two days sifting through books of his speeches to find a reference to the importance of water, but I couldn't find any. So in the end I settled for a quotation about the importance of saving up for the future. Of course I began my speech with the obligatory cliché – "Mr President, may God preserve him ..." But the director who came after me, a spiteful man, used the same phrase but added "... and protect him". This tiny addition pierced my heart like a needle. Why hadn't I said it like him? Why hadn't it occurred to me? That night, I couldn't sleep when I put my head on the pillow, worried about what might happen at any moment. Maybe some new instructions had been issued to add this new phrase, and I hadn't received a copy of them. But how would I prove that if they interrogated me, or made it a black mark against me?'

This man related this story to me as his son served us lemonade in his *diwan*, the formal greeting room for guests. But he showed no embarrassment. He was telling the story as though it had happened to someone else, and he was just a normal retired civil servant sitting in his *jelabiya* at home.

Continual practice makes the citizen eventually believe in his false self. At the same time, the individual despises himself because he does not say what should be said. His personality crumbles, it is the blueprint that prevails. He gets used to forgetting. Everything that is true and authentic goes into a world of oblivion. As this craven man adapts to the necessities of his position a transformation takes place inside him. The hostility inside him reaches the pitch of hatred, a hatred which eats him up because it is rooted in fear and powerlessness. It drives its owner to yet more submissiveness on the one hand, and a countervailing violence, towards children who get used to their father's blows, or the wife who is blamed for everything she does.

Perhaps this mindlessness will explode in a tangled conflicted web of self-expression once the external repression is lifted.

The Information Revolution

Whole generations of Iraqis confronted the enormous bulk of information that had been hidden from them under one-man rule, with its one-voice media. Now it was all spilling out. In the first days after the invasion, I was watching a TV programme about a mass grave which was said to contain the remains of over 70,000 Iraqis killed during the 1991 uprisings. The relatives of those missing were following directly behind the bulldozers uncovering the earth, looking for any bones or other artifacts that would identify their missing children. At that moment my niece, who was thirteen years old, shouted in her mother's face: 'Did you know about this? Why didn't you tell me, you and Papa?'

Her mother was silent. We knew that parents in that time of lethal silence would not discuss such stories even in front of their children for fear that they might repeat it with their friends at school and someone would come to investigate.

That is why a picture was built in children's heads of a ruler who visited schools and sat with the children on study trips, and listened in raptures when they sang anthems and songs praising him. I also asked my sister, how were you able to repress all those stories for decades?

'Fear gripped us,' she said. 'We no longer trusted even the people closest to us. In the beginning we would hear those stories, and it made us hate them more. But it was a powerless hatred which hurt us, not them. We hated ourselves more because we were so weak. When we found no way out, we learned how to forget. We became addicted to it. We became a mixture of despair, triviality and meaninglessness.'

This secret, repressed world was uncovered to Iraqis all at once. A confusing, overwhelming information revolution broke out. The files of the secret police were suddenly scattered in the streets, within reach of the ordinary citizen. The network of secret informers and their reports was exposed. It had led thousands of Iraqis to their deaths and now it was in the hands of the surviving victims, who in many cases had forgone commercial looting to return to their places of detention looking for leads to their torturers, incited by a desire for revenge.

Victims who had once scuttled from hideout to hideout fleeing their torturers now hunted them down. After the famous statue was pulled down, people began to buy their own records and were shocked at how the regime had known their smallest secrets, even family disputes. Alas, they would also discover that the informer was a close friend or relative.

At the start of 2004 we shot a documentary with a British film crew about some of the victims. A sister of a young woman who had been executed showed us the contents of a file which she was opening for the first time in twenty years. The file contained photos of the girl, who had been executed when she was seventeen years old. She smiles in them with the dazzling innocence of youth. Her girlfriends surround her, including one her age who never leaves her side, and has her arm around the girl's shoulder in a sign of everlasting friendship. This is the girl who shopped her friend, as the sister recently discovered when she looked through the official files. The regime was able to poison the most beautiful of ties. The informer no longer remained separate, professional and paid by the state. He was invisible and everywhere. It could be a colleague at college, a neighbour, a close friend, or even a son, 'the eye of the party in the home', as Saddam put it. People told stories about how one brother's report had led to the execution of another, of the wife who taped her husband complaining that the leader appeared too much on television.

People did not only discover their own secrets, but also the hidden secrets of those who had ruled them for the last thirty-five years. After the people's family secrets had been exposed to the regime, the regime's family secrets became known to the people. The private parties, the extravagances of the president's sons, you could buy them all on DVD sold by shouting stallholders. In a strange street market just outside the old Ministry of Culture there were little boutiques which churned out copies of all this stuff. All those disasters that people had heard about, and which had been denied, were duplicated here so you could be sure they had really happened.

These stories became the raw material for the new Iraqi tabloid press. Before, Iraqis had only heard the miraculous achievements of their leaders, how plentiful food was, how readily available drugs, during the shortages and privations of the sanctions. Back then, they had been forced to swallow these stories like unpleasant medicine.

I was with a TV crew in a hotel when an excitable young man approached me and pulled me to one side.

'You're looking for the secrets of the old regime?' he asked.

I shrugged, to make him explain himself more.

'What do you want exactly?' he continued. 'Secrets from the battlefield? I can bring you top officers who were there – only $50 an interview. Saddam loyalists, who carried out beheadings? Just over here' – and here he pointed to a thick-necked young man sitting patiently nearby – 'is one of them. He can take you to places where group executions were carried out. Field trip and interview just $70. Do you want to meet one of Uday Hussein's mistresses who can tell you how he used to get off on torture and sex at the same time? $100, just don't reveal her face or voice on screen. There are also private films about their family scandals which have never been copied. I can get them for you but' – he smiled the smile of an accomplished trader – 'it'll cost you.'

The Hidden Away Emerge

The missing have emerged from their cubbyholes and hideouts, bearded and thin, with wan faces that have not seen the sun in years. They have come out onto the street, bearing the marks of their pains.

One of them is a relative of mine who hid in the cellar of his house for a total of eleven years. I was shocked when I saw him gaunt and bent over, as though he was ten years older than me, whereas in fact I am five years older than him. The strange thing is, he thinks he is in better health than all of us because he followed a strict diet and has lived half his life as a vegetarian, eating uncooked food.

He lived the eight years of the Iran-Iraq war hidden in the cellar. He set up his life in the cellar like a rat in his warren, in such a way that he did not need light at all. He would watch the street from a tiny opening at ground level, seeing only people's feet, not their faces.

'I know how to tell people from their feet, and to know their personalities from the way they walk,' he said. 'I know my friends from my enemies by their shoes.'

He arranged his hideout so that he had an extra small hole that he could just fit into if he curled up with his head between his knees, if a stranger came into the house, closing the opening with a wooden panel perforated by an air vent.

At first only his mother knew of the hideout and on the rare occasions when he emerged into the house proper, he would wear grubby military fatigues as if just back from the front. He wanted to turn this slow death to some use, so he collected medical books and tried to carry out medical research. His perseverance amazed me as he showed me fat notebooks which he had not managed to publish. There was a dictionary of herbs and their healthy and harmful properties, a thick book entitled *Black Poison* about the dangers of drinking tea and another one about garlic. The biggest of all was a compendium of plants with medicinal value. In spite of all this medical learning, he seemed to me to be in the worst health of all of us. His back was curved terribly and his teeth were rotten.

He told me that he had not yet got used to life above ground. His connections to people remained weak and shrouded in suspicion. When there was too much going on and too many people around, he would get dizzy and retreat once again to his safe cellar, which he knew every corner of. Outside was still dubious, scary. He didn't trust anyone apart from his unmarried aunts. And they had to follow the science of the cellar and prepare vegetables, uncooked, and no meat. Lots of garlic and very little salt. Their health deteriorated quite quickly but he stubbornly persisted, ignoring everyone else's warnings.

He asked me if I had ever taken stimulants. I said yes, once, but I had become dizzy from overexcitement. He began to urge me to take sexual stimulants which could perform miracles. But when I asked him if he had tried them, he replied that he had never been with a woman in his life and he did not want to get married because things were still so unsettled.

'Instead of these huge volumes on onions and garlic, why don't you write about your experience of nine years in the cellar?' I asked him.

He dismissed the idea, saying the situation was not yet stable.

'But you could write it for yourself, and delay publication until later,' I said.

He rejected the idea, afraid that the Ba'ath would seize power again and get hold of his papers. Was he really frightened of the Ba'ath, I wondered to myself, or of confronting his own experience?

Hassan was one of the missing who came out of the cellar. But there are others who have not, and will not ever come out – or back. The windows of their rooms on upper floors are still open so that they can look out onto the street, water glasses on the ledge where they left them, their long-sleeved shirts, so neatly ironed by their sisters, hanging waiting for them. Everything around connotes them.

In the house of a communist painter, I saw the picture of a young man set on a chair between his two parents who talked about him as if he was present with us. And here was the young man's easel and colour palette, and the painting of the garden he had left unfinished.

These missing people have not 'died', they simply 'have not come back so far'. The simple reason they have not died is because there is no grave to visit. Every now and then people 'discover', from the urgency of their need and the strength of their fantasies, a hidden prison on a farm, or underneath a government building, or in the cellars of one of the palaces. Rumours fly like lightning and the relatives of the missing rush to the place. A country mother almost running, her arms stretched out in front of her and her black *abeya* flying behind her.

Once there was a rumour about a secret prison right in the underpasses beneath Liberation Square, and fathers and mothers of the missing rushed there. In the tunnel, two young men were stubbornly trying to rip off an iron door.

'We're coming, we're coming,' one of them kept shouting. The echo of his own voice would come back at him and he would imagine that there was someone answering his call. But at the end of a long, hard, disturbing day, nobody came out. Nobody answered the calls of the would-be rescuers.

A Visit to the Prison

I went with a TV crew to Hakimiya prison. One of its former inmates had volunteered to show us around. He had not been there since he had been released and said he felt the same fear as when he first entered it, blindfolded.

A few months before, I had gone to the prison on Robben Island where Nelson Mandela had spent twenty-six years. A former prisoner had been with me then too, a man who had spent seventeen years there. But he too had not been back, not even to the island which tens of thousands of tourists now visit, for over ten years. He remained bearded as he had been in prison. He was pale and extremely sensitive to the light. He didn't smile much and was not a happy man – he had wasted his youth there. As they were getting on the boat his wife had asked him: 'Are you sure you can do this?'

'Of course I'm sure,' he barked back, as much for himself as for her.

He was free. But still his voice quivered when he told us how he had been taken there on this same boat that we were now on. Then he had been bound in chains and held below. His voice became shakier when we got off at the quay. He looked round as though expecting a blow from a policeman's stick. The prison guards apparently would line up on both sides of the quay and form a corridor the new arrivals had to pass down, beating them badly to break their will and make them afraid.

He was panting and looked around. Each time he tried to speak his voice would crack. In spite of that he controlled himself and began to breathe deeply. But when we went inside he started to talk about the moment he had to surrender his normal clothes and receive prison issue clothing. His years of torture surged all at once, and his voice collapsed. This strong man collapsed in the arms of his wife. At that moment cell door swung shut.

Here in Iraq, his 'colleague' inmate, who had spent five years in al-Hakimiya, led us along corridors so dark we could not see where we were going. He tried to guide us by voice.

'Three steps to the left. One more! You'll get to a staircase,' he said. We could not find our way forward. His voice came to us from down the corridor. 'I know these corridors by heart. I went down them many times blindfolded.'

He was ahead of us, retracing his old footsteps. We stumbled in the dark behind him. The darkness made it seem like we were not just in a building, but a secret world, like someone was watching us and the ex-prisoner in the gloom.

I lit a piece of paper to light our path down the passage to the staircase. Suddenly we could see his face, lit up like a bronze mask. I was feeling my way forward with my feet in the faint light. I could hear him ahead of us.

'When I first came down this passage, I was blindfolded. There seemed to be guards on all sides warning me, "Careful, a gap!" When I slipped and fell they laughed.'

By the time we got to the last corridor, we were using each other's voices to navigate, listening to them bouncing on the walls and echoing back. When we finally reached the strong light at the end of the staircase, we looked at each other to make sure we were still all there.

Our guide was quiet, saying only: 'Here ...' His voice trailed off. He had lost his strength, just like his colleague from Robben Island. He slid back the bolt on the iron door of the cell which made a screaming noise. He apologised in a strangled voice. His breath quickened and he showed us into the cell where he had spent five years. 'Here.'

He stopped talking altogether as though he could see in the remains and the gloomy, grey light that thin crouching man, turned towards the door as he opened it, that ghost frightened by the sound of the bolt sliding back, that had been himself.

We also saw the torture chambers. The hooks in the roof, the nails on the walls, the cables for giving electric shocks. How much suffering had happened inside these mute, tight-lipped walls? We saw a back chamber where they took their breaks from torture sessions, surrounded by refrigerators where they stored the bodies.

Some time later, I saw a DVD of a mass torture party held in one of the chambers of this prison, hosted by Watban al-Tikriti, Saddam's half-brother, and his son. An iron door opens and a great mass of people are pushed through it, more than fifty people. Their clothes are rags. Their hands are tied behind their backs, all of them on the same rope. They had hardly got into the chamber than they were surrounded by a cluster of guards and beaten madly.

I was surprised at the zeal of the guards. I looked for one among them who was holding back. But fear of their superiors, and that the tables could be turned, fed their frenzy. Their own panting almost masked the screaming of the victims. To keep them warm, Watban was inventive, lining them up in two ranks and passing the prisoners down the line one by one. They now beat just one man at a time, not stopping even when he had fallen to the ground, motionless, whimpering. The camera zoomed in on the body on the ground so we could follow his last seconds. I never ceased to be amazed at the nerve of the regime. It recorded its worst crimes. Why did they do that? The implementers informed their superiors, and highest of all, the Leader himself, of the abominations committed under their leadership. At what moment in his day did the Leader free himself from the cares of state to watch films like this? At breakfast? A quick break in the working day? Just before bed? As he reached out to touch the body of his mistress? When?

Another time I saw a video of a mass execution of deserters from the army. There was a crowd of people on one side, and a row of blindfolded men on the other. They had been broken by the wait. Only one of them had his head up, trying to look round to catch some last scene of life through his blindfold. Maybe he wanted to say something. But the shots rang out.

I heard ululations from the crowd, as though drowning out shrieks from relatives. In the end a man in civilian clothes went forward, bent over, and shot each one in the head, without turning round to the crowd.

All this secret past had come to life. People who before denied what they had seen with their own eyes now went to the other extreme, weaving a story with their imaginations that exceeded even what had happened. Just opening a conversation with a taxi driver, or a neighbour, could bring stories like this streaming out. The past dominated the present, even though the present was so brutal itself.

Return of the Dead

The dead all woke up at once. The mass graves which previously people had not known existed or which they were afraid to talk about, were now uncovered. Relatives ran to the sites and scrabbled in the earth to find bones that would lead them to the remains of their missing loved ones. I was in Najaf two days after a mass grave was discovered at Hilla, nearby. Saddam has sown the land of Iraq with killing fields. Instead of digging for ancient treasures, or stores of oil, people wanted to dig for the remains of their children. At Hilla, an old man wanted to purge himself of a secret he had stored up for years, afraid. So he stated he had witnessed soldiers digging a trench. His story spread and soon a line appeared of corpses that the Engineer of Death, Ali Hassan al-Majid, had lined up. The killers had got tired of digging graves, and of taking the bodies somewhere else, so they simply bulldozed the corpses into the trench. These death finds had become a main preoccupation of the people. My friend was worried about digging foundations for his new house: 'What if we find a grave with the body of my missing brother in it?'

My uncle, like many others, received a piece of paper informing him that his son had been executed, in his case for connections to the 'collaborationist' Dawa party. But he did not believe the paper because he never got the conclusive proof of the death: the body. As long as there was no grave, his missing son was missing.

My uncle toured the city to look at the notice boards with the masses of photographs and lists of names for a sign that would lead him to news of his son, who was executed at the end of the 70s. He had a feeling that he was still alive. Maybe he had fled to another country and would come back now with others who had been in hiding. Days went past and he never stopped weaving an illusion for himself, which both made him feel better and tortured him. He always said to me as he looked at the lists: 'Where is his body if he is dead?'

The killers did not apologise or ask for pardon. In spite of that, many of the relatives simply forgot about them, consigned them to the past and the judgment of the Lord. More important for them than the past, and its feuds, and the search for the killers, was the search for the victims.

They did not apologise as people who were sorry would, or declare any contrition or give any sign that they would not go back to how they were, or indeed how they still were. They were addicted to power and terror. They were alive, they walked around with the same attitude, the same arrogance towards the victims. But the families avoided them, and consigned them to the past.

This unspoken tolerance took root without any law constraining it, or anyone asking for it. Its duration and scope were not defined: 'Until when? And how far?' It evolved spontaneously, without any conscious decision because people like my uncle were peaceful, and more concerned with their children: where were they, and how could they find them?

To answer this question, the bones of the dead became a traded commodity. There was effectively connivance between the family of the victim and an anonymous do-gooder, who would travel great distances bringing bones with him and announcing he had found the victim. The family who had failed to find anything in their long searches would touch and kiss the bones. In the end, they have to have a grave for their loved one. The do-gooder would consent to accept the consideration set aside for his efforts, although it was clearly understood that he was acting purely from the love of God.

But not only tolerance. There were also victims who emerged, carrying blood that wasn't even dry. They would emerge thirsty from their hiding places, because they had not yet drunk the cup of revenge. They would point with their shaky fingers at the perpetrators and say one word, over and over: 'Give us his blood to drink. His blood.'

With some victims back, and a complete absence of law or punishment, a new revenge movement arose targeting those killers who had been the pawns, the implementers, because the high-ups had already escaped, taking their wealth with them. These acts of spontaneous revenge met the people's need desire for retribution while the authorities did nothing. Those demanding revenge held the names of the killers between their teeth, indifferent to any principle of term limits. They waited for the moment they could wash blood away with blood.

In Sadr City, revenge teams toured the district like census committees. They carried death lists with them with the names, addresses and crimes of those on it. They went round to the houses of former Ba'athists who in the old days had pointed out to the punishment squads where the houses of army deserters were. They knocked on the door politely like government officials, and paid the families 25,000 dinars to cover the funeral for their son, who would be killed at the time they had fixed.

With the new revenge killings, a new flood of corpses arrived at the Holy City of Najaf to be buried. I went out into the bazaar to distract myself, but the long lines of the funeral processions block my vision. Not to mention to ocean of graves behind me in Wadi Salaam. A storm whipped up, driving dust into my eyes, getting under my skin and getting into the goods I'm just about to buy. It blocks up the nose, almost choking me. I feel it heavy and salty in the water I drink. I feel it cracking between my teeth when I eat and bite on a lump of meat.

Fragmented Stories

The Iraqis see, and hear, and live limitless stories from their past, which has not passed. But stories of the past are supplanted by those of the present. Criminals who had been in prison on long sentences had become kings of the back streets, ruling there in place of the authorities. My nephew and guide Yasser and I drove around in a second-hand Brazilian car in order not to excite the lust of car thieves. Every quarter of an hour some story passes in front of me without a beginning or end.

A man with a gunshot wound being chased by another man. I'll never know how and why he was shot or what happens later. The guiding rule here is that you just keep going, to save your own skin in a country ruled by the holy law of the jungle. A woman shouts for help in the street and a car speeds the wrong way up the street, firing warning shots. No one goes to save the woman. Armed men break into a house as we pass. We will never know who they are, why they have broken in and what they found there.

In normal circumstances what happens to you, what you witness, imprint themselves in your memory. The present is linked to the past, informed by experience. But in these days there is no cumulative experience to call on. What is happening is so strange there is no connection to, or precedent in, the past. Also no event gets to run its course in time, to be a present which then becomes part of the past that informs a new present with its new events. Every event is only in the present, and there is no continuity to turn this present into a past. Instead it gets ruptured in the middle by another event which starts before the first one finishes, which effaces it before it is complete. We live a series of disjointed stories which form a continuous present.

At that time I was thinking about making a film about this life of the present by taking tours in the back of taxis. I wanted to draw a cab driver into relating what he saw as he drove around, and what his imagination fashioned with that. These stories would form the spoken narrative but would be completely divorced from the visual narrative, which would be a montage of random events, with no obvious connection to each other, or the soundtrack. I was testing out the idea before shooting, and this is what happened.

First the driver had tried to establish my identity. Then after a period of silence he asked: 'Did you see what happened in that building?'

'Which building?'

'The one we just passed.'

'No, I didn't notice,' I said. I had been watching the other side of the street where a car had just mounted the pavement and it seemed to me like it might explode. 'What happened then?'

'Now they've started ripping the tiles off it, after they plundered all the chairs and tables and computers, and then the doors and windows and electrical cable,' he said.

'So what?' it was on the tip of my tongue to say but at that moment a wailing ambulance heading straight for us distracted our attention. I started thinking about the wounded that must be inside it, and about the gunman who was trying to open a path for himself in the traffic jam by shooting in the air. But he could not clear a path because just then an American armoured vehicle emerged from a side street and took up a position in the middle of the road, bringing all traffic down to a crawl.

The driver, a middle-aged man, had forgotten his story.

'All this, and then they're surprised that Iraq has gone mad!' he said.

His story had been disrupted by a new story which had broken out in front of us. He turned to me angrily and started telling a new story.

'Yesterday at this junction, just before dusk ...' I turn to look at the junction, my ear still with the taxi driver, waiting for his story, for the past he relates to be brought into the present. But he did not continue his new story because American soldiers had now got out of their armoured jeeps and were setting up a temporary road block. One of them had got out of a Hummer and was pointing his rifle at us, shouting, apparently panicked: 'Back! Back! Back!'

'There's something happening up front,' said the driver, sticking his bald pate out of the window and pointing to some place ahead of us. 'A booby trapped car has gone off.' A column of black smoke was being blown east by the wind.

I recall at that moment that something shook the driver's speech, clearly another explosion. It seemed like different times were clashing at the same moment, between the driver's truncated story of what had happened there the day before and the shouting of the American soldiers and the explosion. All these events were bunched up into present time, not sequential. I summoned all the past inside me that I could find, trying to live through these moments with a narrative very different from that of the driver, that was now saying: 'All this is because we killed kings of the line of the Prophet Mohammed. All this, and that infidel Saddam was foretold in the Qur'an.'

How to find meaning in this present, when I am living this vehement clash of three different temporal dimensions? A past that does not want to pass, throwing the entire weight of thirty-five years of a culture of violence into the present, a present where violent groups and individuals have stolen authority and parcelled it out among themselves, a future where every player wants to mould the state, or non-state, that is coming.

All of these times are unfolding now, in the street, in front of my eyes, just as they are building a meaningless chaos inside me. Every new happening poses new questions, when what I need is answers.

At night there are even more questions because I am in my bed, in the pitch black, and can only hear, not see. A woman's scream pierces the night, followed by heavy silence. We will never know who screamed and what happened to her. A quick snatch of gunfire, and we will never know who is the killer and who the victim. The scream and the shots trigger images in my mind, which loom larger and proliferate in the quiet of the night, and the din of my imagination.

Morning comes, and the resumption of life at its most basic level, busy and mundane, effaces the imaginings of the night and what they might mean. I forget about the scream and the shots, and who the killer and victim were. Then our neighbour Um Hassan knocks at the door urgently, warning my sister not to send her daughters to school because another child on our street has been kidnapped this morning.

Every new event finds nothing in my experience to match it. It comes as a surprise with no warning, and is ruptured before it is finished. What I live and see catches me unawares, and this is why past experience cannot help me to explain what is happening to us. Even if I could bring this experience out from the caves of memory into the light of day, there will be no time to find the link with what is happening right now, before it is broken off by something else. So all these events simply clash and do not create meaning. And over time, this build-up of meaningless occurrences drives us mad.

Mad Men in a Mad World

In a mad world, the insane found their true reality after they had taken leave of their senses.

There was no real reason to detain them, since quite simply there was no longer a sane world from which the mad had to be isolated. I met the Norwegian doctor Olaf at the offices of the Red Cross who before the war had been working with Rashad Mental Hospital. Now he was distraught, seeking help from any quarter to get back some 2,000 mentally ill patients who had fled the hospital in the thick of the fighting. He looked for them in vain. They had escaped from their prison when the guards had left, and dispersed in the streets where madness had now become the norm.

Now that mad power had disappeared, power and authority itself became the preoccupation of the mad. In the chaos of traffic, and the tumult that accompanied it, I found a madman organising the traffic in the middle of a public square. Wanting to remind us of the now absent authority of the state, he had donned, above his tattered rags, a traffic policeman's cap and put a whistle in his mouth. Nobody asked or knew where he had found the cap and the whistle. Soldiers and policemen had been abandoning their uniforms and all their official trappings all over the place, as these now held no value for anyone except souvenir collectors.

The cap and whistle define his role for this man. He leaps suddenly from place to place amid the traffic. He blocks a driver who is going the wrong way and bangs his fist on the bonnet of a car which had stopped sidelong in the middle of the street, blocking the traffic. Despite the mockers, he imposed some order on the street. Amid the chaos and madness, the irrationality of people in general or their indifference, this madman seemed to be the only sane man, who had done something useful.

The TV showed another madman, from Kirkuk I think, who had

pillaged a state bank along with the others. He did not smuggle out money out as the others had done. Instead, he stood on the steps of the bank and showered himself with banknotes, as though washing off his poverty. In the business district of Karada, in the middle of Baghdad, another madman crossed the street in large strides, a look of grim determination on his face as though he was a businessman closing the deal of the century. He held the sole of his shoe to his ear like a mobile phone and shouted: 'Just send the goods. Now'.

After he finished his 'call', he put his shoe back on and walked off without turning round.

There is no way to hear what the madmen say as they walk barefoot on the searing hot pavements talking to themselves. The street is too dangerous, in our car we just have to keep going and not stop. We recognise the madmen by their actions, not their words. Their inappropriate actions and weird gestures tell us they have started arguing furiously with themselves because no one listens to their words of wisdom.

A third madman has daubed himself with car oil and sits washing in the fountain. Water calms madmen, giving them a moment of happiness, feeling the world flowing by, and their own movements against the water, like fate. That is why fountains were used as a cure in the mental hospitals of Aleppo. In the infernal heat of Baghdad, the sane use water as a relief from madness. The mad use it as a relief from a mad world.

A mad beggar sits in front of an ice-cream shop on a little stool. He refuses money but asks the charitably minded for an ice cream, specifying the flavour. Someone in the queue told me he guessed the man must eat no less than thirty ice creams a day. When we bought one for him he declined it, saying he had eaten forty-six ice creams so far that day and was feeling bloated.

At the shrine of Imam Ali in Najaf I saw madmen grasping the wooden lattices of the tomb. One of them was looking all around him, stunned, in rapture at all the lights refracted across the mirrors and the crystal of the chandeliers, and the press of bodies kissing the gold on the tomb. Some of them fall into a trance which can be the path to health, or to a silent madness that leads to death. One of them was seized by an epileptic fit, shouting out from some pain in his head.

His village friends tied him roughly to the latticework. It was the last intervention for him. Whoever is not cured here will only be cured by the grave. The sheer number of mentally ill here and their bizarreness caught me off balance.

The madness here is clear and transparent, for the madman does not conceal his condition but breaks convention by declaring it to those passing by. He is on the edge of a wider world.

Din itself is enough to cause madness. The din of hundreds of generators, large and small, churning away in houses, streets and markets, the din of American planes flying low overhead in the middle of the night, the din of bullets and bombs from early morning on. All these sounds are merely the oral register of daily violence in this land of crisis.

The din transforms itself from sound to substance, a substance which has the density and weight of concrete, which makes the very air press on your senses and on your mind. When the sound of the generators stops, it is replaced by a silence which unnerves me, puts me off balance. I float weightless in a void, an internal and external void. I cannot grasp anything. Things slip away from me since the substance that bound us, the din, has gone.

The Ibn Rushd Hospital for Mental Illness gives an idea of the sheer noise that has engulfed Iraq. One of my reporters interviewed a housewife there, aged thirty-five, who said: 'The noise perturbs me so much I have started to feel it even when it is not there. When there are loud noises like American planes or generators, I cannot stay calm. And my panic carries to my children, who scream.'

Amnesia in such circumstances is both an illness and a cure. Another patient, forty-year-old Khaled Mohammed, told my reporter: 'I forget such basic things it becomes embarrassing at work. I get a screaming headache whenever there are loud noises like airplanes, or generators, or the sound of mortars and explosions and rockets'.

Sometimes, there was madness in the nature of some of the family feuds I saw. People who were not able to handle their own hostility to the regime released their angst and anger into family feuds about farmlands, or marriage and divorce. There wasn't a single extended family which did not have some feud which degenerated into sheer evil. And short of that, there were fights about what food to eat, what TV programmes to watch, who could leave the house when, who could wear what shirt. The shouting would break out suddenly, without any preliminaries.

An acquaintance of mine gave his wife a bad black eye. The next day, he went to her family's house to beg her to return, saying: 'I can't live a single day without her.'

The strange thing is she did not even keep him waiting. She packed her clothes in her little case, quickly and silently, put on her *abeya* and left. And yet she knew the same thing would happen again in a couple of days. Torturer and victim were bound together by mutual need, in some weird sadomasochistic relationship.

A friend of mine suggested that Iraq's oil wealth should be deposited in Swiss banks, provided Switzerland would guarantee to accept Iraqis at its sanatoria to cure them of all the mental illnesses spurred by the regime of organised madness.

Across the bridge, on the road leading to the Republican Palace on a traffic island between two roads, another madman sat on a gilded chair with a high back. He wore a silver smoking jacket over his gaunt frame, and sunglasses which made his face obscure and a little alarming. He held a cigar in the style of Saddam and greeted the public in exactly his manner.

'Say hello to those absent for us,' people would say to ese madmen.

Inside the Palace

An Egyptian journalist Mona Abdel Azeem and I went to see Saddam's palace, although both of us thought the Americans would not let us in: 'Praise to God, changer of things.'

The driver we have taken to get us to the entrance hesitates. He says he is thirty-five years old, from a third-generation Baghdad family, and yet has not even seen the road which leads to the palace. He trembles even as we approach the start of the road because in the time of Saddam, the guards would already be zeroed in on us. He gets more worried as we get closer.

'Are you sure you will be able to get in?' he asks.

To get past the front gate, we were using the pretext that there was a press conference, although we know it has been cancelled. After to-ing and fro-ing, the American guard at the gate agreed to let us in, provided he could use our satellite phone to call his girlfriend. We agreed so he opened the road to us, and sent another soldier to accompany us.

We walked through the reception area, dizzy and surprised. It's hard to believe that Saddam's palace has been turned into the American military headquarters. American officers bustled inside the chambers and in the corridors in their protective uniforms. They thumped the marble floors with their boots – we are here – and didn't feel any embarrassment. The world, after all, is their electronic village. We, the locals, were lost.

The American officer in charge of communications said: 'Even we don't believe that we are here.'

I wandered around, looking over furniture which held not an atom of style, nor an ounce of decorum. It was a mixture of the passion of dictators for formal pomp and vulgar taste, belonging to rural classes who have arrived in the city and developed a passion for things bereft of their context, just because they were golden and luxurious. Every chair had backs which were gilded and moulded, rising to a crown which was much higher than the heads of the audience. The arms of the chairs make you nervous rather than comfortable. They spiral up at the end, trapping your hands in the metaphorical fist of power.

There was a chair in the middle different from the rest, at a distance from the other chairs. This is the Leader's chair. This is where he met world leaders, from Africa and Asia and Europe. I recalled his relaxed way of sitting, how he would stretch out his legs to their full extent and splay his arms out on the chair to take up the most space possible, while his guests would be cramped into a narrow space. His way of looking into the eye of his interlocutor, forcing him to lower his head and look away, to listen more than he talked. The ever-present camera, with him even to the moment of death when he turned to it as though he was still in absolute power, even if it was now a fantasy. In the middle of this room is a Victorian-style table with lions poking out from the sides, their fangs bared, seeking to devour those sitting nearby.

Rulers love lions because they give them a greater sense of power and force. The lion embodies both majesty and power, the two characteristics joined together in Saddam's famous phrase 'potency'. The lion was a symbol of rule in ancient Babel, while with the

Assyrians power came to be represented by both the lion and the centaur, a combination of grace, power and wisdom. In the Islamic era palace columns were supported by lions' heads, especially in Andalus.

I once visited a deposed Arab head of state in Damascus and was amazed at the number of lions that were stuffed into his small house. There were sleeping lions, lions with their heads raised on guard, others standing watchfully. Just by the doors there were lions waiting to pounce to defend their cubs. I could feel the silent roar of the lions around me as I talked to him. When he noticed my attention to them he explained proudly that he had collected them while on repeated trips to Africa, and that they were among the few possessions he had carried with him into exile. The lions gave him the illusion of still being in power, here in this small room where his portrait hung on the wall between two swords.

Real live lions had a special place in Saddam's gardens. One of his guards later told the story of his dilemma with them.

'When US planes bombed the palace,' he said, 'they wounded one of these lions. I was in a frontline position as the American soldiers advanced, and behind me was the lion, roaring from pain. He could have leaped on me at any moment. But I could not fire on him for fear of reprisal from the Leader, who loved his lions more than his guards.'

The father passed down his love of the big cats to his eldest son. Uday would attend parties and go to clubs with a leopard in tow. He would reassure frightened onlookers that the leopard only attacked on his command. In fact, he took pleasure from spreading fear wherever he went – son of a lion, master of a leopard.

At the entrance to the main hall, and also perhaps in the information room, where poets who had sung the praises of the Leader would be given their stuffed envelopes, there was a collection of gilded mirrors. Saddam saw himself copied and cloned to infinity in these rows of facing mirrors.

But now a barber called Khalil had gathered them to use them. American officers would sit on the seat Saddam had sat on, Khalil would cut their hair, and the photographer would take their picture in the Leader's chair, amid the mirrors he had now vanished from without trace.

We exited the reception chamber to enter the symbolic centre of the palace, the landmark seen from afar – a dome with four statues of Saddam in different costumes. In one, he wears the headdress of a warrior, perhaps posing as the seventh-century Islamic conqueror Khaled ibn al Waleed, 'the Sword of Islam', a fellow Tikriti. In another he wears the helmet of an Iraqi soldier, a spearhead in the middle of it. In another, an Arab *uqqal*, and in the fourth one his head is uncovered.

All four heads are enlarged to at least ten times their natural size. They face each other, so that Saddam is effectively turning his back to the rest of the world.

So it was not the river which interested him, nor the rich gardens, nor even the bodyguards who were stationed in every corner of the palace. None of that interested him. He wanted to look at himself. He was his own mirror. Those around him had to watch the faces of the four Saddams, and beat back their sense of fear at the man who held the dome.

Everything which pointed to Saddam was here. His statues, his chairs, his mirrors. The intensity of his presence, even when absent. But he himself was gone, in hiding somewhere. His ghost would haunt the city until he was arrested or killed, with all that brought in terms of surprises. Nobody felt safe as long as he was still around.

'Of course he'll come back. He knows his friends from his

enemies now,' said my nephew Yasser. 'He's a genius at escaping from defeat.'

He led me through a crowd and as we passed a lorry, he suddenly said: 'What would you say if Saddam opened that door, said hello to us, then closed it again?'

Every day I would hear a rumour that he had passed here or there, dressed in an *uqqal*. That he had stopped by a drinks stall, taken a glass of juice, and then said to the stallholder: 'Keep hold of that picture of mine, I'll be back soon.'

There were people who swore they had seen him bent in humility at the dawn prayer at the prestigious Nida Mosque, the construction of which he had personally overseen in the 90s. He had a long beard, and after prayers would vanish into thin air. One day a guard at the Red Cross came to see his bosses, swearing blind that an ambulance had stopped at the door of his house after passing up and down the street twice. Saddam, a *keffiya* wrapped round his face, had got out. He wanted to sleep in the house that night but then had suddenly decided, sensing danger, that he would just drink a draught of water instead. Wrapping his *keffiya* around his head again, he had told the guard: 'Tell your superiors that you have seen me, just as I am now, and that I am not afraid. I am touring the city as its president.'

The guard told the story in deep gasps, as though he had seen the king of death vowing to return from the grave.

Every now and then the Americans would cordon off a place he had passed through, or a house he had been in and had only just left, or a mosque where he had stopped to pray.

This is a man who became addicted to danger, to constant movement between hideouts, during his underground work. Normal life came to disturb him. He would be filled with doubt whenever he met any man outside his narrow gang of comrades.

Even when he ruled the country, he would move between dozens of palaces, hidden from the public, catching even the people closest to him unawares as he left his palace for an unknown place, a new room, because he did not trust even his own bodyguards.

His cousin Ali Hassan al-Majid, the 'chemist', learned this cautiousness from him just as he had learned his brutality. I saw him in a video once making an inspection tour of the dead during the 1991 intifada. In the clip, he lands in a helicopter. After looking over the corpses of those executed, one by one, asking their ages and names, he walks towards two cars that are waiting for him. He approaches one of the cars, and a guard holds the door open for him. But then at the last second he changes his mind and gets into his guards' car instead.

During wars and bombardment, Saddam would drop in on ordinary citizens' houses to spend the night, or even just a few hours. Now here he is again practising this constant shifting between houses, leaving them at first light with a generous sum for having put him up. He had always lived on the run, and in fact had imprinted this style on an entire country. The country was in a continual state of alarm and emergency. His people too were constantly on the run, fleeing from one place to the next, fleeing themselves to adopt new selves wherever they were.

They always had other selves, different from their original ones. Just like their Leader, who was confused in his own identity, who sometimes would dress like a peasant with his *uqqal*, at other times the foot soldier in the trenches or the field commander in the operations room, every now and then a cigar-smoking technocrat. He drew his own legend in the minds of an entire generation who still talk about him with a mixture of fear and admiration.

My nephew Yasser was born and lived his whole life under the regime. He knows that Saddam executed his aunt, and as a result his father spent half his life on the front line in the wars, and that another aunt and uncle fled the country. Despite that, Yasser does not hide his admiration for Saddam. He remembers all of his speeches, imitates his voice and body language when he delivers one of his speeches.

'He was our father, our leader, our hero. He was the only man who could make us feel fear,' he said.

On the anniversary of the 14 July Revolution, which ended the monarchy in 1958, I conducted an experiment into the knowledge base of the younger generation which had grown up in Saddam's shadow. I asked them about the July revolution and Abdel-Karim Qassem. One of them, seventeen-year-old Sabeeh Ahmad, replied: 'Yes, I've heard of the July revolution. Isn't that the one Saddam Hussein carried out?'

'No,' I replied, 'it was Abdel-Karim Qassem'.

'The man Saddam tried to assassinate?' he asked.

'Yes, but he failed,' I said.

'Yes, and then there was the counter coup in October in which Saddam was arrested, and then he fled from prison,' Yasser continued.

The history of the country both before and after Saddam has come to revolve around him. For Yasser's generation, Saddam is the key to history, the fashioner of its great events. They know no leader other than him.

After his fall, as political leaders proliferated, the generation which had got used to one charismatic leader was lost. For them, leaders who courted the love of the people were weak.

'We are not fit for democracy,' this school of thought would say. 'We need a strong ruler who can terrorise the people and instil the law by force.'

Freedom was exhausting for a generation trained to wait for orders before acting. When they faced themselves and their own wishes, they were afraid of their freedom and repeated what Alyosha says in *The Brothers Karamazov*: 'a burning need to find someone to surrender to'. Surrender to some power, a dominating charismatic leader. If he could be less brutal than Saddam, or, even if he is just as brutal, if he could be fair, and spread his brutality without favour. And if this restless soul couldn't find a maximum leader, how about a religious authority to issue *fatwas* and be obeyed? The main thing for this mentality is to be rid of the frightening and depressing burden of freedom.

Saddam understood very well this fear and submission. His people kept alive the myth of his return to rid them of the anarchy of freedom. His followers watched news of him on the run and were convinced he would come back like the conquering much-loved hero.

'He could come into this house at any time, with his guards, just as he used to do in other houses in previous wars,' said my friend the writer.

One hot morning Baghdad lit up with gunfire. I had a young man in the house with me from a village near Tikrit, a former Ba'athist who had served in Saddam's personal guard. I asked him, as the firing moved closer to us: 'Are there any soccer games on today?'

Previous experience had taught us that when firing could be heard not only in one neighbourhood, but all over the city, it was not fighting but an announcement: 'There is important news.'

As it turned out, the Iraqi soccer team had not just won a great victory. So I said: 'Well, then, they've caught Saddam.'

The young man shot back: 'Impossible.'

'Why?' I asked.

'There is no master of escape like him. He would kill himself before they caught him,' he said.

We could not check the news immediately because of a power

cut. But when we started the generator and turned on the TV we saw the press conference podium empty. Then Bremer appeared and the then Iraqi Foreign Minister Adnan Pachachi and before he got to the microphone Bremer said: '*We got him!*'

Saddam appeared on screen with a scraggly beard and wild hair, forgetting the camera for the first time in his life as the US soldier inspected his hair and mouth. At this, the ex-Ba'athist fled from the sight, banging his fist on the table: 'Why didn't you fight to the death, like your sons and grandsons?'

His hero had let him down. His ideals were shattered.

Iraq's Literati

Books and Writers

A few days after I had revisited all the places I knew, I needed to revisit the world of books. I went up into the loft of the family house with two young men from our neighbours to bring down the boxes of books I had hidden there before going into exile.

I moved the furniture back to get at these treasures, which now had dust on their covers and pages. The commotion disturbed it, tickling my nose with a sneezing, but I carried on sorting through them. And as on every occasion when I find myself piling up the books around me and leafing through them, I wondered what impelled me to spend my precious money and that of my family on books I already know I won't have time to read? Why create this heavy load when someone like me has to keep his possessions light, knowing that I will leave soon for another place, a new exile, leaving these piles behind me? Why do I need to prove my existence with books, to create around me the illusion of solidity?

Every time I leave the place and another library I remember when in my new exile that I desperately need a particular book. I can picture where it is on the shelves, I know that on the upper corner of the right-hand page in the last third of the book is a turn of phrase, or a piercing observation that I need to elucidate my thought processes right now or to reflect on to bring out a current thought in me. Sometimes I excuse this compulsive hoarding as something the future will justify, making light of it. 'You're just creating the right atmosphere for a writer steeped in all things.'

The guard at our apartment in Bitaween once stood amazed in front of the bookshelves and said: 'Now I know what you do. You sell books.'

When I disabused him of this notion, he said: 'But have you read all of these?'

'Some of them,' I replied.

'If you'd said all of them, I would have asked you when you eat and sleep with your wife,' he replied.

Books have defined my whole personal history and evolution. From the 50s: the whole *Hilal* series, and my own scribbling, and the works of Ihsan Abdel Quddous, and Saba'i, and Naguib Mahfouz, when I just started reading. Then Sartre, Camus, Nietzsche, Colin Wilson, Fu'ad al-Takarla and Ghaib Farman in the 60s, Badr Shaker Siyaab and Adonis and Muhammad al-Maghout, and the quarterly magazine *Hewar*. Then there were the entire works of Mao Ze Dong which I read from start to finish, commenting on every page. This was the time when I was suppressing my personal feelings, killing the intellectual in me to favour the combatant. It was the same with Che Guevara and André Malraux. The writings of Lenin and Marx and Engels and pamphlets by Novosti from the time when I came back to the fold of the Iraqi Communist Party and was trying to immerse myself in the group spirit.

Back now in Iraq after a long time away, I was going back to the beginnings of the Iraqi state with Hanna Batatu, the sociologist Ali al-Wardi and the historian Abdel al-Razzak al-Hasani. Now that we had tasted the catastrophic world of the militias, I became preoccupied with how this state – which I had fled my whole life

– had been built. King Faisal I had become one of my political heroes, along with Youssef Salman Youssef, or Fahd as he was known, the founder of the Iraqi Communist Party, Kamel al-Chadarchi, founder of the Liberal Party and Mohammed Saeed al-Hoboubi, the reformist cleric.

My mother had burned many books, especially all those with a picture of the author with a beard and moustache on the cover. Tolstoy was among the suspect authors now burned, and Nietzsche, whom she had mistaken for Stalin. She burned them understanding instinctively that books define their owners. If ever the Dawn Visitor came, the books would say: 'Behold someone who thinks. He is therefore suspect.'

I re-read the comments I had scribbled on the books as I turned the pages. At some time in the 70s, I had underlined this sentence and put an exclamation mark next to it. But now I was smiling with all the giddiness of a child, wondering why this sentence precisely, and why the exclamation mark? I re-read *The Brothers Karamazov* and was amazed at how slow Dostoyevsky was and how many digressions he made. How could I have read it without being bored? I stopped at another sentence with an exclamation mark, which had dazzled me at the time: 'if God did not exist, we would have had to invent him!' But now I was amazed at my amazement. The text had not changed. I had.

The Cafe of the Tormented

As you pass from Saadoun Street to Tahrir Square, you pass a row of shops, now closed, which once attracted us in to the latest books they had on offer. All these bookshops closed when thieves and murderers took over the street. After the row of shops lies the first alleyway on Saadoun Street. This is where to find the Cafe of the

Tormented, as ordinary folk called it, and maybe even the tormented themselves. It is a very normal cafe. Outside, three benches face the murky flow of the river.

You cannot stop there now. It is one of the most dangerous places in Baghdad, a meeting place for contract killers and kidnappers, grasses, car boot specialists, vengeance exactors.

This is where Monem Azeem used to sit in his eternal sunglasses, and Moayyad 'the dandy' and his followers. Ibrahim al-Zayer, his nostrils flaring in intense conversation; Rahman al-Tahmazi playing the wise man, running his fingers through his beard; Munqidh Shareeda, always either coming from or heading for a blazing row; Waleed al-Jomaa, preaching despair to the table and no doubt insulting someone. Shareef al-Rabai was the only man Waleed feared. He had a tongue as sharp as a knife and a knack for sarcasm which fully matched Waleed's perorations of despair. Abdel Amir al-Hussairy might be stood in front of the bar but he won't stay long as he knows with the keenness of the addict that he won't find anyone in this bar of the penniless to stand him a round. He hurries off into the night to find other bars to conquer, just as he has spent all day in them.

This is the ideal place to take a snapshot of the 60s generation of intellectuals. It is a generation formed out of the disasters of 1963, when Abdel Karim Qassem was assassinated and the Ba'ath came to power for the first time, and which ended scattered between death, exile, and humiliation by the regime.

When the Ba'ath took power for the second time in 1968, Abdulillah al-Naimi commented: 'Let them take the whole country. Just, leave us this alleyway!'

For here was everything we needed to be self-sufficient. Just next to our old cafe there were three restaurants, a little stall selling gum and Palestinians who sold *fool* and *falafel* for next to nothing. There were at least three boarding houses with cheap rooms and right in front of the cafe was our barber, Abu Kamiran. Two bars at the end of the street and just a few metres away the Gardenia bar. And if we were completely broke, there was always Um Katerina, who would sell you a bottle in the street. If you needed privacy, there were the little rowing boats that would take you to one of the islands in the middle of the river where you could smoke hashish in peace, and there were the street booksellers who laid out their stocks just after the turning into Saadoun Street.

The apartment which Moayad al-Rawi and Anwar al-Ghassani lived in was at the end of the ally on the left, and my own apartment on the Mashjar Street, just across from Saadoun Street.

We never asked for each other's addresses or phone numbers. Every day we had a date in this cafe at dusk, and each of us knew that the whole gang would be there. The cafe was the point of departure. We would gather around the air conditioner that sucked the fetid smoky air of the cafe in and pump it back out again, moist.

As the heat went out of the day and evening fell, we would gather up whatever money we had between us and go bar hopping.

Many times I made resolutions to change my life, to break the habit of going to the cafe and get my brain moving. But somehow, I don't know how, I would find myself crossing the bridge and lying to myself like an addict. I just need to get that book back I lent to one of the guys, to get my own back on the guy who had insulted me in our cups, or to recapture a thought which had flitted across my mind in mid-argument the day before, or to find out what somebody thought about an article I had written. In the end, I would find myself in the same place with the same gang.

One day, my feet dragging me to the cafe as they did every day, I was shocked to find it was shut. There was a sign on the door: 'Closed for health reasons'. I felt I would lose my friends for good, not knowing where they lived or any other place they met. As the evening set in, we gradually gathered in the alleyway and looked at each other: where could we go?

During the time of the National Front, the pact between the Communists and the Ba'athists after the Ba'athists had taken power again in 1968, Baghdadi intellectuals of the 60s were split between the Writers Club and the Cafe of the Tormented. I never felt at home in the Writers Club, although colleagues urged me to go to their evening readings. I found the atmosphere of watchfulness, the uneasy truce between the Communists and the Ba'athists, wearing. So I preferred the Cafe of the Tormented. There I would find like-mindedness, a depth of debate, and intense suspicion of this uneasy truce. Listening to the fears of our gang, I found any illusions about prospects for the Front stripped away. Monem and Rahman were the doomsayers for the disastrous end of the pact.

I went to the cafe just before I went into my long exile. I was on crutches because I had just been in a car accident and had left the apartment in a state of alarm. I was sure *they* were watching me. A car would pick me up and take me to some stronghold of the security forces. In spite of that, I went to see the cafe and the old gang. I could read the astonishment on people's faces. The Ba'ath had resumed their old language and style, and had spread the word against me. But in any case I had come to say goodbye more to the place than to my people in it. Rahman and I went out for a stroll, forced to whisper to each other. Shaker Lu'aibi walked past, pretending not to notice us, afraid to be seen with us undesirables.

Mutanabbi Street

The magic of old friends and of the books that brought us together drew me to Mutanabbi Street. So I went out one Friday morning with Yasser looking for both of them. In the 70s, Mutanabbi Street had contracted, become a place to look for old books, frequented by academics and researchers and antiquarians fleeing from the present. Tahrir Square became the centre for new books.

Now the street had recovered its former role as thieves and murderers had taken over Tahrir Square. I got there in the hot late morning. I was torn between the books laid out on the pavements, and looking at faces I thought I knew. Opening the book, I would find that personal dedications had been either scratched out or ripped out. These were books from libraries that people were ashamed to sell during the sanctions of the 90s.

The books were laid out horizontally on the pavements, and vertically inside the shops, in a way which made you want to acquire them, not just browse. But a little patience and a little luck, and you can make a rare find, something quite unexpected. I loved the books that other people had read and dedicated. One of them was a gift from former British Foreign Minister Douglas Hurd to his Iraqi counterpart Tareq Aziz, minister to minister.

I bend over like a peasant in the field to get a closer look at the books, which have been laid out on the bare pavement. Inside the bookshops I put my hands on them, weigh them and feel them like a buyer feeling merchandise in the bazaar. The books on the ground are actually more engaging. I can follow another reader's journey, stop where he stopped and underlined a passage and put an exclamation or question mark, or some critical comment.

The market here affirms for me that Iraq has not lost all its culture, as we in exile had imagined. Many books and translations were published while we were away, part of a continuous movement against the isolation which the old regime sought to impose. Now all the forbidden and copied books have come out of their hiding places.

One of the booksellers recognised me and said: 'I've got a present for you.'

He saw me return in the programme which had aired on the *Al-Arabiyya* channel, and had kept hold of the last two photocopies of old books of mine, one on fascism, and the other notes taken in the mountains.

I wandered between the books and the faces of the other browsers. I was leafing through a book by Fahmi al-Mudarris, a famous journalist from the first days of independence, when an American journalist approached me and asked: 'What are you reading?'

'A book about the 20s,' I told her.

'The *20s*, and here we are in the twenty-first century?' she asked.

'Yes!' I said. 'We're now in the *20s* for the *third* or *fourth* time, attempting to build a state from zero. Except this time the people are less innocent.'

While browsing, I lifted my head and caught sight of the face of a man. He looked at me for a moment or two, then we each turned away, hiding in the books while we search our memories – where do I know him from? I know him. Lord help me remember. Then our eyes meet again.

'You're Malek al-Mutalebi?'

The same smile which made his eyes narrow.

They passed before me, one by one, my old friends and colleagues, searching like me among the books – 'Denar al-Samarrai? You haven't changed a bit'; 'Ahmad Khalaf' – his tense face relaxed a little; 'Hussein al-Husseini, the unrequited lover'.

Hussein Hassan

Standing at a grubby window set in an old frame, outside Aref Agha Cafe, I saw a face I could not mistake – Hussein Hassan. He was confused for a moment when I greeted him, as I guessed he would be, his lower jaw open and his blue eyes wide open, boring into my face. Then he shouted my name, bursting into tears.

The entire cafe stopped to watch us as we stood in an embrace. Our emotion had touched some of them. The backgammon piece stayed in the hand, suspended in mid-air, of the man whom Hussein had been playing with. His body, frail and tired from so much alcohol, collapsed into my arms. We sat down facing each other, looking each other straight in the face, astonished by the damage that all that time had wrought on us.

We were the closest of any two men of our generation. We read the same books. Once, we had written a poem together. Our stream of thoughts mingled so strongly we could no longer tell who was who when we talked. We loved the same girls, and our girlfriends would complain about one of us to the other one. Each of us could imitate the tiniest mannerism of the other.

Hussein was raised by his mother alone and had taken on some of the softness of women and their emotiveness. He had wasted much of his life drinking and had failed to achieve anything significant, despite the fact that he was very widely read and had highly developed poetic sensitivity.

Together with Ibrahim Zayer, we formed a trio that could not be parted. We had a daily drinking schedule. We scoffed at the fact that we were always broke, making up long stories about then president Abdel Rahman Aref's trip to France and his broken English conversations with De Gaulle, or an imaginary trip to Iraq by Jean-Paul Sartre, and how the crusty old presenter Fuad Jameel would introduce him on television: 'There is in our midst one of the Frankish atheist heretics, who has taken the woman Simone unto himself as a chattel against the law of God, ...'

I used to have a watch that we would pawn to buy a plate of kebabs or chicken in a restaurant, and then buy back a few days later. Once I pawned it to Jabbar Abu al-Shabrat for over twenty days. When I came to redeem it I found his son wearing it. When I asked for it back, he gave me a story about how the owner had died or gone travelling.

Hussein was the least easy to embarrass, he was the most adapted to our poverty. So we would send him to borrow money. One day he explained his philosophy of borrowing.

'Don't beg and don't beat around the bush,' he said. 'Use a voice of command and impatience and get straight to the point, as if you are in a hurry and don't have time to wait. "I want a dinar!" The impatience doesn't give the lender any time to reflect. His hand will go straight to his pocket. It's only later he'll regret it.'

Hussein also had no hesitation in borrowing money from women, and they were very generous to him.

Ibrahim Zayer had mastered the art of persecuting Hussein, who was his perpetual victim. I will never forget the time Hussein stormed out of a restaurant leaving half a chicken on a plate, only to storm back in again, blind with rage, snatch the chicken up and leave again, shouting all the while at Ibrahim.

Another time, he threw himself in the gutter and said: 'Bury me!'

Hussein was a lover from another age. He had a series of unrequited loves and wrote the best love letters, masterpieces. Women enjoyed this kind of love and would egg him on, while wary of his emotional turbulence. In any country other than this brutal Iraq, Hussein could have become a master love poet. As I looked into his worn, beaten face I felt heavy pangs of guilt that I had left this delicate man in a country without mercy.

My friends who had stayed grew old together and saw the gradual whitening of each other's hair. We were the surprise factor, we who had come back to them from exile. We looked into each other's faces in astonishment. What had happened? Had time really done all that? We were each other's mirror and time was the surprise.

Youssef al-Sayyegh

I had been determined to see Youssef al-Sayyegh since I first came back to Iraq, for two reasons. First, my old friendship with him. But second, to know what had caused his conversion to eulogist of Saddam Hussein. I was shocked when I saw him for the first time after twenty-five years. He looked as if he had lost what he had had before, rather than gained anything. His gaze wandered, his attention scattered. Later on, he told me that he saw things now as though through a broken mirror, with everything fragmented into pieces.

Before I heard his voice, I could hear his heavy breathing, crossing the room as though he was crossing a mountain. I saw his oxygen machine before he came into view. When he put his hand out to greet me, he missed me and his words, when he could get them out, were short and rough and seemed to hurt his throat and squeeze his heart.

As we talked, I didn't know, and maybe he didn't know himself: was he criticising the old regime, he who was undoubtedly one of its victims? Or was it the new order he held to account? There were those who blamed him for his compromises and eulogies of the Leader. How would Youssef settle his accounts with the age that had abased him?

Like many others, Youssef did not see the new era as the ideal substitute for tyranny. On the contrary, the dictatorship, albeit without a dictator, had stayed in people's being, and the stain of violence, and the regime of constant war. But added to it now was the humiliation of occupation. So Youssef expressed no regrets, nor any joy for the new era. But he did have a remarkable curiosity to see all our old friends and listed their names, one by one, as if he was saying them for the first time in years.

Youssef had been in my mind the whole time I wrote *Terrifying and Terrified*. I had tried to follow, from a distance by then, the whole story of his relationship with the Dictator. It was a connection that by stages moved from hatred and fear through submission and reverence, to love and worship – a story that contained sex and religion and the subjugation of the lowly intellectual before the man of power. I was certain that he had not read the novel and I had no wish for him to read it now. I take no joy in kicking a man when he is down.

He asked me about the others, one by one. When he asked me about people who had stayed inside Iraq, among them Dinar al-Samarrai and Alfred Samaan, I was surprised he had not seen them in the last two decades. He still had the same old sarcasm in his voice, asking me how I found everything, as if to say: 'Is this how you wanted it?'

His young wife sat beside him, his junior by forty years. She looked at me in consternation. 'You came very late, friend,' she seemed to be saying as she waited for a chance to bait me. She asked: 'How did you get back in?', expecting me to say I had come in with the American forces. I disappointed her:

'Like any ordinary citizen. I came from Jordan after taking an Iraqi visa in Amman,' I replied.

'On an American passport?' she asked.

'No, British,' I replied.

'What have you come to do here?' she asked me sharply.

'If you mean me personally, to see my family and visit the grave of my father,' I replied. I tried to work out why she was upset. Maybe it was because I was talking to Youssef, not to her.

Youssef said when she was out of the room that he had exhausted himself in the short time since he had known her, with sex and daily drinking and smoking.

I had written about Youssef, or more particularly about his work *The Last Confessions of Malik ibn al Raib*, when I was on Mount Lolan in Kurdistan, with clouds floating by beneath the level of my mud hut. I tried to estimate the long days Youssef must have passed struggling for words. In reality he was struggling with his past, the convictions and sacrifices that he had made to wipe all of it out and follow new convictions. Now, he listed all the people who would attack him and then dismissed them: 'They have no right to judge me. Who is it that decides right from wrong?' he said, clouding the issue.

Interestingly, solidarity and betrayal, and the relation between torturer and victim were a major preoccupation of Youssef Sayyegh's work. He plays with it in his novel *The Distance*, mixing heroism and betrayal. The hero ends up torturing his former comrade, while protesting his ideological purity. Meanwhile, the comrade who has remained pure wonders, on the torture table, how mere thought can resist pain, which is so real and sensed. Youssef loves contradictions and moves between them, mixing them up. But these two characters remain embedded in the old communist conception: they are two separate people. Instead of the reality: one individual who is both victim and self-torturer.

Youssef is an extremely complex man, as is his art, his poetry, painting, novels and criticism. He has a febrile talent which jumps from one thought to its opposite, from one kind of creativity to another, leaving a path of warmth behind it.

He asked me about specific names, Saadeq al-Sayegh and Ibrahim Ahmed, and I understood at once he sought to save himself by judging others.

His frailty had not removed his argumentativeness. Provocation had always been Youssef's weapon to resist what was stronger than he was. He was provocative in the way he wrote when he resisted, and then again when he submitted, as if he wanted to drag everyone along with him. When I read his last 'confession' and his more recent writings, it occurred to me that Youssef had written with his own life the story of the failure of the intellectual. It was not by chance that he left to us a long poem in which he addresses himself, '... you have sullied yourself ...', finishing it with the start of a new conversation: 'this is my second last confession'.

Later he told me that he had praised Saddam because his whole life he had always loved strength and adventure. He also told me that he had simply continued the old poetic tradition of eulogising the ruler, and that there was no compulsion in this tradition because both the ruler and the poet agreed on it.

On a second visit, Youssef was asking for something, this time to join the team at our newspaper *al-Mada*. He claimed he would write a 'counter-confession'. Salwa and I tried to persuade the owner Fakhri Karim. But Fakhri was more concerned by a man's positions than his talent. When it came down to it, I agreed with Youssef. Who decides right and wrong? What would have stopped Fakhri or me being in the same position if we had faced the same inevitable choice?

Moayyad Neema

Moayyad Neema still had style. A sports jacket and a silk scarf, all clean and carefully ironed. And his manners fit his style. He didn't talk much, and if he did it was about work things. He said a lot with few words, words which stuck to his teeth as he said them. Everything about him screamed aristocrat. Only one thing spoiled this image, a smile which by its nervousness revealed the cartoonist who sees in the normal scenes of everyday life things which fly in the face of reality, and which have a resonance which transcends them. I remember one cartoon of two men of power embracing, and each one has his hand in the pocket of the other one. What struck me was the expression on the men's faces, thoughtful and deliberate. Each of them was thinking: where can I put this money I am stealing and how will I spend it? The ordinary citizen was never Moayyad's target. On the contrary, he was human, whether good or bad, and knew what he was saying and doing.

He was just like his drawings. Inside this calm, elegant man who looked as though he couldn't harm a fly, was a savage who showed himself in cartoons with lines as sharp as knives.

For a time, Moayyad used to send me cartoons at *al-Mada* which had severed heads in them, and chopped off hands, and other body parts hacked off in some horrible, evil way. Why don't you stop with the stuff about Saddam and the Ba'athists, I asked him.

'I want to purge something inside me,' he said. 'This is the brutality I had to live but could not express. Well, now I've found my chance. I want to earth the brutality that snuck inside me.'

With each new cartoon, I would worry more about Moayyad. He syndicated his cartoons in three newspapers and was settling scores with the various agents of violence all at the same time.

I was actually surprised when apparently, he died a natural death in the end, a heart attack. If that story is true, Moayyad had cheated hordes of enemies who were sharpening their knives for him, each unaware of the others.

Suheil Nader

I could never confuse Suheil Sami Nader for anyone else. I found him in the Hewar cafe, just how I had left him, sitting on the edge of his chair so that his short legs could reach the ground. His eyes widened in utter surprise for a few moments before he greeted me. I was young when I was introduced to Suheil for the first time, by Umran Qaysi as 'my guilty conscience'. They had got out of prison together a few months previously and bonded through their shared experience of torture and the absurdity of life inside. During a long drinking bout, Suheil suddenly jumped up and ran off and Umran took the opportunity to whisper in my ear. 'He's a little bit mad, you know.'

When Suheil hummed a symphony of his own creation to himself, or talked in the persona of a character in a story which he wouldn't write, we left him to his own devices. Then he would come back to us in his full senses. The place I was meeting him in now, Hewar, was Suheil's place, where he moved freely and knew all the regulars. Nobody knew Suheil's real value except this close group of friends. He was one of the generation wasted by a depraved, wounded country because it valued violence over the intellect. Suheil was one of the victims of that, and his perpetual feeling of disappointment made him a prisoner of his thoughts. He did not appreciate himself, and for that reason his output was limited to one book and hundreds of scattered articles.

If Suheil had been in another country like Egypt or Lebanon it would have been another story.

Riyad Qassim

Between Suheil and me, Riyad Qassim took the role of Umran Qaysi. Whereas Suheil took no care even over his friendships, Riyad viewed his friendships as more important than literature. The age-old orphan complex pushed Riyad to always be seeking friendships. He would develop them to the point where he became embedded as part of the family. The concerns of friendship took for him the place of those of the writer. Like many of his overlooked generation, Riyad put no value in being creative in a country which placed thought and culture under the heavy boot of power. He would always laugh it off if we ever mentioned the first verses he had published in *Hewar*:

> *We were together, behind night's curtain,*
> *We sought something and found something else,*
> *A ship that denies its passengers,*
> *And a knight who curses the tip of his spear.*

He would dismiss it with a gesture, that far-off painful past. Riyad is a strange mixture of light-hearted frivolity and passionate emotions. He took a great delight in ordinary things. One minute a vagabond, the next an ideal father who brought up his daughters himself, trying to make up for the loss of their mother. He could be chaotic, with no boundaries, and yet hold fast to firm customs, and the ties of family and friends, and fixed habits and schedules for eating, drinking and sleeping. He could be both reckless with his life, and fearful to the point of profound pessimism.

Riyad's ideal in life is the aristocrat who takes an interest in form and style, the way to eat or take a first sip of wine. After an evening with Riyad, I stay merry and laughing for a long time for the jokes flow from him like poetry, ironic about everyone around him, and about himself. Some of the best times I have spent with him have been when, in a party, he would work up a storm of laughter about one of the gathering. I have never felt a sense of friendship as strong as I have felt with him.

The 60s generation that I grew up in is almost extinct now, what with death and exile. The new generations dominate the literary scene now. Consequently, I feel strange whenever I go to a literary gathering. Everyone knows each other except me, I am the stranger. Everyone turns to see who the newcomer is, they stop for a few moments, and then surge forwards towards me. I am in my element now and I want to stay with these people, to ask their forgiveness for having left them in the hard times. I too will forgive them everything. We were all victims of a time that was wrong.

Everyone lives in a state of alarm and confusion. We did not make this change for ourselves, it was made for us and now we have to adapt to it. This new space of freedom has surprised everyone because we did not seize it, it was given to us. Chains restrained an entire generation and deprived us of any ability to take the initiative. We wait for some authority, either the authority of power, or that of ideology, of the political parties. A history of being pushed aside any spirit of creativity. We were born and raised as critics. Even if we want to, we have no power to destroy the old taboos. The old power has gone but we wait in the void for some new authority, even if we don't know what.

The public at large, which was totally abject, has now started to exercise its freedom to the limit. To steal from a government office, to drive a car the wrong way down a street, to take over any apartment or building you feel like, to kill who you like and take revenge on anyone ... but we are agonised by a sense of responsibility. We want to do something but put our feet forward timidly, frightened of stepping off the edge. We are full of fear and determination at the same time, the will to do something and fear of that same will as we have not experienced our own willpower for such a long time. Everything seems possible and impossible at the same time, easy and hard in a city ruled by thieves and killers. But all us intellectuals can do is sit and talk and urge each other on.

'We have to do something!' we tell each other. But we don't know what.

To Work

Al-Mada newspaper

A group of us, including Suheil and Salwa, met in the garden of Hewar cafe, which had become the meeting place for intellectuals. Fakhri Karim had called the meeting to discuss what we should do amid this chaos and destruction. Fakhri's idea that he should lead some kind of cultural project was well received. We had in front of us a man who could solve all kinds of problems because he had two distinct characteristics: a sense of initiative, and money.

In this heady atmosphere, Fakhri was generous in his offers of money. His idea was to get hold of the old army barracks and turn it into a cultural centre. But later we discovered that the area would need more than forty iron gates just to protect it from criminals.

It was here in the garden of Hewar that the idea of *al-Mada* newspaper was born.

I was listening to suggestions for the newspaper that Abdel-Zuhra Zaki had prepared when Fakhri whispered in my ear: 'What do you say to taking this on and becoming editor?'

Everything here was new now, a clean slate to start again with good intentions. I nodded yes immediately. Fakhri told me after the meeting broke up of how he had come back to Iraq without his wife and family because he missed it so much, and so was determined to make his efforts count with some cultural project. He convinced me to be his right-hand man. The newspaper's management was made up of Abdel-Zuhra Zaki, who led the discussions on the constitution and editorial policies, and management structures of the newspaper – I don't know in the end how faithful we were to the original goals we drew up. Then there was Qassem Abbas, who was entering the print press for the first time after a long time in the book industry; Hussein Muhammad Ajeel, who had come out of a long period of isolation and had first taken part in a project to find lost cultural artifacts; Suheil Sami Nader; Salwa Zako; and me.

Time, place and exile separated me from this group and I wondered how I would work with them. Plus, I had never been boss in my life. I was always a doer, that was my strength, and it allowed me also to criticise decisions when it became clear they were wrong. So I had always preferred to work in the team than to be at the top of the pyramid.

Fakhri left Iraq again and left us to get on with it. We had established general principles about targeting the educated, middle class, leftist, liberal and open-minded. Our goal was to spread a spirit of tolerance among different groups that had lived in their own ghettoes, both victims of the climate of violence and contributors to it. We wanted to open real debate, spread the language of dialogue, and open the newspaper to a review of the past, which, unanalysed, had not really passed, and to debate about the future.

I found offices for the newspaper in an old money-changer's shop that belonged to a relative. We started meeting there without any fan or air conditioner, in the infernal heat. Leading intellectuals flocked to us there. It became a commonplace that the project had attracted the best minds. A little later, the young, bold intellectual Haidar came to us as editor of the opinions page, argumentative and iconoclastic. He would write his column for the front page as though he were writing his last will and testament. The stern Jamal al-Umaydi also came and became one of the pillars of the newspaper as the editor of the front page.

My idea was to gather a store of good material, and get a decent staff together before we published the first issue. We only had one telephone, a Thuraya satellite phone. I would go onto the roof under the hot sun because it did not work inside the building. While the sun roasted me, I would raise my voice over the bad line until I was screaming to Fakhri to send his money.

Fakhri, sitting in Damascus, hurried us on in his usual manner, which relies on using sheer willpower to do it quicker. We should just start, he said, and solve our problems on the fly. Each time he fixed our publishing date we would postpone it again. We wanted to mark out a place for ourselves among all the flood of new newspapers.

Three Generations

As we got the staff together there were three separate generations. The first generation were educated before the Ba'ath took power, generally leftist, critical and humanist at the same time. The veteran journalist Salwa Zako, Suheil, the critic Fadhil Thamer and I were of this generation.

The second generation's perceptions were formed when the Ba'ath was at the height of its powers, totally dominating all aspects of cultural life. Some of this generation had made concessions to survive in this era, part of them were actually part of the state power machine. Confused now, these people would try to adapt, and searched their past for points of disagreement with the old regime. There were Ba'athists who had abused power, but who knew the art of adapting lies in debasing what is lofty and aggrandising what is base. They infiltrated into the new newspapers and changed their language, and who they praised, to the new situation.

The third generation was made up of those who began to work in the cultural field as the apparatus of the state started to fragment after the first Gulf War in 1990. They were less afraid and less venal. This generation had begun to distance themselves from the state, even if they earned a living from it. There were also others who had compromised themselves before with the Ba'ath who redeemed themselves when the state began to run out of money and power, and to cause trouble in one way or another.

We worked with all three generations and had trouble reconciling them from the start. Those who had suffered and been tortured, and had remained silent and resisted, felt doubly let down when those who had humiliated and tortured them lost nothing in the new era but in fact took jobs that they imagined should be theirs. They would reproach us almost to the point of threats: how could we accept people like this in a leftist newspaper? Some of them showed us files they had kept for a day of reckoning with articles others had written in praise of Saddam and his wars. Others warned us of the deeply rooted conspiracies and coup-making tendencies of the Ba'athists: 'We know them. They'll push you aside and take control.'

Salwa hesitated to work with these people. Suheil tried to solve the problem with a formulation. In the end, we agreed that everyone was a victim, in one way or another, of a whole period that was wrong, and that we needed to offer through work the chance to put that right, especially to those who were talented.

Fakhri got hold of a headquarters for the newspaper through his network of contacts, an old Baghdad house on Abu Nawas Street which had belonged to some Jews and then been confiscated. There was an open garden at the back, some palm trees, and a cabin. An ideal place for one of the Abu Nawas bars. We tried to remember the name of the bar that had been in that house, but couldn't. The cabin in the back became a cafeteria where writers and journalists met more frequently than in the official writers' union. The food was cheap and cheerful, and there was a place to sit and discuss a little removed from the killing and car bombs.

In fact, it was always a dilemma for us, whether to stay in our editing offices or come down to see our friends who had come to the cafeteria to meet us. The foreign journalists who could not travel far from their hotels, the Meridien or the Sheraton, came to search for news, and to chat with ordinary Iraqis. These kinds of social relations took up most of our time.

Insiders and Outsiders

Work in the cultural sphere had spawned a new sectarianism, that of the insider, who had stayed through the Saddam years, and the outsider, back from exile. This was not entirely artificial, nor one of the conspiracies of the occupier. It was a genuine issue among Iraqis who are prone to internal division, as Hanna Batatu described so well in his book *The Revolutionary Classes of Iraq* in a chapter 'Two Iraqis, Three Political Parties'.

The Sunni-Shia division is not the only one. There were divisions among the intellectuals. The young would complain that the old guard were blocking their paths to advancement and had laid their hands on all the prestigious posts. Older intellectuals in their turn would complain that the resentful young wanted to short-cut their path of learning and experience, to have it all before they had even cut their teeth.

Then there were those insiders who had remained silent, found ways to avoid compromising, and now felt cheated because the Ba'athist intellectuals had returned and were now at the forefront.

Meanwhile, the Ba'athists would accuse them of not having written anything in the previous period, of ending up encased in their hiding holes like mice. There was the division between intellectuals from the provinces who would complain that the Baghdadis had taken over all the cultural institutions, while the Baghdadis dismissed them as parochial.

But the division between insider and outsider evolved into the main one. Insiders felt disappointed and a sense of injustice because the cocky outsiders arrived with their dollars to scoop up all the important staff jobs, while they, who had lived through the wars and endured the privations of the sanctions, ended up working as freelancers for peanuts. They were right up to a point because most of the chief editors of newspapers and heads of cultural institutions were returnees.

What was perhaps more dangerous was that the high state positions were the prerogative of returnees, and particularly the leadership of political parties based in the diaspora. These men did not offer any kind of example of democracy, either in what they achieved or in the fight against corruption. They lived cut off from the people, either always travelling or hidden inside the Green Zone. Because of the constant staff turnover, their state position represented, for every one of them, the moment of plunder.

In the first days I went for an appointment with a friend at the Sheraton. The fingers of the US soldier who had searched between my legs were still imprinted on me as I entered the foyer. There I met a crowd of political hacks and it looked as if they had been mapping out the shape of the new government.

One of them asked me: 'Where have you been these past few days?'

'Here?' I asked.

'What have you been doing?'

'I'm with a TV crew. We're capturing the reality before it fades into memory.'

'What?' my interlocutor cried with astonishment. 'What kind of film can you be talking about when your name has been mentioned three times in connection with a senior post? And you haven't been there.'

'I think there's a misunderstanding. You mean my relative Mufeed al-Jezairy,' I said.

'No, I mean you,' he said. He was a man from my home town and there were bonds between our two families. Then he said, so there could be no mistake: 'Put your hand in the pot. You might draw out a nice fat piece of meat!'

He was joking and serious at the same time. To many of the returnees high office was just booty. Not a project to renew the country.

The returnees looked on the insiders in general like they were the whores of the previous regime. Intellectuals in particular they considered the apologists of the maximum leader and the marketers of his wars. Even the best of them, according to this view, had remained isolated from the latest developments in science and culture. Abroad, many Iraqis had learned the importance of energy, being proactive, practical and getting results. Back in Iraq, however, results had remained linked to political power alone.

Both groups held preconceptions about the other. Every now and then I would return to London and face a barrage of questions there from Iraqi friends there, infused with a deep sense of injustice.

'What about us? Who have been scattered into exile and suffered here?' they would say. 'Our places of exile spurn us and so does the homeland. Our marriages have come under pressure, even our children can no longer read what we write. It seems we have become nothing after everything has moved back inside the country.'

Their sense of injustice only increased when the Ba'athi intellectuals, the 'apologists', moved back to the forefront.

Then I would return to Iraq and face the accusations of those inside, that the returnees only came for the festivals and big occasions and then left again, petrified they would lose their privileges there.

This kind of factionalism increased in direct proportion to the shallowness of the intellectual concerned. It was not built on creative output. Both sides had suffered alienation stemming from the same source. Both were victims of the same regime.

After over four years back inside the country, I no longer know where I stand between the two sides. I have found a niche among a certain elite group that see in the divide between inside and outside a source of self-challenge and completion.

The atmosphere we lived in at the newspaper, and the kinds of orientations it produced, laid a burden on the three of us – Salwa and Suheil and myself – to right the wrongs of history.

Salwa had spent the last twenty-five years keeping a low profile, buried in professions other than writing. Writing would have cost her compromises which she wanted to avoid. She had worked as a copy editor and teacher and had renounced writing completely. For this reason she always started out nervous and hesitant before any new step, or new person placed in front of us. The years of self-effacement had taught her to be wary of anyone she did not know, and could not be sure of. Her caution served us well, enabling us to avoid hasty decisions. It also played out as she sat staring at a blank sheet of paper, which she had abandoned a quarter of a century before. When she offered her first column, about Abdel-Karim Qassem, Suheil and I stopped and looked at each other. The clarity and precision of the language were astonishing. She used to chain-smoke as she sat with paper in front of her, waiting to write. But all barriers would fall away as soon as she put pen to paper. It was as though the words had been imprisoned inside her, waiting only for the blank sheet of paper to be free.

All this time Suheil busied himself with backroom tasks. He edited others' articles, improving the language, never adding his own name. He hid himself behind others, plunging into office work. He had no great desire to propose and plan features, but he needed these articles to continue his chosen craft, editing other people's work. He would take some of the stories home with him in a battered old case, and forget them when he left in the morning again, or the afternoon, to be more precise. In this, he had not changed since I left him in the 70s when he was editing the letters page on the *TV and Radio* magazine. Once he had left a case full of letters in the back of a taxi. The next day the driver, a distinguished old gentleman, had come to the magazine offices asking for 'the father of the house' insisting on meeting him alone on a matter that concerned his honour. He thought that the letters belonged to a flirtatious young girl. He had come to return the scandalous briefcase, and tell her father to scold his daughter.

Suheil was a very versatile thinker, and could turn his hand to pretty much any subject we wanted to broach – given an editorial commission, he would come back the next day with a long article he had stayed up until dawn to write. His smouldering mind was as sharp as a knife, and the language he used brimmed with anger. He wrote editorials in which the boiling and buried past appeared in the present.

From the very beginning I wanted to lay out the culture of violence that prevailed in the country as a legacy from the former regime. In the trenches, in the training camps, in the atmosphere of total militarisation, three generations had grown up inculcated with the idea of violence as a form of self-expression and protest. They were unbound by any law, or even any social norms, such as going out into the streets to demonstrate, unless it was under force of compulsion. The sanctions imposed on Iraq in the 90s reinforced this culture of violence by diminishing the position of the educated middle class, who had been the leaders of modernism and progress in the country. Under grinding economic pressure this class slipped a few rungs on the ladder. Meanwhile, marginal sectors of adolescents and young men, youngsters without any academic future or dream of self-development, youngsters whose defining experience was the street, where they gained their strength, unconnected to school or family, these marginal sectors sprang up, ready to commit violence and crimes.

The anarchy that followed the occupation, and the dissolution of the army and security forces, unleashed the forces of violence and crime onto the street. Street violence became the way to express freedom in a society which had never known freedom. Security replaced democracy as the overwhelming need of the people. What use was a pluralist media, pluralism in politics, if it came with a security atmosphere so tense that the citizen felt in danger even in his own home, if his children were at risk just by going to school, or he himself if he went out to work, or to the market? That was the reason the idea spread that Iraq was not ready for democracy, but needed a strong leader instead.

We knew that the state's role in protecting citizens was still just embryonic. For that reason, we thought very carefully before publishing news about the blowing up of a mosque, the killing of a cleric, or pictures of a slaughtered kidnap victim. Our society had a built-in bias towards blood, away from professional objectivity. But this information would not be just information by the time it reached someone who was unemployed and imbued with the culture of violence. It would have been transformed into feelings of fear and vengeance.

In the same way, professionalism did not just demand including the opinions of the various warring parties. It also involved airing the opinions of those who had no voice, the ones caught between the combatants and had no interests in the fighting, who wanted to swap the fighting for some less destructive mechanism of settling disputes. I would push the features section on every possible occasion to go down into the street and collect public opinion on every controversial topic. I wanted to substitute a conflict of words for one of bombs and bullets.

There was an unspoken consensus that we were in favour of change, and of state building, but we adopted the role of constructive criticism. We knew that every social change brings anxiety. The quelling of that anxiety depends on the wish of the majority for change. But even if the desire for change was absolute, it was important that reform should start on the basis of culture. Fear of the future, and the wish to stick with the past, are born in ignorance. Once the desire arises to participate in shaping the future, the need also arises for broader information about the political parties that have entered the scene after the collapse of the single party, about the new leaders who have arisen after the one leader.

The Present in History

I was fully absorbed in the daily routine of the newspaper. Yet at the same time I was reading up on the history of Iraq. I read Hana Batatu for the fourth time, *Iraq between Two Occupations* by Abbas al-Azawi, the works of Kamal Mazhar and Longridge. I even went back to Sumerian times. There was nothing willed about this, I simply found myself pushed towards history under the pressure of the Now. I committed to memory the history of a country which has burned and wrecked its own history. These latest fires were simply the symbolic seal on three decades of an authoritarian culture for generations who had grown up with the idea that history began when the Ba'ath took power.

I was caught between history and the present. Between on the one hand a time which stretched back as far as when writing began, and on the other a present time in which each new moment starts history all over again, and abolishes what we knew before.

History taught me to devalue present suffering – these cries were as old as time. This destruction had happened repeatedly. Baghdad had been consumed by fire and pillage many times over. The spirit of history said to me, frighteningly: 'Why all this screaming and shouting?'

Everything I have lived through will be summed up in a few lines in a history book:

> Anarchy broke out after the fall of a ruler who was brutal and unjust, but who had through three decades built a state to be feared and gone to war three times against his neighbours and the world.

That's it! That's all it will say about our current time. All the detail of our current suffering will be lost.

And yet the present also frightens me. This present which says with its chaos and its myths that the history that you read in books is just a series of random events, like what is happening now, and that historians of today have simply constructed their own narratives to make sense of it by their own belief systems.

It was by reading history that I realised how isolated the Iraqis are from time. They live each moment as if it is the last. They want something to happen now or not at all. They live their ordeal as if it was the only one which existed, ignorant of the fact that both the human past and present are full of phases such as the one we are passing through. Like any people who have lived under tyranny for a long time, the Iraqis are very impatient after regime change. The years of oppression, the broken promises and the yawning gap between people and elite have sapped all their energies and faith in the future. That is why the tone of hysteria rises during these transitions. The present moment is to win or lose, absolutely, a moment of either life or death, not a point in the progression of history.

Reading history gave me the feeling that destruction, and escaping from destruction, were the destiny of the Iraqi people. After all, they have not lived through a phase of stable construction. I would always think as I went to the newspaper in the morning, to follow the news of the day: 'How can we fit these moments into the long train of our history?' And by the end of each day I would find the question senseless. Those to come will write our history. All we can do is record these brief passing moments.

The Oil Coupons

The newspaper leapt to fame when Fakhri put into our hands a list with 275 names on it – Arab and Western – of people who had taken oil coupons from Saddam. There were presidents, ministers, parliamentarians, Christian and Muslim clergymen, publishers and writers who had shuttled to and from Baghdad during the UN sanctions regime in the 90s, or, to be more precise, the five-star hotels in Baghdad, where they had struck deals while flaunting their solidarity with Iraq and the children of Iraq under the vicious sanctions regime.

When we published it we did not realise what we were getting into. Correspondents from the international press began flocking to the office, with their bodyguards and fixers and photographers. Whenever the receptionist told us about the number of journalists waiting downstairs, each one of us would try to make the other meet them. We were all bored with answering the same questions. I would have to break off work to go down into the garden with a camera crew or a reporter asking me: 'Can you show me the original document?' seeking further explanation of something everyone already knew.

Ambassadors would come to make enquiries or remonstrate because important politicians had been named on the list. I asked a French diplomat if he was surprised by the naming of French politicians, including a former interior minister. He said on the contrary, he was surprised by the absence of names he *knew* had taken bribes and asked if there was another list.

Appeals came in from people abroad, affected by the revelation, threatening us with legal proceedings or with violence. But the only American the affair interested was from Fox News and he asked, in a tone more of menace than curiosity: 'You guys know how legally dangerous what you're doing is, right?'

'It is our luck as journalists that in fact there is no law,' I replied, provoked by his tone. 'I know the normal curiosity of journalists. But this is not that because you are not one of them. You're from the CIA, aren't you?'

A few months later we got a call from the US embassy in Baghdad with the news that a US Congressional delegation wanted to meet with the management of the newspaper on a very important matter to do with the 'Oil for Food' list. We agreed that the meeting should be at the newspaper, not in the Green Zone, and told them that. The next day the doorman at the newspaper called up to say that a group of armed Americans had just invaded the lobby. I went down to see what was going on and met two of these private security guards, in fatigues and sun glasses, carrying automatic rifles with their fingers on the triggers and microphones in front of their mouths. They didn't reply to my question about the reason for their intrusion, but brushed past me to search the rooms and passageways and terraces, speaking to each other on their microphones in coded language. I had no doubt they were from the infamous Blackwater security company. The whole thing lasted no more than twenty minutes; they searched the building both inside and out, and stared us down with hostility. Then they left the newspaper without saying a word. We still had no idea why they had come or why they had left, just a general sense of powerlessness as citizens before this invading force.

Two hours later, the US embassy phoned to tell us that 'after an inspection' it was clear that our premises were not secure, and so we would have to go and meet them in the Green Zone.

There are few places whose nature conflicts more with its name than the Green Zone. There is almost nothing green inside those concrete walls. It occupies more than three entire districts, from Qadissiya and Kindy in the west to Republic Bridge and the Zora Gardens in the north, a total of 20 square kilometres, bounded by the Tigris to the east and south. So it takes up pretty much all the area that used to be the district of Karada Maryam, and Tashree' and Um al-Azam districts, and also a large part of the Zora gardens, the largest public park in Baghdad, and the public festival grounds that include statues and theatres and cinemas and exhibition halls. The Qadissiya highway is also part of the zone, and the Rashid Hotel tunnel, and the hotel itself.

Those concrete walls cut off the Green Zone, which includes ministers and parliamentarians and ambassadors, from the real, red world outside them. They also cut its residents off from each other. You can't actually look for more than a few metres without running into those concrete walls in the cement nightmare known as the Green Zone.

I didn't really understand the nature of life inside it until one of its British residents complained to me of isolation in what he called a 'cement container'.

'In the beginning I had promised myself that I would write a book, a kind of diary to chronicle the historic new period that we had begun in Iraq,' he said.

The diaries of the British during their first occupation (Gertude Bell and her contemporaries) had become a source for us on the formation of the Iraqi state. So, genuinely fascinated, I asked him: 'Why didn't you write it?'

'What would I write? I have not seen anything of Iraq in the year-and-a-half I have been here except this district, where I am a prisoner. I don't know any Iraqis except those I work with, and my protection detail. How could I write about a people I don't know, houses I have not visited, cafes I have not been to? I haven't even been to an exhibition, as diplomats classically do,' he said.

'Have you never been out of this container?' I asked.

'Even if I have, we never see anything,' he replied. 'I go out in an armour-plated car with blacked-out windows and a security detail that everybody runs from.'

An American diplomat I met at a conference in Amman told me that he had once thought of leaving the Green Zone to go and visit his colleagues in the Iraqi Foreign Ministry, only a few metres away from the main gate to the zone. Just as they were leaving, his security guards, who were from Blackwater, ran into two civilian cars.

'I told them to turn us around and go home immediately,' he said.

Despite professional obligations, I had not been to the Green Zone more than three or four times. I never got in without breaking a heavy sweat, both from the amount of time I had to walk under the burning sun, and from the hassle of being searched so many times at checkpoints by troops of different nationalities.

At the first checkpoint, which is Iraqi, they will ask you for your ID card, and if you have an appointment.

At the second checkpoint, they take the battery from your mobile phone. Then they ask the same questions as at the first checkpoint and ask for two pieces of identity. Then two soldiers frisk you, from in front first, then behind; starting with your shoulders and arms and pockets, and moving down to your legs and waist.

Once I was on my way to see the then deputy prime minister Rooj Shawash but was stopped by an American soldier who demanded another ID card in addition to the journalist ID I had already offered. I decided not to wait for a long time, or to call his secretary, but instead just asked for my ID back and returned to the newspaper.

Despite big reservations, four of us from the newspaper attended the US delegation meeting. Before us was a group of Iraqi politicians including Dr Ahmed Chalabi. Their meeting was curtailed to twenty-five minutes to allow more time for ours. I don't remember the names but I remember there were both Republican and Democrat congressmen there and they wanted to ask us about the accuracy of what we had published about the oil coupons, and also an article we had printed about corruption among US officers who granted contracts after taking fat commissions.

They began by praising our newspaper – 'one of the most intelligent Arabic newspapers', lauding its courage in criticism. One of them, the press attaché to the US embassy I think, told us that they daily took at least twelve stories from the newspaper, translated them, and sent them to the higher-ups.

After the flattery, they came to business, asking about the accuracy of the list of names that we had published. One of them, I don't remember his name, said that Kofi Annan believed that Ahmed Chalabi had worked in some names of his own advisers because he held a grudge against him. We told them we had checked the names with senior officials in the Iraqi state oil company, who had confirmed them. Besides which, some of the names listed had openly confessed their involvement, and some even justified it on the grounds that it was helping Iraq when it was under sanctions.

We spoke openly about the corruption of American soldiers. I told them: 'This is not a complicated question. Just a few metres away is a queue of secondary Iraqi contractors. They know exactly who they need to bribe.'

We came out of the meeting a little disturbed, but also relieved, because we had said what we believed without mincing words or prettying it up.

Friends would call from abroad to tell us about the storm we were creating among the competing political parties by publishing the list.

Meanwhile, Iraqis who had known all this was going on but never possessed proof, asked us if there were other lists. They urged us to publish everything we had because this money offered to the bribe takers had been snatched away from their mouths during sanctions in which the regime would even trade in the coffins of children who had died from malnutrition and lack of drugs.

A nurse who had worked in one of the hospitals told my sister Ilham that the state had hired professional mourners who walked behind sometimes empty coffins, shrieking and hitting their own faces as though the children who had died of hunger were their own. The nurse said she had once seen one of these mourners screaming with rage because another one had received the same pay from the secret police as she had but without putting in the work in her opinion. The other one had walked behind the coffin, but had not wailed or torn at her face.

There was no noble emotion, no spirit of empathy that this corrupt regime did not debase.

The coupon system during the period of sanctions was not confined to high-level bribe takers. Tariq Aziz was once rumoured to have said: 'There is no one who can stand against corruption, period. The only question is what his price is.'

Each time the newspaper brought out more details – and became more influential – we came under threat and increased our enemies, from among the elite of the old regime, and old and new militia forces, and even from tribal leaders.

Once someone came to visit wearing the high, white *uqqal* and *keffiya* of the tribes of the west. He introduced himself with his full clan title, and also as a general in the ex-army. He told me that his brother's name had been mentioned in our newspaper as the leader of one of the insurgent groups in the 'triangle of death' south of Baghdad. He had the family lawyer with him. His tone at first was diplomatic. He let the lawyer lead with warnings of prosecution if we did not retract the story in our own names. In the end the sheikh stormed out with the lawyer, but not before he had approached us, shouting in a rough, threatening voice: 'If diplomatic means don't work, we shall resolve this by tribal reckoning.'

Another time, a militia leader phoned to protest against a story we had published. He insisted that I tell him the name of the person who had leaked the story to us. When I refused he said that he was tired of holding back the furious crowd around him, and if I continued to be obstinate an angry crowd would devise an end for me.

One day we came to the offices and discovered that the UN guard which had been garrisoned just next door had pulled out to avoid the danger of being nearby.

A Katyusha rocket came fizzing into the compound as a kind of warning. It overturned the chairs in the meeting room and went through some walls, but miraculously did not detonate. It fell to me to quickly vacate the offices of our staff, comprised of alarmed young men and women. I assured them, and before that myself, that the missile had targeted the Green Zone on the other side of the river and had struck us by mistake.

We carried on working in this atmosphere of fear. We hid our individual fears by believing in our group destiny. We would meet every day in the garden, which came to resemble one of the bars of Baghdad from the old days.

But we had started disagreeing a lot among ourselves, and I began to count the days until the end of my contract. All my working life as a journalist I had worked in newspapers which belonged to political parties. I would stir trouble and sometimes worry at their taboo subjects, always calculating from what I knew was their programme and their alliances for years to come. I learned how to create a margin of freedom within a general system of constraint. But Fakhri's taboos were more complex, his friendships and animosities personal. This meant he was closer to the changeable moods of an intellectual than to the cold but calculating tactics of a politician with his enemies.

To be fair, Fakhri put up with all my transgressions. He wanted me to be stricter with the staff at the newspaper and in order that I should be serious, and project authority, he cut me off from the rest of the editors with three rooms of my own. There was my own office, the secretary's ante-chamber, and the meeting room, all apart from the rest.

But I have never liked hierarchy in the workplace. I prefer a team spirit. I favour friendship over discipline. I would always leave my own office and wander around my colleagues, engaging them in debate to get a feel for their views. We were operating in a mine field of sensitivities, and I felt that we needed everyone on board; we needed to know all the difficulties. I felt collegiality and friendship were a better way to influence the staff. But this was in a culture in which many people know only the dynamics of command and obedience.

I was counting the days until I could leave. The day I knew it was the end, I quietly gathered my papers and suppressed a deep sadness because I was leaving a dream and a project in which I had invested so much. Once again I would have to rely on my skill at losing, and starting again.

On 12 November 2005, I handed the keys over to the secretary and left.

A Ballot in the Box

I never knew who put my name on the list. But I found myself a delegate to the national conference. Its first session, for me, was the last.

It is rare to find all that amazing diversity in one room. Sunni headgear and Shia headgear, black turbans and white ones, Kurdish scarves from Soran and Bahdinan, rough, southern *uqqals* on chequered *keffiyas,* smooth northern ones on white *keffiyas*. Veiled and unveiled women – Chaldean and Assyrian Christians, Yazidis, Zoroastrians, Shia and Sunni Turkomen. How had Iraq gathered all this astonishing diversity? King Faisal I, who came from the flat desert and a homogenous Bedouin society, had every right to be alarmed at this variety and to regard it as his bad luck.

After the president, Ghazi Ujail al-Yawar, and the prime minister, Iyad Allawi, and the speaker of parliament, Fuad Masum, had given short speeches, the entire assembly erupted. Twelve people at twelve microphones spoke at once. Everyone was shouting, demanding the others listen. And nobody could hear anyone.

It wasn't so much talk as people coughing, clearing their throats, and shouting, speaking so fast they were swallowing their own words.

All those pent-up thoughts, wanting to express themselves – 'Now! Now! Not tomorrow!' And the voices merged into each other until we could not tell who was speaking and what he was saying.

The chair of the session, Fuad Masum, a master of patience, let it go until the chamber reached absolute chaos, like in a Fellini film. Then he tapped the microphone three times. It was as though Saddam had come out of hiding and commanded silence with one, abrupt gesture. There was a strange moment of quiet, and then the voices began again, low this time, and everyone raised their hand politely for permission to speak, and waited until the other guy had finished.

As we approached election day the walls were plastered with faces and promises. How would Iraq, which had lived for thirty-five years under one party and one ruler, have space for all these lists and parties? There were 285 party lists competing for 275 seats in the parliament.

'Before its time,' I said to myself as I watched the flow of posters on the walls. This one promises to keep Iraq united, that one will end corruption and create jobs for the unemployed. Another one raises his finger to promise me strengthened independence and the withdrawal of all foreign troops, and of course there are others promising to end terrorism. 'Before its time,' I repeat to myself, for the Iraqis will not vote on the basis of electoral pledges or programmes, but first on the basis of identity, sect, tribe and town. But as polling day got closer I started saying: 'Let's just try it and see, even if we pick the wrong paper.' As the date drew near and the contest heated up, accusations replaced promises. The Shia coalition accused the sitting prime minister Iyad Allawi of concealing secret negotiations with the Ba'athists. Allawi in turn accused their 'List 555' of leading Iraq into a civil war.

Spread across a huge wall was a picture of Allawi: 'A man for all Iraqis'.

A taxi driver asked me as we passed it: 'How much money do you think they spent on that?'

'Millions,' I replied.

'Why didn't they spend it on giving us a bit more electricity?' he asked.

As the day drew near, curiosity increased as everyone wanted to know each other's secret. After 'Hello' the next comment was: 'Who are you going to vote for?'

It was a historic day for Iraqis: 15 January 2005. A day full of fear and hope, the day we put our ballots in the boxes for the first time.

I was hesitant and fearful. Who would dare to go to vote after all the various threats of recent days? Bandits on the roads lying in wait for voters on their way to the booths. Terrorists dressed as policemen watching those who participated to settle accounts with them shortly afterwards. Booby-trapped cars in police markings waiting at the gates of the polling centres. Armed groups who would shortly carry out house to house searches and cut off every finger blackened by the indelible ink from the booths.

The fear-laden atmosphere that had prevailed in the run-up to the election, and the sound of mortar bombs exploding since the early morning, persuaded us that it was impossible. Who would risk his life, amid all these dangers, to vote for a list of people he did not know? But then my cousin Ali, who had crept out onto the street, came back to us with the news: 'Our neighbours have gone!'

My neighbour Abu Mai was the last person who could be described as courageous. But he had left with his family, in their best clothes, to go to the polling centres, so we felt ashamed of our fear and as though we had to go too.

I went up onto the roof after another mortar attack. I was surprised by the long lines of those heading towards the election centres. My sister Dhikra and I decided: 'Let's go!'

'Change your clothes,' said Dhikra, muttering a prayer for those about to enter danger.

'I will go,' I said, 'wearing our father's *dishdasha*. For more than fifty years of his life, he never once voted.'

Jamal had come to our house the day before, tired of being cooped up in his own house. But he was loyal to the boycott by Ba'athis and many Sunnis of the polls and had decided not to take part in the game.

'Try just once to take a decision for yourself!' I said.

But he said what I think were the views of many: 'You believe in the ballot box? Bremer has already prepared the list of winners.'

My brother-in-law, and my nephew Ali advised us to wait until after 10.30 AM. His refined instinct for security and experience told him that most of the car bombs would explode between nine and ten-thirty in the morning. But when he saw how determined we were, he asked us to wait while he changed. We knew how long it would take before he was ready in his accustomed style. But we still waited for him.

We walked quickly when we left while he walked behind us, on the look-out for danger. Where would the bandits stand? Where would a mortar come from? On which corner would a booby-trap be placed?

All fears were possible. The continual explosions and the rattling of gunfire told us that our fears were not just idle. We sped up even more in response to them, to conquer our fear. We try to summon the will that their Project of Fear would banish from us. Every step was a decision against fear. And then we had passed the point of return, and the swelling lines gave us the security of being part of a group. Women veiled in black carried children on their chest. There were old men on their last legs.

'We want to experience it, to taste freedom,' one of them said. 'Then we can die in peace!'

There were cripples in wheelchairs pushed by their grandchildren, middle-aged men dressed in their finest clothes as though they were going to a party where they were the guest of honour, after so many parties for other people – entire families, the old, the young, even children.

'We want to die together, so they are not left as orphans,' one said.

There were no cars in the streets. Young boys beneath voting age were playing football in the middle of the street, occasionally stopping to direct a passer-by to the polling booth.

People did not know the party lists they were voting for. Most of the names on them had remained a secret until the last moment, apart from the party chiefs. And most voters had not read the programmes of the parties and were not voting according to political beliefs or their own self-interest. Rather, they were voting according to their identity, religious or tribal, or their first affiliation. Many would vote according to the *fatwas* of the clergy. But at least for the first time they would be exercising their right to choose, even if they did not really know who they wanted.

I wanted to vote with all my heart. I put aside my traditional allegiance to the Communist Party, afraid that the party could come back to play the part of despotic power once again if it succeeded. Democracy in the party remained a slogan, not any kind of culture. I wanted to vote for the list of Iyad Allawi because it was secular, and because he was the only one we had tried up until now. I wanted to give him a second chance despite what I knew about his autocratic tendencies.

But in the end I did vote for the People's Union list, which represented the former Communists.

I did not vote for them because they were the 'Party of Martyrs'. We have seen too many martyrs for that to be a bond. Besides many martyrs have also been wrong. I no longer hold martyrs sacred because of how many they were, or how brave. On the contrary, I consider them no differently from the living, and am even sceptical about their 'martyrdom', including Fahd himself.

I did not vote for them because they are 'the builders of socialism'. The bastions of socialism have fallen due to the corrupting power of the state which owns everything and makes the people their vassals. Communist parties only gave lip service to socialism. I did not vote for them because they are a progressive party. Being progressive has become complex these days since the rise of religious fundamentalists which offer forward-looking programs – 'let us build an Islamic state'. While the 'progressive' parties rely on their past.

I voted for them because my nature is to side with the loser. And because the Communists have lost their superpower backing, and ideological impregnability and so are guided rather by current realities on the ground. They have become the party closest to reason and secularism.

I did not vote for them when I voted for the People's Union list. I voted against tribalism and sectarianism. I voted for them because they are not tribal or sectarian, but in fact represent national and religious diversity in Iraq.

After I had put the ballot in the box, I breathed a deep sigh of relief. I had banished my fears and the long history of repressed will.

Before I left the booth a blind old man called out, asking me to check that his young grandson had put his own cross on the list which he had chosen – 144, Iyad Allawi's list. The grandson was laughing because he had been teasing the old man on their way to the booths that he would make him vote instead for List 555, that Ayatollah Ali Sistani, the spiritual leader of the Shia Islamists, had endorsed. Clearly, they disagreed about politics but the young man had indeed put the old man's cross in the right place.

He was delighted when I told him the young man had acted in good faith.

'You don't know him, he's a cheat!' he said.

'Well, uncle, the cheat was honest today,' I replied.

The grandson and I together took that old, gaunt hand and led it, the paper trembling, to the box. When we left the polling station I felt as though what I had done was a lot more than just putting a piece of paper in a box. We had done something historic.

In the street, I asked my sister Dhikra who she had voted for. I was certain (given her great religious faith) that she would have voted for Sistani. But she surprised me by saying that she too had voted for the People's Union.

'I can't believe it. You voted for the "infidels",' I teased her.

'I voted for the least crooked of them,' she replied.

The South

The Marshes

At the river, give me a flood.
In the field, give me more wheat.
In the orchards, give me more dates and grapes.
In the marshes, give me more grass and cane.

from *The Journey of Nana to Nafar*

It was as if I saw the beginning of creation, as I sat on the raft amid the reed thickets, in the great marsh. It was in 2004 and I was shooting a documentary on the return of water to the marshes. For it was on the waters of the marshes, between the thickets, that the Sumerian Creation myth was born. In this story, the water is in fact two waters, the upper and the lower. And the god Analil parted the waters with a word: 'Let there be a skin between them'.

The water here is the lower kind. The raft which cuts through it is the same as my Sumerian ancestors used. It makes a kind of swishing sound to tell us we have entered a magical world, Analil's world, where silence has precedence over speech. The sound of the boating hook as it plunges into water is muffled. As it rises again it sprays us with drops, reminding us of where we are. If you lean over the side, you can see the whole picture, the two waters, above and below, mingled in the ripples of the surface.

Man has not changed nature in the marshes. He has not trimmed or uprooted it, but left it as it is. Just, he built his houses on little islands made of its material, mud and rushes. He took his vitals from it: fish, the milk of the buffalo, birds. And man himself was not changed. The man steering our boat, roasted by the sun, looks like his Sumerian ancestors with his big beak of a nose, broad forehead and knobbly legs.

The Babylonians' descendants still use the same wooden boats sealed with tar that Gilgamesh had travelled in, and Anana the god of spring, and Nana, goddess of the moon. They use the same hooks and oars and fish with the same spears and nets and live in houses made of reeds, on islands in the middle of the marshes called *yashan* where the remains of their ancestors can be found. And as for their ancestors, water is the source of life.

When Misbah al-Saadi sings, his voice comes back, broken, across the water, as though travelling through time. This voice in the empty wild touches me deeply, although I can't understand the words.

Birds flew out of the reed beds in the distance. Then we saw another boat gliding across the water. I think Mudhaffir al-Nawwab knew him, calling him 'the old man'. Just then Misbah al-Saadi called out: 'Ho! Mister oarsman, ho'. His voice skidded across the water like a stone.

Misbah was motionless at the front of the boat, his eyes following a fish darting to the right. He readied his three-pronged spear, then struck. The boat rocked with the force of his movement. In the space of a second, I saw the silver fish skewered on the end of his spear. As he moved it in, I could see the pain in the gawping of its mouth, the thrashing of its tail. Behind him, I saw the figure of the Sumerian fisherman, his smile of victory.

And yet his harshness seemed innocent, primordial compared with what other fishermen did. They used explosives and poison and electric currents, killing the small fish the fishmongers won't pay for, along with the large.

'If they carry on fishing like this, there won't be any fish left in the marshes,' said Misbah.

'Who are *they*?' I asked.

'Our people,' he replied. 'The Saadis. The Bu Muhammad are better than us at respecting nature. They only fish for their needs, with spears and nets. We became brutal when fishing became a business and it was no longer about subsistence.'

The Sumerians and Babylonians knew the value of water as the source of riches. Here was the first place on earth that edicts were issued, to regulate irrigation, determine who got what flows and how to invest these water resources. Hammurabi issued his famous code to govern the use of water, and penalties for those who infringed.

We followed the marshes back to their source, the Tigris and Euphrates rivers, where the water seeps into thousands of rivulets and channels and into this basin which stretches across 6,000 square miles – from the town of Amara on the Tigris to the Iranian border, and then again west to the Euphrates between the towns of Hilla and Suq al-Shoyoukh. Water stretching out to the horizon, swept with reed beds, and reed huts dotted here and there. This paradise was one of the largest extents of fresh water in the world, if not the largest.

Among the reed beds and matt huts in the marshes, a dystopian vision once flourished in the minds of a group of communists, that it would be possible to 'liberate' civilisation from this harsh environment. From the same spirit of sacrifice and self-negation which bewitched me in my youth, there were intellectuals who left their universities and offices and comfortable European cities to test their will here. With extraordinary determination, to make the dream of freeing Iraq from these rough reeds come true. In Baghdad, my colleagues and I swapped stories and pamphlets about them in the cafe, and waited for our turn to come to join them. The Ba'athi coup occurred before the experiment came to fruition. The dream was stolen by the tank which entered the palace. And so the destinies of the fighters of the marshes became material for novelists, rather than historians.

War in the Marshes

When Anki, the god of Water, rises
The waters rise with him,
Fear trickles into the depths,
And alarm rules the great river,
The wind of the south takes the waves of the Euphrates.

Barbed wire extends wherever we go, an affront to the atmosphere and tranquillity of this lost paradise. There is no tiny patch of land that Saddam and his barbed wire have not penetrated. We followed a long line of trenches and small dams, crossed by stretches of barbed wire fencing off the reed beds. We saw upturned, bashed-in helmets scattered here and there, and around them the casings of shells. The remains of the eight-year war with Iran. These shallow waters had seen the fiercest fighting with Iran.

The soldiers who had shared in this war showed us some of the locations. The Iraqi army had neither a plan, nor the skills to fight in the marshes. The Iranian army used the natural difficulties of the terrain to launch a series of offensives they called *Allahu Akbar – God is Great –* in 1984. They seized the Majnoun islands, with oil reserves estimated at 220 billion barrels. The Iraqi army, untrained in the use of small boats to fight in the marshes, established two dams, *A* and *B*, to distribute its men along these long lines. They established minefields, placing mines in the water, and barbed wire.

'Our children became food for the mines,' one of the marshmen told me. 'Our government used them to explode the mines the Iranians had planted in the path of the Iraqi army. The government did not tell them about these mines, so that they exploded when they went out fishing. Fish in the marshes got noticeably fatter because of all the bodies they were eating.'

The marshes during the years of the last war also became a refuge for deserters, and armed Islamist factions, and tribal groups in rebellion against the central government.

Towards the end of the war, at the same time as the Halabcha attacks and the *Anfal* campaign in Kurdistan, the Iraqi government issued its plan to target both the people and the environment in the marshes. On 30 January 1989, they published a document called *Work Plan for the Marshes*. It contained elements such as strategic security considerations, controlled explosions, poisoning the water and burning houses under the pretext of a worsening security situation. An amnesty was offered to army deserters and those who had avoided conscription if they agreed to kill the hostile political groups hiding in the marshes. There were collective punishment and deterrent operations carried out systematically against the populations in the marshes, who were ranked among those 'who collaborated with the saboteurs'. These operations included destroying houses, imposing an economic blockade on all areas where rebels were active, a ban on selling fish, and the harshest measures against those caught smuggling food into the deserters and outlaws and rebel groups. There was also a ban on all forms of commercial traffic into these districts, and the deployment of a wide network of hidden informers to find the locations of deserters and other hostile groups. Attempts were made to lure them out of their hiding places so they could be arrested, and army helicopters and planes were used in the operations to pursue the army deserters. Thought was given to the idea of resettling all the villages of the marshes elsewhere, on dry land, where they could be easily controlled, and roads were built to reach the most remote parts of the marshes.

Like the rest of the south, the marshes took part in the *intifadah*, or uprising, of 1991. They were the last stronghold of those who fled the towns after the uprising had been crushed.

When all the Shia towns had been taken after the uprising, the sectarian face of the Ba'ath regime appeared in a series of articles: *What Happened at the End of 1990?* and *Why Did What Happened Happen in 1991?* The central party newspaper not only attacked the Shia right in the stronghold of their beliefs. They also classified the Sumerians, the ancestors of the marsh Arabs, into the category of second- or third-class citizens. In one of the articles, the party newspaper described a general class of people who were 'the centre of base duplicity, serving treacherous elements that spread across southern Iraq and the towns of the central Euphrates during the last events'.

'If we know all this and more,' the article continued, 'we know that some of this class of people in the marshes of Iraq came with the buffaloes that Muhammad Qassim imported from India. We know that their most salient characteristics are stealing the possessions of their rivals, burning the reed huts of those they are fighting or in struggle with. So it is easy to explain a lot of the incidents of plunder, destruction, arson, and rape that these hired criminals have undertaken.'

This contempt has its roots in the long-held disdain the Bedouin have felt for arable farmers, considering them soft because they exchanged swords for ploughs.

This depiction, which devalued the foe and made him sub-human, became the pretext for massacres by the army. Most of these units were from the Republican Guard, or other companies where most of the men, or at least the officer corps, came from the same tribal backgrounds as Saddam.

The regime chose its most brutal man, Ali Hassan al-Majeed, to clear out the pockets of resistance in the marshes from the uprising with campaigns of collective executions. The town of Jabayash alone saw 2,500 men executed, either locals or others who had gone into hiding there.

I had seen some footage which had fallen into the hands of the opposition, shot by the cameraman who accompanied Ali Hassan al-Majeed on this campaign to clear out the marshes. In it, there are rows of people on the ground, helpless, their hands tied behind their backs, their eyes covered with blindfolds. Normally, you would expect that this position of helplessness would afford some sense of comfort and achievement to the victors. But there is no real victor in these scenes. Both sides are routed.

You have citizens and some soldiers, whose spontaneous and uncoordinated rebellion has been smashed by what is left of the regime's repression machine, and the regime itself, which has just been defeated in an external war and would like to wipe out its defeat with a win that gives some self-confidence back. The enemy within has become a peg for them to hang the humiliation of their external defeat on. The more heavily the external defeat weighs, the more brutal the repression of the internal enemy. A British TV programme said that the number of casualties was four times greater in the internal fighting than it had been in the war over Kuwait.

And yet the victory gave the regime no assurance. In this film, the acts of the victorious soldiers over their own people reveal a sense of unease and nervousness – brutality. They are teaching them a lesson, as they kick and beat them lying on the floor because these people almost won. And they know that they would have been in the same position, and felt the same degree of hatred. It is fear which expresses itself in their brutality. In order to prove to himself that he has escaped from this nightmare, he keeps up the beating.

The officers are standing directly behind the men, who have no chance to step back, to pause, just to watch. They have to break indecision by action, to keep at it, to cut them off from any sense of humanity which might stop them. The violence becomes worse as the victims become weaker. They put their boots on their heads, as if to say these are not humans, but some lower thing which doesn't deserve to live. They must abase their victims before killing them.

Ali Hassan al-Majid is in the background, sometimes the foreground even, giving orders, talking constantly, lapsing into silence only to erupt into some act of violence. His self-appointed task is to wipe out an entire body of people from Suq al-Shuyukh down to Basra. In this region there are no innocent parties and guilty ones. Everyone is condemned and must be exterminated. That is how the towns of the uprising were dealt with.

The names given to the campaign changed, as did the name 'the marshes'. After the National Council approved a motion in April 1992 to relocate the citizens of the marshes, the campaign became known as 'land rehabilitation'. Then, when no land was actually put to use, they called it 'operation dryout'. The term 'marshes' disappeared from official vocabulary, replaced by 'rehabilitated lands' and then 'dried lands'. This change of names actually matched what was happening on the ground, for with the air and artillery bombardment and the burning of villages, the Marsh Arabs were pushed, by force and fire, across the border into refugee camps in Iran. Men who had opened their eyes in the morning onto an open sky and expanses of water which stretched to the horizon, found themselves inside tented compounds, surrounded by barbed wire, on desiccated land in Iran. Those who did not manage to escape were taken to execution grounds in northern Iraq, just as other victims of the *Anfal* campaign in Kurdistan were being taken for execution in the deserts of the south.

After the marshes were emptied of their people, they were emptied of their water. At a time of the international sanctions, tens of millions of dollars were spent on creating new 'rivers', Qadissiya River, the Mother of all Battles River, Pride River, the Crown of Battles River, the Leader River. These were rivers with a perverse purpose, to dry out the lands instead of to water them. A series of dams were also built between the Tigris and Euphrates rivers stretching 600 kilometres from Qurna to Makhfar al-Shayb to prevent water flowing back into this sanctuary which the leader now wanted to be pure salt. Some 80 percent of the middle marshes and 94 percent of the Hamara marshes were turned into crusts of salt land. Only the Howeiza River was left, the source of which was the Karun River in Iran.

When the regime fell, the water leaked from these dams which were no longer maintained, into the salt depressions. It brought with it the reeds, and fish, and water buffaloes and some of the Marsh Arabs, who had come back to their ancestral lands. And yet the possibility of the return of the waters also brought fear of water to the people of the water. Many still lived in settlements on dried-out lands. They were afraid the levees would collapse completely and flood them.

When I went, we set out in our Land Rover to reach the marshes before dawn. With the windows open, we listened to the chirping of millions of crickets and birds, welcoming the sun along with us as it gradually infused the heads of the tall reeds with a grey green colour. Before we got to the second barrage, I saw a light like I had never seen in my life, a mixture of yellow and rose and purple. Then, all of a sudden it seemed, the sun leaped out like a ball shot by the god Analil. It felt like we had just missed the moment of creation.

The Bu Muhammad

In a guest building made of reeds, on a piece of fissured dried-out land, I met one of the oldest tribes of Iraq, the Bu Muhammad. The Bedouin who migrated from the Arabian Peninsula before the arrival of Islam had left their language, religion, culture and lineage to this tribe. Some of them settled arable farms on lands stretching from Amara to Saleh Castle, while others became Marsh Arabs, living by fishing.

The Bu Muhammad trace their name to a love story some fifteen generations back.

'Our ancestor Muhammad fled his own tribe,' one of the elders told me, 'because he had killed his cousin in a fight. He took refuge among the Fereijat clan and lived among them as a stranger. He was sad and love struck, and was the first to sing our song, the Muhammadawi dirge. He loved the daughter of leader of the Fereijat tribe, Mahtaya. He loved her like he loved the marshes, and asked for her hand from the sheikh. The sheikh demanded in turn Muhammad's sister as his third wife, quid pro quo. After they had exchanged women, Muhammad realised on his wedding night that he had been tricked. The sheikh had married him to his ugly daughter, not to the one he loved. But our grandfather swallowed the setback, and decided that this was his destiny. And from this fate, the Bu Muhammad tribe were born. From him, we, the grandchildren, learned love and endurance of misfortune'.

As I listened to them, I searched for my own roots among them, for the Beni Asad, my own clan, are traced back to the Bu Muhammad and the al-Jezairy are one of that clan's town-dwelling branches. The story is that the 'Jezairy', or 'island-dweller' in our name, refers to the islands in the marshes.

They have a distinctive way of talking which I identified with. There is nobody like the elders of the Bu Muhammad who have mastered the art of speaking with their hands and mouths at the same time. They know how to start a conversation with an arresting phrase, raising and lowering their tones rhythmically, in a way which matches their subject matter. The hand movements add a question mark, a note of hesitation, an exclamation mark. Even the rosary in their hands is part of the conversation, saying something or listening.

Like the other Marsh Arab tribes, the Bu Muhammad people were forced to leave the water and come to dry land during the war with Iran.

'I went to the governor to complain,' the elder said. 'Water is our life. Water is our earth and our air too. I told him that our animals had died from thirst and now our children are beginning to die. You promised us you would bring us water in tankers. I told him our children were in the front line, in front of all the soldiers, during the war. They cleared the paths for you, they blew up the mines with their own bodies. Is it fair to abandon us now in this state? There was an intelligence officer sitting next to the governor, a Tikriti. He looked me over while I was talking, showing obvious disdain. And every now and then he would shout at me "Lower your hands while you're talking. Lower your voice!"'

He paused.

'You know us,' the elder continued. 'The Bu Muhammad, we talk with our hands as much as our mouths. Plus, we only know how to talk loudly.'

Umm Ouf, a middle-aged woman, recalled the verse from al-Jawahiri when she received us in her ramshackle lodging. The smell of bread baking was mouth-watering. I asked her if we could film her while she baked and talked. She said confidently: 'film? Why not?'

She was not ashamed of her dwelling. Her poverty was out in the open, uncovered as though a reproach to the corruption of the world which had brought her to this state.

She said she had never been to town except to go to a funeral. She lived on fish, and the flour from her rations. She sleeps in the hovel with the cows and the chickens. 'We live with the animals, and get rid of the gnats and mosquitoes by burning their manure.'

Her daughter sat beside her, peeking out at us from beneath a burqa. I asked if they had any problems between them. She said no.

'What would we fight about?'

I asked if her husband would bring a new wife. She replied: 'Let him first figure out how to put shoes on his feet.'

The strange thing about this poverty is that it is happening on some of the richest lands on earth. There are huge oil deposits which hardly even need discovering since the black gold oozes out of the ground and colours the earth around it.

South to Basra

I was distracted as we drove south, part of a delegation invited to take part in a poetry competition, torn between words and images: the words of my neighbour in the car, whom I was meeting after a long time apart, and the flow of images passing as we drove along. I tried to reconcile what I was now seeing with the images in my head. When I had been at university in Baghdad, I had taken this road south back home to Najaf so often I had been bored stiff by it.

The best ideas had come to me on this road, at the time when I was just starting to write. I blocked out my memories to look at the scene now, and what it all meant, the dusty palm trees in the distance, and the flat expanses of salt which had now eaten up the rich black earth. There were the corpses of old bits of farm machinery, lying on their sides, broken beyond repair, and abandoned fields with ruined, old ploughs lying in the middle of them. What war had the farmer gone off to, never to return?

The long exhibition of Iraq's ruin proceeded without a break. It would never end.

Children seemed to come out of nowhere, running alongside us, barefooted, the wind billowing their *dishdashas* out. The energy and fun of childhood shielded them from their poverty. They could not get to the road in time to touch us as we passed. We left them behind, only to see another wave of children coming after them, out of nowhere again, or the remains of brokendown houses strangled by the encroaching salt in the fields.

This procession of poets moved south. Meanwhile another procession was coming the other way, bearing black and green and red banners, indefatigable, moving towards the tomb of the Imam Hussain at Kerbala, a few days before the anniversary of his death.

Beside the road, some also walked barefoot. These people were remarkable. They had many tragedies behind them and under their feet, and their dead, slaughtered in the series of wars or in massacres, whispered in their ears. They had tragedies ahead of them, the booby- trapped cars that waited for them at the gates of the Shia holy cities of Najaf and Kerbala. But they forgot their own tragedies of the recent past and the near future. All their focus was on reliving the tragedy that had happened 1500 years before.

These are my people. But I find it hard to understand the motivation. I could say that they are looking for group identity in a tragedy that happened in another time and place, to relive it together every year. The tragedy that gives them an identity they could not have during the years of oppression. The rhythm of the march gave them strength beyond their weak bodies. Their eyes were fixed on the horizon in front of them, sometimes rising up on tip toes to see if they could yet snatch a glimpse of the Golden Domes of Kerbala. They looked for a meaning to transcend their poverty, a story to unite them.

An old woman, dressed in black, tires and sits down by the side of the road. Her daughter, a young widow, looks after her. She is going to mourn a husband taken from her by the wars, no doubt. There is no time to see more. We pass another gaggle of women, their *abeyas* floating in the wind, and then a group of barefooted young boys, brandishing their banners at us, and then older men, who have gathered up their robes in their hands to preserve them and are marching steadily towards a hospitality tent where the host is already gesturing to them, and the smell of food wafts out to welcome them.

There are such tents all along the road, with plates of food set out, hosts beckoning them inside to eat and drink and rest. They come out onto the street to beckon us also inside. We wave to them as we carry on south. The other procession continues, unabated, north. Distance and the desert and the barren fields stretch out between the two caravans.

Pictures and Guns

Having arrived in Basra, before the poetry reading, there was an exhibition of photographs of old Basra, just out on the street, to be opened. I am caught between looking at the dead photos and the very live weapons. On the one hand, snaps of Tanuma and Um Baroum Square. On the other, armed men who patrol among us, looking stern and pointing their guns in all directions. I go up close to a picture of the old square, clearly recognisable today even with all the banner ads for Samsung and Orascom. Then my eye is drawn beyond the photo up to the roofs of the houses surrounding us, and the figures of armed men up there. I hear the poet Muwaffaq Mohammed talking to me about his operetta *Inana*, reciting some verses from it, and at the same time compressed talk over the walkie-talkie systems: 'All the side streets have been blocked off. More attention'.

I look for an old picture of Sindbad garden where two women once promised to meet myself and the photographer Jassem al-Zubaidi and never came. But as I do, the guards brush me out of the way of the governor who has come to open the exhibition. Then I look for Qaysaria district, which we walked through drunk one night back in 1967. We fell in with a doctor, who'd also been drinking, and his wife had thrown him out of the house for the evening. He took us to party in his clinic. I'm just looking for the clinic when the guards push me inside the hall. These guards are not interested in old photos. The security emergency in the city is their thing. They cut short our browsing as if to say: 'It's useless to look for this past. It's gone. There's a different rhythm now in this city, under emergency. There's a new story every minute, a story which never ends because it is replaced by another story as sharp as a knife.' Meanwhile, our hosts would like to freeze this time of emergency with words, with poetry.

The presenter opens the reading. Thanks to the band, and welcome to the poets! And he speaks of the past with all the details of its woe to hand, but stops short of the future, which remains unknown. The new atmosphere of freedom has not managed to temper the dominant tone of despair in our poetry. Despair over the martyrdom of Hussein, 1500 years ago, or the mass graves of Saddam Hussein, or all the friends who are gone. Some of the poems wallow in the massacres with a detail that is titillating, to the point where the poet's own power to conceive bloody images has exceeded that of the torturer.

Many mocked the poetry of the previous age. Nevertheless, although the object of their praise has gone, the praises remain in this new era. Poetry has reverted to its first function: praise of the tribe, praise of oneself, or of the saints Ali and Hussein.

In the taxi the driver asked us: 'Who are you?'

'Poets,' we replied.

'All the armoured cars and protection and the closing off of the streets ... that's for you?' he asked.

'That's right,' I replied.

He asked derisively: 'Are we at a poetry festival, then? What's the occasion, the birthday of the Leader?'

In the mind of this man, who must have been about thirty-five, born and weaned in a culture of praise for the Leader, poetry was inextricably linked to public occasions. And these public events could only relate to the Leader himself. Muwaffaq Mohammed explained to me, with his customary drollness, how poetry festivals had been organised for the birthday of the Leader. The event organiser would ask someone in the party beforehand how many poets were required, and of what rank. Then he would price the whole package, the room and the food and the poets.

The audience at this recital was different from the kinds of audiences I had known in the 70s. It was noisy, people talked during recitals more than they listened. It was an anxious, impatient audience. The poet would be forced to raise his voice, which added to the rumpus.

It was my bad luck to be sat next to Aryan al-Sayyid Khalaf, known to friends as Abu Khaled. I had not known how popular he was with the younger generation. Every five minutes a young man would come up and beg me to give up my seat so he could sit next to Abu Khaled and have his picture taken. Afterwards, no doubt, he would show it off to his friends, maybe his girlfriend. I never felt as much jealousy towards someone more famous than me as I did sitting there next to Aryan.

There was a different public outside, the public of the Mahdi Army. They patrol the streets in their black shirts, worked up, likely to flare up at any moment. And with them was another mass, that of the unemployed. The city was far from poetry. It was taut, nervous, fingers were on the triggers. Could poetry change this heavy atmosphere?

We went out that night, Kowkab Hamza, Aryan al-Sayyid Khalaf and me. We left the hotel looking for a bottle of *arak*. Getting hold of alcohol in Basra is a task which requires a genius in secret operations. We sounded our driver out, to find out what side he was on. As a joke, we asked him if he knew of Kowkab Hamza. With him sitting in the car, he answered: 'No, by God I don't know her. May God protect her'.

After we had introduced ourselves, in the end he agreed to get into it with us on condition that he did not have to touch the bottle of *arak* with his own hands. I won't relate here the tortuous means we had to use to get the *arak*, through three intermediaries, or the code we used to convince the seller, his eyes bulging. But we got hold of a bottle in the end and drank it with the great pleasure of breaking a taboo.

Flight from the Centre

Basra is looking to reclaim itself, far from the centre in Baghdad. The speech of Governor Wael Abdel Latif at the opening of the recital focused on the burdens the city had had to bear. The wars had started from here, and ended here and had left lines of poverty etched in the city's face.

The city had been systematically and atrociously debased. This was captured for me in a scene I will never forget. There was a small raft fashioned from old oil barrels, tethered to wooden posts in the middle of a stagnant, green pond. And on this boat, in the middle of this stagnant pond, people were sat whiling the evening away as though they were in some corner of paradise.

Basra and the South were the main subjects of the poets from Basra. They described its *khans*, its streets and squares, as though they were in exile. The recital had begun with readings of dead poets from Basra: Badr Shaker al-Siyaab, Mahmoud al-Bureikan who had died just a few days before, stabbed by a thief he did not know, Mustafa Abdullah who had died in exile in his forties. Basra was being proposed in opposition to Baghdad.

Was this a reaction to the centralisation of the centre? My friend Qassem was troubled by it, seeing in it a thinly concealed desire for secession. But I saw it as the natural reaction to centralisation by a regime which wanted to erase all regional particularities. The Dictator would sit squarely on top of a pyramid the base of which was even and uniform, without distinction.

Now the pyramid has collapsed and everything is reverting to its first identity. A religious sect recovers its sectarianism, the tribe reaches for its tribal dress. A neighbourhood returns to neighbourly relations. A city closes its gates to be with itself. Is this fragmentation, or is it a return to the source, to reunite later in a different way? Basra is like every other city on the sea, far from the desert which separates it from Baghdad. It has all the features of a Gulf city state. It has more inhabitants than any neighbouring Gulf state, and it has beaches and oil, and great cultural heritage. But despite all that, it knows its position as Iraq's opening to the world.

Siyaab's Exile

We're walking along the corniche at Basra, where Muhammad Khaddayir's heroine walked past all the onlookers. Every ten metres there is a plinth to one of the many heroes of *al-Qadissiya*. Thieves had stolen the statues, leaving just the plinths as a token to what is missing. The slogans of the new age, post-Saddam, were sprawled on them in graffiti: 'Every place is Kerbala, every day Ashura', 'Hussein is from me, and I am from Hussein', 'This place is reserved for Falah al-Karbasi', 'Saddam is a donkey'.

Amidst the long line of empty plinths where statues to Saddam's officers once stood, the statue of the poet Siyaab remains. His frame is gaunt, his clothes loose, a notebook in his pocket for writing poetry. Ironically, he is turned with his back to the Gulf. Siyaab left his beloved Basra to go to Kuwait, which is within sight of Basra. And yet he still cried: 'I shout to the Gulf! O Gulf! Oh bestower of good and bad.'

He did not know that in the black time to come, we Iraqis would be scattered much wider, from Yemen to Australia, to the farthest corners of the Scandinavian countries. The tombs of his contemporaries would be found at the Sayyida Zeinab shrine in Damascus, where al-Jawahiri and al-Bayyati rest, the ice of Moscow where Ghaib Ta'ma Farman lies, and Highgate Cemetery in London where Boland al-Haydari and Zahed Muhammad lie. Although Siyaab is here on the Shat al-Arab, near to his village, he still seems embarrassed, as though in the wrong place and time. He seems dazed by his surroundings, the empty plinths, the destruction and chaos. An oil slick floats in the water behind him. A scene of urban desolation.

Someone has put a bouquet of plastic flowers in the fingers of his statue.

Later, I am shopping and shut my eyes to sniff for the spice market between al-Qaysariya. There are shirts wrapped in plastic. Prayer carpets made of plastic, big 'mahogany' chairs made of plastic, fruits sprayed with water, clocks with ballerinas dancing in time to the mechanism, all plastic. I move to a different passage, seeking the smell of incense which has eluded me. Bunches of tulips, pomegranate flowers, and myrtle branches spill out towards me. All plastic. Vases and serving bowls with pictures of *houris* of paradise.

The markets of Basra are smothered by this world of plastic, with nothing scratched in it, nothing imperfect.

Nothing real.

And yet in this market I hear the word *'haboubeh'*, which I had not heard for a long time. Looking down the alleyways, I see upper stories of the houses leaning into the middle with their wooden balconies. Just for a moment, I glimpse the spirit of old Basra.

Najaf

The whole way back to my city, Najaf, I asked myself what remains of it in me, and of me in it. I grope towards the vague certainty that I contain its contradictions, the mutual attraction of the desert westwards towards the Nejd, and the gardens on the banks of the Euphrates.

It is a thirsty city. It is placed beyond large expanses of salt fields and desert dunes, within a stone's throw of the Euphrates River, and yet it does not drink its waters. It wants to achieve a religion of desire by abstention, an art of precision by intention.

Full of paradoxes. Najaf knows both the most hard-line obscurantism, and the most radical free-thinking. It is familiar with religion turned priggishness and atheism turned creed.

The city vaunts its place as Iraq's port to the desert and the first port of call after the Empty Quarter, just as it vaunts its role as spiritual home to the world's Shia Muslims. But it does not possess the means to back its pride. Its people are poor and ashamed of their penury. They consider it a shame, to be hidden by appearances. The city, like me, sates itself with words just as it sates with words all its followers around the world. It has spiritual authority to counter Baghdad's authority of power.

I come back to my city Najaf afraid of three things: that I will have forgotten, that I will be blamed, and that I will die.

As we pass through Kufa, nearby, I put my head out of the window, panting like a pilgrim to see the sparkle of the golden domes so he can become cleansed by the mere sight of it.

If the houses of Najaf and Kufa ever meet, says an old proverb, it is a sign of the Day of Judgement is near. Now, out of urban growth, it has happened but in spite of that, people are moving about as if the Day of Judgment already came, or comes every day.

Nobody in the city will know me after all this time. The old sons of the city fled it for Baghdad, leaving the city of the Word for Baghdad, the city of the Dinar. But those that stayed might blame me for leaving them in the hour of crisis and returning too late, when it is all just dust and funerals as pious Shia from all over the world come to be buried here. At the entrance to the city I saw people cutting down eucalyptus trees, the city's *green belt*, with axes. They cut them down in haste and anxiety as though the desert was the only possible backdrop for all this death.

I didn't find the city as I knew it. I didn't find anyone I knew, as I had hoped to, and so went to stay in a hotel. No one blamed me for that, not even the hotel owner whom I got to know who was, purely by chance, a distant cousin. Nobody blamed me for staying in a hotel because the whole city had become a refuge for strangers after most of the original townsfolk had left.

I wandered around the city torn between two desires: that I

could grasp the city as it is now, to expunge my illusions of it, and just the opposite, that I could expunge the present and find in the city what would strengthen my memories.

As I walked round the town, I tried to recover the details of the city directly from my mind's eye, not from memories, or the memory of memories. But it would not come. The city withdrew into itself, away from me, and in this short time I could not find the common ground. I am deep in an illusion of time and place, and the city provokes me with its new shape and its new people.

In the two marketplaces I looked for faces I knew, among the cloth sellers or people from the big old Najaf families, such as the House of Ajeena or the House of Mudaffar. I asked in a shop about them but the shopkeeper shook his head and turned away to serve other customers. I looked for the Helw Bookshop where in my childhood I had kept a weekly appointment, 11.30 AM on Thursdays, when *Samir* magazine arrived, and where later I became a regular customer for all my books, and for *Helal* magazine.

The Najaf I knew is no more. The old Najafi families, and especially people of my generation, left it for Baghdad. I had seen most of my generation from Najaf, in fact, at various parties in Baghdad. What I saw in Najaf were the descendants of those who had migrated into the city from further south.

I had not been here to follow the transformation in the city's architecture stone by stone, so the difference seemed enormous and gaping, and I was left wandering around like some archaeologist, seeing the skeleton of the past lying underneath the city of the present. Beyond my mental map was another city altogether, choked by a belt of new suburbs that the Ba'ath had named after their own special manner: al-Ba'ath District, Jerusalem District, Leader District, and the Mother of Battles. New people lived in them who lived and died for the party, not the city. Within these new bastard suburbs, which did nothing for the integrity of the city, only two areas were left of the old city: al-Howeish, and part of al-Mishraaq. I never really knew al-Howeish that well, beyond the entrance to it from Timma, where Baqir, whom we nicknamed 'little Buqairy', always stood selling legumes and the pickles that went with it. And of course there were also the crunchy flies that had fallen in and got fried too.

But the city had retained its landmarks, in spite of the immense changes: the shrine and tomb of Imam Ali.

We went up onto the roof of one of the hotels to get our bearings, the director Abdel-Hadi al-Rawi, the TV crew, and me. The Haidari Dome is the heart of the city. Around it were placed the four old quarters of the city, al-Howeish, al-Mishraaq, al-Buraaq and al-Amara. As boys, we would enter the dome from one of the gates that led to it from our quarter of the city.

But the shrine and the dome were not only the link between the older parts of town and the newer districts. It was also the link between past and present. Like a river of light and gold. We stayed on the roof following the movement of the light on the domes. The light changed, from the white heat of midday to cream tinged with gold. When the sun disappeared from direct view, we could still see it reflected on the domes, and then a fiery orange started to glow. The light which had projected onto the scene now became the scene itself, and with it the pilgrims we could see in the precinct, in the distance, were transformed into strange creatures of light and fire and gold. We could see them and they could not see us. We could hear no sound but the Qur'anic recitation, which rang out from among the mosques and domes but placeless, as though it arose spontaneously from the scene, or the light.

As the last ray of light stretched across the sky, I felt a deep sense of awe thinking about my family who were connected to this place.

My aunt Salma, badly treated by her brutal husband, would come to the shrine every day after the midday siesta. She would kneel on the white marble floor, grasp the golden latticework around the shrine, place her forehead against it, and listen to the prayers, including the *da'i kameel*. She would close her eyes and weep until the coolness of the marble and the golden lattice entered her heart and gave her a strange calm. Then she could forgive the world its brutality, and return home in a state of grace.

These golden minarets dazzle those who approach the city. Bedouin crossing the desert to get here would be astonished by this amazing shrine. Entering this city which spurns them and their camels, they would move around in town, trading with the artisans and merchants, but never ceasing to be amazed by the crescents on the minarets which flashed the gold of the sun back at them.

Artisans and peasants would come from the south to receive grace at the grate of the Prince. Their hands would grasp grates, and feel the cold of its silver. Touch was then hearing and vision, and their hands, normally just work tools, abandoned their everyday function to become ears, hearts beseeching the Hidden and the Present to relieve them of an illness, or a fatigue, a personal disaster that had befallen them. If their intercession did not work, they would stay on to be close to their tombs in Wadi Salaam, men and women barely older than fifty.

Poor Iranians came, some of them on foot across the deserts and mountains having collected all the money and strength they had to get to the shrine. Tears flowed from them as they kissed the doors to the shrine. Afghans came who had mastered the art of baking *Taftuni* and *Nakhuni* bread. Pakistanis filled the khans of Najaf, and Indian dervishes who stuck themselves with knives. Our mothers terrified us with stories about how they kidnapped children and ate their hearts. This strange crowd would gather around the Shrine, the point of reference for Shia Muslims around the world.

From the roof of the hotel, I look for my old neighbourhood al-Amara. I close my eyes to see it in my mind's eye, the start of al-Amara *suq*, the cafe on the left, and Qasim's barber's shop on the right. I can see the leaders of the Bu Kalal clan, with their thick moustaches and wide *uqqal*, stocky bodies and revolvers at their sides to protect them in their feud with the Bu Amer clan. And Qassim the Stalinist barber who moved around his customers, ceaselessly talking politics. He moved jerkily, his darting eyes split between the heads of his clients and the movement in the street, some secret worry pushing him.

In the *suq*, there was the tall, lean, clean Baghdadi with his *uqqal* set high on his head and his rough Najafi manners, able to hold a clutch of plates in one hand, which had only four fingers. Also, there was the Baghdadi's shop that sold the best pickles in the city. And Hussein Abu Thalaj, who sold curdled milk. My father would stop there on his way home from the school to pick up some curds. One day two men were arguing in front of his shop and one of them threw a shoe at the other one. The shoe flew over the head of the other man and landed in the whey. In a flash, Hussein had retrieved the shoe, wiped it on his *dishdasha* without anyone else seeing, returned it to the man who had thrown it, calmed the fight, and resumed his market cry: 'Cold milk for sale!' I was the only one who knew where the shoe had been. I never drank his milk after that.

After the *suq*, in an alleyway after Jabbouri the baker's, was the house of Alwan the Bird. There was nobody who had tried to fly, escape the boredom of the city, like Alwan. He looked like an imbecile with his mouth always open and his lips hanging. You would never have guessed this was a boy who dreamed of flying. But he tried many times from the roof of the family house. He tried with wings made of wood, then fibre and rubber, then cloth stretched onto a rubber frame. He would flap his wings with all the strength in his arms, standing on the edge of the roof which looked onto a thatched passageway. He would close his eyes and tilt his head up, desperate to escape the confines of this boring city. He flapped his wings, faster and faster. And in that brief moment he was in the air he would dream he had left the earth. Then open his eyes to find he had landed on the thatched roof of the passageway. He was still in the city. He had not soared above the golden minarets.

One day Alwan came along with both an arm and a leg in plaster, limping from the pain of his broken limbs. He had tried to fly using an umbrella, and fallen onto the little storehouse where Jabbouri the baker kept his charcoal. He was lucky to survive. From then on, everyone in the neighbourhood called him Alwan the Bird, more a reference to the way his brain had taken flight than his body. Later on, no one seemed to know if Alwan continued in his attempts to fly, or had to satisfy himself with flying only in his dreams, like the rest of us.

Instead, it is the whole district which has flown away, as if that part of my life that I lived in these alleyways – the ones I can walk through with my eyes closed, with houses and people I remember house by house, individual by individual – had never existed. The space between the gate to the Shrine and the first shops of the al-Amara *suq* is empty, cleared as far as the salt lake. The Ba'ath regime cleared it with bulldozers after the 1991 uprising.

I could now encompass this district, which had once been my whole world, with one sweep of the eyes. Could it really be, I asked myself, that the neighbourhood, with all its alleyways and passages and houses and diverse personalities, had been so small?

I would always hurry from al-Amara to my grandfather's house, for there was a brutal war between the boys of the two districts. There was daily fighting between the graves and the quarry with all the tactics of war – flight, counter-attack and intimidation. But in this war, everyone knew the name and family and clan of each enemy.

Each day there would be new casualties, and when they went to school they would be punished again by the teachers, who knew from their bandages or cuts that they had been fighting. And yet there was an unspoken agreement between the two sides to stop fighting and run away whenever the police cars came round. My foes in Mishraaq would block my way as I went to my grandfather's house, so I used to go at midday, when the heat was most intense, to avoid them.

The Two Old Maids of Najaf

After thirty years Sabeeh and I went back to the house of my grandfather in Najaf, setting out from the Eastern Gate inside the city. I asked Sabeeh to leave me to figure the way out on my own. I set the direction guided by the old mound of dirt, which now had a hotel standing on it, crossing the same alleyway that had blue domes and the tombs of the Jawahari and Bahr Uloum families bursting onto it from either side.

I followed the steps of the young boy I had been, coming from his house in Amara district to the house of his grandfather in Mishraaq. I half expected to see my boyhood foes standing by the turning to the alleyway, or on the doorsteps of their homes. They would be ready to fight in the same old way, and I'd feel their eyes burning through my back as I walked past them. But the alleyways were entirely empty. The path was clear.

I reached my grandfather's house, which the late Sayyed Mohsen Hakim had bought off him, part of an enormous property empire which his sons and grandsons were now inheriting. Nothing remained to our family from the great old compound except the cottage attached, in which the two daughters of my aunt Manahil lived. When we got to the house we knew it by the old, chestnut-coloured wooden door, and the ornate knocker. As I slowly lifted the knocker I wondered what memories would come flooding back, which ghosts of the past would reply.

'Who's there?' a voice behind the door asked.

'It's me. Zuhair,' I said.

'Zuhair? Which Zuhair?' the voice said.

'Zuhair al-Jezairy, the son of Ali,' I said.

There were voices inside sounding like they came from the bottom of a deep well, and like I was in a word game with ghosts. The voices came closer. I dug into the past again.

'Open up. It's the Zuhair whose mother was Amira,' I said.

The magic word did its work. The door opened a crack and inside four eyes peered at me from the gloom of a badly lit corridor and behind black *abeyas*. They were wide open with surprise and a little scared.

I entered the house. The eyes followed me: what's brought him here after all these years? Has he come to claim some property or demand a share in the house? I felt unsettled in front of these eyes which ran up and down me. I sat down on a bench. The faces came a little more into view, the *abeyas* pushed back a little. I was looking for which one was Hasiba and which one Azzat, to warm the atmosphere up a little.

So I asked: 'Which one of you was it that picked nits out of my hair, and to distract me, because I hated it so much, would tell the story of the *jinn* who jumped out of the well?'

I had a look at the structure of the house, the lower and upper rooms. I was talking about the past but the two sisters wanted to talk about the present. The elder one complained that when Hakim had bought the main house and was doing it up he had also absorbed part of the cottage where the two women lived. The second one took me to see what the latest fighting between the Americans and the Mahdi Army had done. A Mahdi Army missile had punched through the roof of the house and shattered its walls. It had settled on its side in the middle of the room.

'We didn't get anything from the government in spite of their promises,' she said.

I asked about her brother Adel and what he was doing about the problem and she said that Adel had not come to see them in a long time. So nobody took care of the two old spinsters, and nobody came to break the crushing monotony of their lives in this house, which seemed like a well. Our visit had given them a story they would talk about for years. Leaving the house, I felt a great sense of numbness. I did not turn back. When I shut the door I said to myself it would not open again on another visitor for long years to come. Nobody would remember them, as they simply curled up from loneliness and boredom. I thought about how much they must have longed for love and marriage and children, how much they must have waited for someone to take them out of the loneliness and monotony. But they had stayed here, embroidering the hems of their *abeyas*, stitch by stitch, until time ran out on them.

The North

Tikrit: Oppressor and Victim

In contrast with Najaf, which disowned me, Tikrit welcomed me
like an important guest. We crossed a number of American and Iraqi
checkpoints before we reached the town. At one of these checkpoints
they made us get out of the car for dogs to sniff us, and masked men
to inspect us. Our bodies were supple and pliant as they frisked us,
as though we had no bones or muscles.

My host, who drove us into town, said: 'See for yourself. What
marks it out from other towns?'

He said that because he knew the rumours that this town had
beggared the country, scooping up all its wealth.

And in truth, there really wasn't anything to distinguish this town
from the others. The markets were just like in any other town except
perhaps for sporadic new buildings here and there which took away
from its authenticity and flooded it with plastic goods.

The Tigris river twists and turns through this region, passing by
the town like a wayfarer stopping to see. On one of its bends, Saddam
had set up a complex of palaces on a stretch of land formed in the
shape of the Arab world. And on each piece of land was a separate
palace for an Arab head of state.

This atrocious sense of style, drawn to symbolism, imagined that of course the Arab leaders would come to visit the town Saddam had been born in. At that point they would not have any sense of being in the wilderness, or longing for their own countries because the Leader had thought for them, and prepared for them a house and a map, so that they could imagine that they were in two places at once, in their own country and in the town of the Leader.

As we crossed the iron bridge that spanned the map, a high steel wall prevented us from seeing into the palaces. A statue of Saddam wearing the *uqqal* and *keffiya*, astride a horse, stood at the entrance of the large palace complex. He must have chosen this picture to recall his own journey of flight after the attempt as a young man to kill Abdel Karim Qassem, one of the key pieces of Saddam's lore.

There was a widespread belief back in 2003 that Saddam was hidden away in some place in the town, and that he would again make the journey of flight. But to where?

The Americans have taken this palace complex and all the houses on it as their base. They have done this, and left the statue of Saddam upright, as a deliberate symbol: we are here, in his house and in his town.

Symbols have played a huge role in this conflict. Just as the statue of Saddam tumbled in Tahrir Square, *al-Arabiyya* put out pictures of him 'live' from Azamiya district (a short distance away) surrounded by his supporters. During the inspections for weapons of mass destruction, the regime put a red line around these palaces which it called 'the symbols of Iraqi sovereignty'. They were the only place forbidden to the inspection teams. Apart from that they could go anywhere they liked: to army barracks, public and secret factories, universities, mosques, ministry buildings. The main thing was that sovereignty would reside in these palaces alone. In return, Bush Jr insisted precisely on the inspection of these palaces, as part of the war of symbols. After the regime had collapsed, the civilian governor Bremer made Saddam's bedroom an office, leaving the bed in its place.

The people of Tikrit deny that Saddam is from their town. They point to a patch of land after a bend in the river, where the village of al-Aouja is now fenced off with barbed wire, 7 kilometres away from the centre of their town, and to a group of luxurious palaces stretched on the river beyond it: 'Those are the mansions of his clan.'

When we got to the home of my host, well-wishers had gathered. They were all from the same tribe. The style of honouring was straight out of the traditions of Arab hospitality. As the guest, I had to sit at the top of the table with the elders. The young men sat in a different place. They were expected to pay attention to what was being said but not to speak themselves unless they were asked a question. It was a reception with two purposes: they could explain their true situation, and dispel some myths, and they could find out from someone working in the media how things were shaping up.

While the elders had stored up some wisdom from everything they had been through, the younger men seemed to me to be lost. As officers in the Republican Guard, and Saddam's private guard, they had enjoyed a certain power and position. Now they complained of the humiliation they suffered at American checkpoints. The elders are sometimes cynical with them: 'That's nothing to what you yourselves have done to people!'

The elders complained to me that they had lost their children some time ago. They had been taken from the homes and farms of their parents when they were small, to become soldiers and officers in the armed forces.

'They were kidnapped,' one man said to me. 'The military detachments they joined became their new families and the president became their father and uncle. They left our parental control and came under his. Some of them have killed their own brothers and cousins on orders from the president.'

They took me to their rich lands just by the river which were now unkempt. Orchards of pomegranate and date and citrus trees were dense with undergrowth.

'Look! These farms have no one to look after them after we go. Our sons were cut off from agriculture when the authorities took them. Here they are in the pride of their youth and yet they do not know how to dig an irrigation ditch or prune a tree.'

The young men replied in turn. 'What do they envy us for? We have never travelled outside the country. We were denied education and spent our entire youth in a state of emergency, sleeping in barracks, resisting Iranian attacks.'

Time stands still here, the same rustic scenes recurring slowly. A chicken pecks at some corn. A car passes and all eyes follow it with curiosity and suspicion. Idleness wears the nerves of the young men who were cut loose when the army collapsed. They walk through the village in their *dishdashas*, bowing their heads when women pass by in shame at their unemployment. Theirs is a small world, shuttling between the houses of their brothers and cousins, exchanging gossip about the latest clashes between the American forces and the resistance on the main road. At the same time, they are accused of collaboration with the Americans because the sheikhs of the tribes have made a deal with the Americans, undertaking to prevent sniping from their villages.

Some of them don't want to believe that his time has gone, never to return. They fantasise that Saddam will return just as before. Others wait without knowing what they are waiting for. Perhaps things will settle down and the features of this new world will become clear. The one real thing to do in these villages is to marry and procreate.

I was amazed to think, as I experienced the kindness of the people here, how all the crimes of the regime had been laid at their door when they were victims too. Just as people were afraid of them, they were afraid of him.

Kurdistan: A Topsy Turvy Return

I was returning to Kurdistan through the front door this time, in an official convoy protected by guards from the Presidency. The convoy sped along the asphalted road that, during the time of the Peshmergas, we had run across at night on highest alert. The tarmac road was our enemy then, bringing the tanks and armoured cars of the regime and army guard posts planted on both sides of it.

The convoy travelled along the government road from Erbil to Dohuk, passing through Barzan. The guard's eyes were fixed on the mountains that had once been our refuge. Kurdistan Workers Party (PKK) fighters, Kurds from Turkey, are still holed up there, watching government cars pass, just as we had. But I did not feel any sense of danger from them, or triumph in being in the place of the government I had fought. It was not us that liberated this land but them.

I had the feeling as we passed along this road of betraying my old friends the mountains when I had come down into the city, as though I was in the wrong place. I was in the wrong time and place.

The Peshmerga that I fought the regime with had become the new government.

I go into their office and they come round from behind their big power tables, in their big black suits, buttoned up, neck ties, unsure whether to smile at the reunion or stay serious, to project the gravitas their new position needs.

Masoud Barzani has kept his traditional Peshmerga clothes in order to emphasise his old charismatic role, not his new official one.

'It's hard for us to build a state,' he says. 'We learned how to blow up bridges and roads. Now we need to build them. We used to make war on the government and now we have become it.'

The time in the mountains was not constructive for the political parties, or their urban cadres. The urban-based party guerrilla, for example, does not need a safe fallback base. He blends into the city, stays with friends and relatives, lives off party income. Other party members in the city live off their everyday jobs as workers, petty traders and government officials. But the extreme campaigns of repression turned the party rural, escaping the regime's cities into remote stretches of countryside.

There it was the rural members, at home in the environment and among the tribes, who prevailed over those sections who came from the towns and were estranged. Tough guerrilla action also came to be valued more highly than intellectual work, now the plaything of urban elites, of no interest to the fighters in the mountains. Among the fighters themselves, a culture of tribal and military allegiance took precedence over the debates and ideological values of a party.

It was a different time and place now, but the men who had come down from the mountains still felt angry towards the effete city and its technocrats. We would find this tension between the men of the mountains and men of the cities wherever we went in free Kurdistan. The technocrats and intellectuals of the cities called the mountain men the Old Guard of the party, and attacked them for being against innovation and hogging all the sensitive posts to do with security and money and politics. 'They are repeating the mistakes of Algeria,' one of them said, citing the alienation caused by the National Liberation Front (FLN) guerrillas after they won power from the French in the 60s but stayed too cliquey. The Old

Guard accused the men of the towns of having served the Ba'athist regime, and working their way into new posts by exploiting the weak knowledge of the Peshmerga in matters of state.

The old custom of settling differences by internal fighting had put the parliamentarians in a delicate position. When fighting broke out between the two Peshmerga groups in 1996 most of the parliamentarians had condemned it and camped out in the parliament building in protest for 110 days. The combatants had not entered the building during that time. Dr Rooz Showesh, the speaker of parliament, showed me the places where the different factions sat inside parliament, and then the window through which they had watched the street fighting of the Peshmerga. They debated among themselves and watched the news on TV while outside matters were settled in the traditional Peshmerga fashion.

Sometimes you could find both sides of this divide represented in one man. For when I met some of the men from the mountains who had now become officials, they would come to shake my hand, uncertainly, apologetically, embarrassed, as though we had let our father the mountain down and become city dwellers, and the men of power that we had once fought. I could see the dye they used to cover their greying hair, to remove the hardships of the mountains. It seemed like they wanted to take root here in their offices. Maybe for them the corruption which appeared with the rise of the new state was some kind of compensation for all their trials and deprivations.

I would try when I met these men to remove the distance created by protocol and begin talking about that life long ago in the mountains. When we began reminiscing, the serious one tone would go away, to be replaced by a joyful smile. The feeling pervaded us that that was the real time of innocence, and the present, with its dark suits, neck ties and dyed hair, was simply what was imposed by the necessities of governing.

I could not help reminding one of the leaders when he invited me to a restaurant, of the times we had eaten *hommous* in the mountains off little camping tables, three Peshmerga to each dish.

'That was then and this is now,' he said, embarrassed, as if he would have wiped out all those memories if he could.

I mastered my emotions and apologised. There was no escape from this kind of compromise in order to build the state the Kurds have dreamed of. I tried to define my position with them as someone who has fought their battles with them and shared their triumph, and also a critic.

Arbil and Barzaan

Fawzi Karim and I left the Jawar Jara Hotel, escaping our bodyguards, into the heart of the city of Arbil. Fawzi asked me doubtfully: 'Are you sure you know the way?'

I nodded, smiling, figuring that sooner or later a gap in the alleyways would show us the citadel on the hill, and then we could orient ourselves. We went to Majko cafe, hang-out of the intellectuals, and drank tea, trying to assimilate the fact that we were actually in a part of our own country, everything seemed so alien.

I was taken back to another time. Here, somewhere between the citadel and the maze of *suqs*, was the hotel where I had slept on the roof with my father as a boy. I could not sleep in spite of the tiring journey we had made from Baghdad. My eyes fell on a shaky old man, who was slowly progressing up the narrow path to the citadel. I decided I wasn't going to go to sleep until I saw what happened. I was convinced he wasn't going to make it. Lying on my side, propped up by my elbow, I watched him progress step by step for one, maybe two hours. I could see him breathing in time to his steps. In the end he got to the top, and I slept at last, relaxed, as though I were the one who had made the ascent.

Later, when I grew up and lived as a guerrilla in the mountains here, the Kurds taught me the wisdom of this old man in climbing mountains.

'Get yourself into the rhythm of your feet,' they would say. 'Feel the solidity of the ground with the end of your toes before you take each new step, like the mountain goat. Stay within yourself, conserve half your energy for when you reach the top.'

Now I went up the hill to the citadel using the old man's technique. I look behind me to see how far I have come, not ahead of me to see how far is left. Below me is the amazing criss-cross of Arbil's *suqs*, a mish-mash of smells and colours. One *suq* leads to another, the goods changing from one street to the next. Smells mingle, goat-skin carpets, spices, cheeses, and an array of colours. No one likes bright colours as much as the Kurds and the traditional dress of their women reflect this affection. Shelf after shelf of colour in the stalls dazzles me. It seems like all the feast days have come together in the dress of a woman.

My eyes wander over the markets, the bustle and the traffic. At the same time, an inner sense tells me to think about where I am: 'You are climbing to a place inhabited by six separate civilisations built on top of each other over six thousand years'. The children who run up to me have no idea of this, nor the woman emptying her bucket of dirty water in the street, turning away from me, that her water will seep down to an ancient city beneath her feet that she does not know.

In contrast to Kurdistan's abandoned villages, its towns are crowded with country folk, whole armies of youngsters who have left their villages. They just hang around, or hawk smuggled goods.

There are armies of middle-aged men too, sitting splayed out on cafe chairs, endlessly fingering the beads on their rosaries, or the ends of their moustaches.

Why have they left such fertile countryside, I ask? On the twisty mountain road between Arbil and Suleimaniya, Hadi Hassan Mami, a man in his fifties, told me what had happened to the generation of men who had been brought up in forced settlements.

We reached the town of Barzan by the road where before we had laid ambushes, the old asphalted road where we had waited for armed columns of government forces. In those days, the way to Barzan was across the mountains, passing through villages where the seven Barzan tribes lived. The villages in these valleys are still in distress. The women have grown old waiting for men who went away and didn't come back. No word came, only rumours that they had been used for experiments with chemical weapons. Sons had grown up without seeing their fathers. Once on a visit when I was taking supper in one of these villages, a woman stirring a saucepan furiously leant over to the man sitting beside me.

'Ask this Arab beside you. Has he got any news about our men?'

My Kurdish companion answered her: 'Where would he have got news from? He doesn't even know about his own family!'

'Ask him anyway,' the woman replied. 'Maybe he knows something.'

I felt embarrassed, as though I was somehow implicated in the abduction of those 5,000 men, all taken on the same night which must have seemed like Judgement Day, when helicopters dropped from the sky like the armies of Gog and Magog. The men were led away blindfolded, the women forbidden to scream. The last soldiers poured kerosene on the houses and trees and storehouses around them.

'The last time I saw him, they had already taken the house. It was burning, smoke rising from it,' the woman said.

We passed through all these villages in mourning. We carried away their stories, along with the food the widows cooked for us and then ascended Mount Shirin, and its desolate, volcanic summit, which looks over the town of Barzan. Then we came down the slopes and entered the town. I had stayed here once before, in 1984, when we guerrillas had lived a brief and troubled truce with government forces.

I asked where the settlements were that 'we' had withdrawn from in 1987, fleeing from chemical weapons. My young companions, from the Barzan tribe, did not understand what I meant. They were from a later generation of flight. They grew up in refugee camps and knew nothing of those days except a few scraps from the talk of their elders. Even Hassan, whose father had died in a government prison during the offensive against the Barzan villages.

The town of Barzan has a special status. The historic Kurdish leader Mustafa Barzani is buried here, under a pile of stones, without a headstone. The place is under protection and it is forbidden to hunt. Birds sat chirping a few metres away from us, paying no attention to us.

My companions had never crossed the mountains on foot. They have never drunk water from these wells, or slept out on the slopes. They come to their ancestral town in fancy cars on made-up roads. They listened to my stories about the old days like they were fairy tales.

Suleimaniya, Town in Rebellion

On the way to Suleimaniya, we stopped at a roadside cafe. One of my old Peshmerga colleagues took me by the hand: 'You see that series of grey peaks? Behind that mountain directly ...' – I could just make out two adjacent peaks shrouded in fog and darkness – '... is Kandeel Mountain'.

I left the group and the tables groaning with food, the fountains, the lines of cars behind me, and went to the edge of the terrace. I looked for those peaks, shaped like cows' udders, and cast my mind back to 1983 and the time I was fighting with the Kurdish Peshmerga against the Saddam government. I could see myself trudging through the snow up to my waist, Wadi Beshtashan behind me where bombs were falling, bullets whistling, fires raging. We had left behind many dead, and hundreds of comrades whose fates were unknown. The images of that day, which still sometimes come to me in my dreams, came back: the fall of Liyuja, then Zewa, then the encirclement of Beshtashan. Burning our papers, exploding our ammunition dumps, and then the retreat to the mountains.

Now, we came down to the plain, closer to that mountain we had once climbed with the desperate determination to cling to life. I later wrote about it in my novel *Preferred Towns*.

As night fell, I could no longer make out the detail and was left with a vague outline. My exhausted body, plunged deep into the snow, could no longer grasp any thought except my obscure, nightmarish existence, and the impulse to get up again when I stumbled and keep going. There was a thick fog in my head which made my fantasies more real than reality. I lit a match and entered a cave, which stretched away like a horizontal well shaft, only to come to an abrupt end. I fall onto a bed of ice. I stir myself: 'What's the matter with you?'

I try to master my body, lift my head up. I see one of my comrades on the ice, face down, his mouth open, eating the snow. I see another digging into it with his fingers: 'I left a piece of warm meat here.' He whimpers like a child when they carry him away from that snow. I can see a fire lit at the end of the cave, hands fluttering around it to get warm, like birds. I walk towards it, past comrades stretched out on either side of the tunnel. I step over one without calling to him. Another one grasps my hand. I move on and see someone cry out violently from his dream: 'You will die!'

A third one grasps my hand. I am losing the will to live. I drop onto the snow and cannot rise when they call me. I started to count the seconds: one, two, three, and close my eyes to find peace. The rocky outcrops and snowy peaks were slipping away, the remains of colleagues who had reached there before me and dropped, the endless mountains, the stumbling, the brutal marching, and the weight of life which we were carrying like donkeys. Hypothermia came, a trippy kind of fatigue. The pain retreated, first from the end of my finger tips, then my feet, then up to my knees. I could barely hear even my own cries for help, or my own little grunts, or any voice of will. My internal thoughts and worries faded, all that was left of life was a burning sensation on my tongue. I could see my body turned into ice, lying there until the spring rains thawed it out.

I looked around in the car to find someone who had shared this experience with me. Only someone who had lived through it could understand what I was going through, looking at those cows' udder peaks.

I looked at the faces in our escort and wondered which of them, in the other Kurdish groups then aligned with the Baghdad government, had pursued us then across the mountains, killed our colleagues as they lay in the snow? Then I brushed away the thought, telling myself: 'What are you looking for? This is how history goes, fighting then forgetting. Those who hunted us down then are now our hosts. The bullets have become bouquets.'

We approached Suleimaniya, nestled under Azmar Mountain, the spiritual home of the Kurds. This city was always in revolt. The regime could not pacify it and so instead turned it into a big prison.

Once, in the 1970s, I had visited it as part of a delegation of journalists. Our military escort said: 'Do not trust this city. It's a big trap.'

He took us to a big hotel surrounded by soldiers and sharpshooters on the roof. And, even then, he warned us not to sleep on the bed. 'Sleep on the floor,' he said. 'It's safer. Brigands come down at night from the mountain and infiltrate the town. They could shoot through the windows.'

During the day, they took us to the market and whispered: 'All of these traders who seem so innocent, they are all collaborators with the brigands. Stay close to us'.

The old regime, skilled in the science of enclosing cities, was inspired to build a perimeter road in the 60s. The army was then able to move units out of their barracks and position them along the length of the road, surrounding the rebel city in minutes. Twice, they used this manoeuvre to isolate the city from the surrounding mountains and the armed groups there. The model implementation was in 1985. The ruling party in Suleimaniya, the Patriotic Union of Kurdistan (PUK), had been in alliance with Saddam's government but the agreement broke down. The army surrounded the city in minutes, and then arrested 6,000 members of the PUK. Before the city could even realise what was happening, they were greeted with the spectacle of 150 party members executed, their bodies hanging from public places, as part of a terror campaign. The same manoeuvre was repeated, but even faster, after the 1991 uprising.

Suleimaniya had changed since those days. There was relative security now, despite the occasional car bomb. There was uncontrolled development. There were a clutch of foreign-looking buildings thrown up along Salim Road which cuts through the city. They looked like they were made of plastic, big windows with shaded glass, the mark of luxury and privacy. These were alien buildings with no connection to the nature of a mountain town. Plastic goods had flooded the local markets. A phony cosmopolitanism. A city which was fleeing itself, trying to become something else.

The intellectual elite here have broken away from the modernising movement in Arab culture. They are moving towards a cultural secession which is more thorough than the political secession. Writers in the city want no connection with the Union of Iraqi Writers. They have founded their own association. Kurdish journalists want no connection to the Iraqi union of journalists since they founded their own unions. This is in contrast to the political leadership, which wishes to influence the centre, having secured complete control over the Kurdish region. Kurdish intellectuals, aligned along fault lines of clan and party, have chosen to concentrate on the Kurdish national question rather than any deepening of democracy beyond the two traditional parties, the Kurdish Democratic Party (KDP) and the PUK.

Every time I met them, they mentioned my writing. I felt embarrassed and caught short. I have been following the most distance cultures, remote in space and time and experience, and am ignorant of that closest to me, the Kurdish culture.

The last time I travelled to Kurdistan I came from a Baghdad where forty headless bodies were found in a single day. I reached there and the worry of car bombs was behind me. It was hard to relax. I noticed how fast construction was happening, so much change since even my last visit. Foreign companies were setting up all across the city. There were lots of foreigners staying in the top hotels.

It felt like two separate eras were unfolding. The era of Kurdistan, where state institutions were solidifying, with all their faults, and towns and factories were being built. There was relative security, and yet the region is surrounded by imperial powers that hate the Kurds. By contrast the era of Baghdad is one of dissolution of the state, encirclement within the Green Zone, where the last facets of our culture were being demolished by car bombs and militias and the rise of fundamentalism which, in all its various brands, wants to create an Iraqi Taliban where joy is forbidden. I felt calm as I sat in the hotel garden watching the water in the fountain, bracing myself against the mild cold of the evening. I put Baghdad and its news out of mind. I knew that I would be back there in two days.

Who are we? Sunni and Shia

I awoke on the morning of 26 February 2006 to the sound of thick gunfire. I stayed in bed a little while, trying to figure out what was happening by determining the direction of the shots. 'It's not a local incident, for sure, because some of that fire is coming from armoured vehicles,' I said to myself. I was supposed to get up and go to work but a colleague called me.

'Stay at home. They've blown up the shrine at Samarra,' she said.

The Satanic genius of al-Qaeda had found how to strike the Shia at their very heart of hope. They had chosen the shrine which was the final resting place of the tenth and eleventh imams and, even more importantly, the spot of the last sighting of the final imam before he disappeared, the imam the Shia have been awaiting for 1100 years to return and remove the yolk of oppression from them.

I wanted to go out just in my tracksuit to the nearest Internet cafe but my neighbour, peeping out from behind his door, stopped me in my tracks: 'Where are you going? The world is on fire!'

Hardly were the words out of his mouth than a convoy of pick-ups passed on the main road at the end of our street. Young men dressed in black hung off the back of them like angels of death, their rifles trained horizontally, not aimed at anything in particular.

Some of them loosed off short bursts. One of them screamed at the bystanders: 'They've blown it up!'

The bystanders took a step back involuntarily, as if they were under suspicion by mere fact of being onlookers who had not joined the fray.

With a speed that pre-empted any words of wisdom, young men armed themselves and slipped away from their fathers to join the counter-attack: 'Revenge! Revenge!'

Al-Qaeda sought to trigger a war by everyone on everyone, in a society where the chain of action and reaction is mechanical, in a spiral of ever-increasing force and scope. The strategy of Abu Musa al-Zarqawi, who had lost his popularity in the Sunni areas, was to push in the direction of total civil war which he could use to infiltrate into more places, and gain more room for manoeuvre. The other political players, wittingly or unwittingly, were playing into his hands.

At the nearby roundabout, the convoy of men in black circled twice, the screech of their tyres piercing the silence in-between bursts of gunfire. A masked man sat on one of the bonnets waving a sword.

There was no clear place they were going. The force of destruction inside them was just looking for a symbol of the *other*.

This was not just a show of strength. In the hours that followed, Sunni mosques were burned down, houses of prayer, with worshippers on their carpets and Qur'ans in their hands. Nothing was sacred, nothing could escape the fire.

Violence was born of fear. Moqtada al-Sadr had called for a peaceful demonstration in a society which knew no form of non-violent expression. The state stood paralysed before the rise of the armed militias, or rather, the police were in total sympathy with the Mahdi Army. These demonstrations were not just a show of numbers; they were a show of power, allowing armed groups that had floundered for a while to find the momentum to overcome their previous inactivity. They came out with weapons and the weapons demanded action. Fingers were on triggers.

Within days the streets began to take on the aspect of civil war. Our car passed through al-Aamil district like some nervous animal, slow and cautious as it weaved through the tree trunks and tyres placed across the road to block attacks by the other side. By day, the streets were empty, the young men asleep after their night watches.

My journalist colleague Abdel Sittar al-Baidani, who lived in the neighbourhood, was with us to guide us, showing us the route with the fewest checkpoints to his house. 'All the boys of the neighbourhood have seized their guns to fight against any armed groups that try hit-and-run raids. Everyone reveres the Mahdi Army as their protector in the absence of any power from the state,' he said.

I sit in front of the television to see what the government says. Its authority has vanished behind that of armed groups and militias. Official TV says nothing, as if nothing has happened. There is some old mullah talking about the virtues of the Prophet Mohammed. I remember that this talk had already been broadcast on the Prophet's birthday. The rerun shows the government has nothing to say. It is running away from these events, perhaps afraid to speak the truth.

When the government's voice is absent, rumours start to spread.

'Over 100 al-Qaeda fighters came to our district yesterday, running the streets for a couple of hours. It wasn't clear what their target was. They daubed marks on some of the houses.'

'The Sunnis have tanks and fighter jets left over from the days of Saddam, hidden away in the orchards of Ramadi.'

For its part, al-Qaeda was sharpening the knives of civil war that were already keen. They had figured out how to provoke total war, which was to strike at the poor and unemployed. Car bombs no longer targeted the government's institutions and its leaders so much, or American convoys. They targeted poverty where it was aggregated. Public transport depots thronging with the poor on their way to or from shanty towns, the maze of stalls and carts on big public squares, the long queues of journeymen waiting to be picked even for a single day's work.

On one day, 23 November 2006, six car bombs and mortar attacks produced a tally of 215 dead and 275 wounded. The funerals became protest rallies: 'Revenge! Revenge!'

Daily life in the poorer districts became dangerous just by walking out the front door. The threats, both real and imagined, created a collective fear which became an impulse to strike back rather than just to sit there afraid. In a society so pervaded with violence fear leads not to bunkering down but to attack. Reason retreats to the house and hysterical violence takes to the street: 'Revenge! Revenge!'

The bloody hero Abu Dara' arose in this atmosphere of the poor seeking refuge, and someone to put things right. A criminal who escaped hard labour in prison when the Ba'ath regime fell, Abu Dara' formed a small army of revenge seekers in the Sadr City districts of Baghdad. They would launch lightning raids into Sunni areas and abduct whoever they came across, indiscriminately. Then they would execute them at once, no questions asked.

To increase fear, Abu Dara' would always leave one of the abducted alive to return home and recount the horrors of the massacre, the story always carrying the signature of its author, Abu Dara'.

The revenge squads that worked under his banner never looked for particular individuals – that was the work of prosecutors and judges. As long as the *'other'* could not be identified by individual, the perpetrators they sought were anonymous. Therefore everyone on the other side was guilty. Revenge became collective. One group killed another group and the perpetrators were always anonymous.

Abu Dara's deeds – execution by sect, arson and sabotage – were not condemned in the Shia community. On the contrary he became a saviour, the avenger, a popular hero.

Our neighbour's son came screeching up on his motorbike, skidding to a halt, panting: 'Over there ... behind the piles of old tyres in the park ... Abu Dara's men killed five Sunnis ... Each one of them took a shot to the head ... They didn't let us watch ... But we heard the shots ... The bodies are just lying there.'

His father stopped pruning his roses. He was clearly upset but made no comment on this. He just shouted at his son: 'Shut up and get in the house – now!'

Militias and armed groups took over the street. They were the protectors and the avengers. They showed themselves everywhere, announcing their presence. As the armed groups rose, the forces of the state vanished, or became token. The groups carried out their attacks in government uniforms, using official cars and prisons. The people came to fear those who were supposed to protect them.

A young friend of mine, M., twenty-two years old, saw, from his bedroom window, a group of armed and masked men enter the house next door at night. He told me the story:

I lay on my bed and watched them moving about. Sometimes they were carrying heavy sacks and once I saw them take a man out of the boot who was blindfolded and bound. Without telling anyone in my family, I went to the police station on the main road and asked to see the station chief alone. He came into the room, closed the door and the two of us talked. I began to worry after nothing happened the next day. Or the day after that. On the third day some police came but they found nothing, not a single trace of any armed group. A week later, someone shot at the front door of our house.

'Why did they shoot at our house?' asked my father. Then he tried to reassure us. 'It's a mistake. First of all, we're not Shia. Secondly, we don't have anyone connected to the state in the family. So it's some kind of error.'

The next day a hand grenade thrown in front of the front gate shook up the house and everyone in it. We quickly gathered up our most precious possessions and left under cover of darkness, like thieves. 'Why us?' my family wondered.

I am the first person to know this, and you are the second. I didn't even tell my family because after that I trusted no one. From now on, I'm not going to tell anyone about anything, even if I see a massacre in front of my eyes.

My sister went out shopping and came back with an empty basket. The baker had not opened; the greengrocer had not laid out his produce on the pavement. There were no shoppers in the streets. She said, in-between catching her breath: 'Only gunmen are out on the streets, the masters of it, and even they hurry. As I was walking along I felt like I was in a nightmare with all avenues of escape cut off. I was walking home with no idea what would happen.'

I wanted to call out to one of my nieces but found my voice stuck in my throat. I went downstairs and tried to joke with her.

'Why didn't you go to school?'

'What school, Uncle?' she replied. 'The streets are empty.'

'Well, you should still go to school in spite of that,' I said.

'Our neighbour said the schools will probably close for the rest of the year,' she said.

'It's better,' I said. 'We'll marry you off to your cousin after you've learned how to cook and do the laundry,' I said.

The girl, twelve-years old, was not taken in by my feeble attempts at humour. She said: 'Uncle, you've gone pale.'

Her tone, afraid of my fear, shocked me. I felt my face drop and busied myself with the roses in the garden. I am a prisoner of this house, and of my fears.

We wanted to install a satellite dish so we could follow the news. We'd been looking for a workman to do the job for some time but my brother insisted we could not hire anyone whose origins we did not know.

'I know someone we can trust, from our corner,' he said.

'What do you mean, "our corner"?' I asked.

'He's a Shia from Najaf.' Hiring Ma'moun or anyone else in this world of sectarian fear was now a matter of their identity, not their attitude or performance.

I followed people's fears of the 'other side' as I listened to ordinary conversation.

'They (the Sunnis) have more military expertise than us. They were the officers of the army, we were its grunts,' one man would say.

'If the Americans get tired of supporting our side, they may support a military coup led by some of the Sunni generals and then we Shia will be back to zero,' another said.

The sectarian cleansing created fear, as did the closing-off of entire districts.We had a past filled with memories of intermingling, but it was being erased. Citizens were divided according to their sectarian militias.

Our own family experienced this divide. My sister Hoda used to go with her husband Jamal to visit his village in the governorate of Tikrit. There you could feel at peace, far from the clatter of gunfire and bombs. Her son would go to play with the other boys in the fields surrounding the village.

As things got worse, Jamal went for a visit by himself, He had not seen his family for months. While he was there Sunni and Shia checkpoints sprang up all along the road between Tikrit and Baghdad. For three months, Jamal could not return home for fear of the Shia checkpoints near Biji, and his wife Hoda could not join him in the village for fear of the Sunni checkpoints near Tikrit.

'They will slaughter you and the children if they find out you are a Shia from Najaf,' said Jamal.

The mobile phone became the only meeting place for these families split on both sides. Jamal would ask to talk to his two sons. One of them, Hamza, with that simplicity of childhood, asked: 'Why don't you come in a plane instead of a car?' Or another time he suggested: 'The guards will go to sleep at night. You can slip through then.'

Every time he talked to them, Jamal promised he would come home soon. But stories of killings at the checkpoints kept him in the village.

Over time, we got used to the huge cement barriers that sealed off the government, and the parliamentarians we had elected, and the government departments we needed to frequent. We were successively amazed, then angry, at these walls which went up around our universities, then our mosques and churches where people prayed. While the car bombs openly targeted places where civilians were gathered, the walls crept quietly into our lives, choking us.

Some walls closed off marketplaces, separating goods from their customers. The walls round schools and colleges meant that our sons were lost to a world of cement. There were walls which closed off streets, and bridges, and junctions.

Our government wanted to make these walls a fact of life so

they asked artists to paint gardens and clear blue skies and fields across the horizons of these walls, to break the monotony of grey. They wanted to soften the hardness of the walls with colour. But the cancer of cement was quicker than they were. Walls enclosed Azamiyya district, cutting it off from the nearby markets.

'Is there no other way?' I would frequently hear.

'Without them more people will die,' would be the response.

'It would be better to die than to live in this cement nightmare!'

'I am a Shia married to a Sunni woman. It's got so I'm afraid I might wake up one morning and find a wall down the middle of the bed, cutting me off from my wife!'

Together with a sense of fear there was a general feeling that the armed groups of both sides had entered the realm of madness, and if things carried on like this, they would drag us all to hell with them. But the militias' own hunger for power fed on itself, far from such cautious logic, so that it spiralled out of the control of their leaders when they called for a truce, or to back off. The armed groups had atomised, each one subordinate to the interests of local and tribal leaders. Fighting within the two sects had also arisen, with victory going to the group that was prepared to use the most ferocity and ruthlessness.

The militias might battle each other to the death. But they agreed on turning our neighbourhoods into little 'Talebanistans'. The marginalised and rural migrants who made up the bulk of their members asserted the authority of weapons over people. They banned the sale of alcohol by throwing hand grenades. Our local wine dealer had taken to opening his door just by a crack and keeping the shop open for not more than an hour, just around dusk. You had to specify your order ahead of time and have the right money ready to speed the transaction up as much as possible. A car could pull up at any moment and a masked man jump out to lob a grenade through the open doorway.

Even that didn't last very long. Soon the shop was shut and we started buying alcohol secretly, via an agent who knocked at the door. He would have a black plastic bag filled with vegetables, the bottle hidden inside it. Buyer and seller would meet for no more than an instant.

The reign of terror was not confined to alcohol. It spread to hairdressers. Shots would be fired at their shops without warning because they cut beards which according to fundamentalist ideology should be left to grow, or they cut hair too short, making the head 'naked'.

Women's clothes shops were targeted if they sold anything other than the Islamic cloak which covers all parts of a woman's body, and of course the *hejab* scarf. In Karada souq I saw a female mannequin used to model women's clothes in the shop window lying in the gutter of the street, mutilated. The torso was on the pavement, the ripped-off arms in the middle of the road and the head, crushed, lying by the shop door. I have never liked these plastic mannequins. For me, they are a travesty of art. But looking at the severed head and limbs I felt like I was mourning a real creature. Its frozen features gave me an eerie sense of the difference between life and death.

I asked the trader, who had glistening eyes and was swallowing hard, what had happened: 'A patrol of masked men passed. They did this in the blink of an eye.'

Women, whom these men could not have, were their easiest target. They would wait outside the gates of universities and high schools to harass them: 'A woman's place is in the home. The home only.'

Everything connected to modernity was forbidden by force of arms. This terrorism was itself the bloody fruit of the inability of society to embrace modernity, the failure to find a language which could embed any kind of progress. Confronted by this idea of modernity, the mind which cannot adapt posits instead an impossible paradigm of the past it wants to return to, and to take with it all of society which it brands 'the new age of ignorance', by force of weapons and accusations of apostasy. And the more it was impossible to reach these goals, the greater the need for sacrifice. Death and destruction became essential in their own right, as a form of purity and a means of ending corruption.

Ameriyya district became an example of this kind of nightmare life under an Islamic emirate. All forms of decoration were banned in shops. Street lighting was banned, to guarantee secrecy of movement. Public gardens became open graves for corpses, a favourite hang-out for wild dogs. All local amenities and services were banned, and even if they hadn't have been no state official would have dared to enter this no-go zone. People disappeared from the streets. Death became the only permissible public spectacle. Even then masked men would strut at funerals as if to say: 'This is our emirate!'

After the mujahedeen and al-Qaeda took control of Ameriyya, they began to expel the Shia from the area according to a well-concerted plan. Zulfiqar, aged twenty-six, told me: 'They would take a young man from the middle of his family and kill him right there in the street. Then they would order people not to bury him but to leave the corpse there, to terrorise the family.'

The bodies stacked up in the streets and alleyways and a huge stink began to pursue people wherever they went, whatever they were doing, eating or drinking, going out or coming in to the house. The smells would rise until they were nearly choking people at the height of the day, then they would weaken as the day passed, spiralling out into the sky. But you could still smell them in the calm of the night. They polluted even the marriage bed.

Mothers would cover their children's eyes when they went out in the morning to protect them from the gruesome sight of corpses eaten by dogs and rats, or severed heads. But in the end they would find they didn't have a clue, as the corpses had become the stuff of their children's conversations and nightmares.

'When killing by ID card started my brother and I left the neighbourhood without any belongings in order not to attract any attention,' said Zulfiqar. 'My mother and father stayed in the house, believing the killing targeted only the young, not the old. This was the first time our family got separated. But then one of the neighbours, a Sunni, persuaded my father that we should stay and there was no need to fear. So we came back. Two weeks later, my father was just starting the car when he saw a bag held down by a large stone. The bag contained a bullet and a printed death threat. "Oh apostates, you who have sold your religion for profit in the world, it is clear that you attack the mujahedeen by your thoughts and your actions," it said. At the end, the threat was that we leave the area in three days or "just punishment will be meted out". Our neighbours found about the death threat and came to ask us: "Will you go?" They asked with great sadness and helped us with our things. My mother went round touching everything in the house and crying. Even my father only just held back his tears as he gathered up his papers and left food for the cats.'

He continued his story.

'We left the house with as little as we could make do with and lived in the house of my uncle in Huriya district. We were all in one room. Every day my father would resolve to go back. He'd say, "I am an old man and they won't kill me. Even if they do kill me I will go." In the beginning, we thought things couldn't go on in that way for long. But this was just a baseless hunch because in fact everything was turning in the other direction. Masked gunmen fired five shots at my brother as he sold electrical goods in the University district. He lay still and they left him for dead, bleeding on the ground. That was when we realised that it was going to go on like this, and that more Shia families were fleeing, like us, or their sons had been killed without warning. So we rented a house in Dola'i district and thought about how to get our furniture there from the house in Ameriyya. No driver would help us move our things. If he was Shia, he would refuse to go into a Sunni district. If he was Sunni, he would refuse to enter the new Shia district where we lived. Also, no driver would move the household goods of a family that had received a threat. We decided to move our stuff ourselves, on the quiet. We knew that the gunmen who had closed up our house considered everything in it to be theirs. So we decided to "steal" our own possessions.'

I asked him how they managed to do this.

'We went just before dark and the curfew, when al-Qaeda moves off the streets because they are afraid the Americans will shoot them on sight,' he explained. 'We had made an arrangement with our Sunni neighbour, and parked our Kia car in his house. Then we broke down part of the dividing wall between his and our own house. The first thing my father did when we got into the house was to feed the cats, who had gone skinny in our absence, water the roses, and cry, saying he would rather die in this house he had built with the sweat of his own brow. We started to move the furniture, in total darkness, like thieves. My friend, our neighbour's son, went out into the street to act as scout. He would send us a missed call on the mobile if there was any unusual movement there. Just before the curfew ended, in the early morning, we left in the car, taking the back streets. But when we got to the main road, the Americans ordered us to turn back, after firing warning shots over our heads. Oh my God! What to do? If we went forward the Americans would fire on us. If we went back, al-Qaeda would pursue us. As we sat there, someone came to ask what the matter was. We said we were a Sunni family that had fled a Shia area. The guy was clearly al-Qaeda because he said: "Why are you so upset? There are plenty of empty houses here the Shia have left. Come and take one of them!" We said we wanted to live with our relatives in Jihad district.'

He paused. I encouraged him to continue.

'It was now about 8.00 AM. We pulled up outside a house which looked onto the main road. A young woman looked out at us, suspicious. She started to ask my mother questions and it was clear from her accent that she was from the Sunnis of west Baghdad. My mother could no longer contain herself and told the whole story. Soon the young woman was crying with my mother and insisted that we enter her house. Later that morning, we tried to approach the Americans to persuade them to allow us to leave the district. But they fired shots over our heads. In the end we decided just to leave the car there and escape with our skins. But the young woman told us to park our car in the garage of her house until we could work out what to do. Just then an ambulance pulled up. My father went up to it and talked to an American officer, who said, "No one can leave this district. Go back to your home. We'll be searching the district shortly and then it will be the most secure place in Iraq!" My father's rage boiled over: "You've been here promising us security for years and just look what's happened." We went over to the other side of the street where some Iraqi army units were pulled up. My father talked with the Iraqi commander and showed him the death threat. The commander sent a lieutenant and a translator with my father to the Americans but their answer remained the same: "we will open fire on them if they leave in a car." We left our furniture in the woman's house to get away from the blockade and the bullets whizzing over our heads. In the days that followed the young woman would call us from time to time to tell us whether the road was open or closed. Then we sent a friend of ours to her, a Sunni, to get the car back. When he got there she denied that she knew us or that she was storing furniture, and then called us to tell us what had happened. When we reassured her about him she handed over the car to him, and my father met him at the entry to our new district. Our furniture was all there, untouched.'

I asked him when they next returned to the house.

'My father returned to the house from time to time, to feed the cats or water the flowers. Sometimes he would sleep there and leave the next morning at dawn. My mother was ill but wanted to go with him. Every time he came back he would relate horror stories of the bodies in the street, and the piles of rubbish built up, and how al-Qaeda members strut around even without masks. He said the residents were alarmed at the style of this new Islamic emirate. They were torn between wanting an end to the dominance of al-Qaeda and at the same time wanting them to stay and protect them from the Shia militias. When we were living in Dola'i a messenger came to inform us that there was a Sunni in the neighbourhood who wanted to swap houses after he had received a threat from the Shia militias. He would hand over his house in Dola'i in return for our house in Ameriya. We accepted the offer as it seemed better than if they just blew our house up or al-Qaeda lived in it. And so we moved for the sixth time in a year. Twice out of our old house, once my brother and I had lived in an apartment, once from my uncle's house and once to a rented house. In spite of everything, my father still waited for an improvement in the situation so we could go home.'

The home is a storehouse of memories. The ghosts of ancestors stir in its corners at night. Often in the Iraqi tradition an animal has been sacrificed in its foundations, its blood mingling with the earth. Grandfathers remember how they built it, how the staircases went up step by step. The poet Badr Shaker al-Siyaab evokes the patter of shoes on the stairs and the squawks of children captured between the walls of his house. A constant theme in Iraqi songs is longing for the happy house you have left, the symbol of happy times.

This home, which the family had assumed was the last redoubt of safety, became a source of danger to them. They left it under threat in the darkness of night, carrying the lightest of possessions. Displaced from their homes, displaced in and from their own towns, they flee their own homeland. Families split up, with the sons in one place and the fathers in another place, the women in one place and the men in another.

Every time I leave Iraq I find the brightest technocrats and businessmen in the airport, leaving the country in flight from fire and death. There is in their faces the anxiety of those cut loose, heading towards an unknown fate, a distraught tear in the eye perhaps. They try to console each other: 'It won't last long. It's just a dark cloud that will pass.'

Once as I entered the airport grounds to check in, I was among a group of passengers who escaped two mortars that targeted one of the checkpoints into the airport. Sitting in the lounge, recovering after this experience, there was a middle-aged man sat beside me, on the plump side, who was panting. He gathered his family around him. He turned towards me, loudly praising God because he had escaped certain death twice in one week.

'I know about the second one,' I said. 'What about the first?'

'A hand grenade thrown into my shop.'

'And why you?' I asked.

'Because of the name of my shop. I had been the victim of an attempted abduction in my old shop selling building materials in Sheikh Omar district so I moved to a new shop on Republic Street. I chose a name for the new shop which would protect me and my livelihood, "The Shield of Hussein". Twenty days later I received a threat under the door: "We will blow you and your shop up if you don't change the name". Safety was the top priority, so I changed the name to "The Shield of Baghdad" – maybe it could save me from what the "Shield of Hussein" couldn't. Last Saturday, a hand grenade was thrown into the shop, just a few minutes after I had left to go and pray at noon prayers. Neither the Shield of Hussein nor the Shield of Baghdad saved me.'

His wife was still trying to recover from the two mortar bombs while his daughter shivered and chewed her fingers.

'Why didn't they just poison him in prison and finish this disastrous trial?' she said.

I was at a loss for the connection between Saddam Hussein's trial and the mortar attacks. But the husband explained that he had decided to leave the country at exactly this moment because the trial was coming to a close. It had gone on too long, and the closer it came to ending, the more Saddam's diehard supporters would try to prove to the people that his rule had been a paradise compared with these days: 'The Iraqi is killing himself or his neighbours.'

I was constantly amazed as a journalist at ordinary people's ability to analyse the news and act on it.

'It's as though it is our fate,' said the wife, 'to live under his regime of torture while he is alive, and now he is torturing us more as his death approaches, and heaven knows what will happen after the sentence is carried out.'

Now I understood why she wished he had been poisoned at the beginning and all this was over.

This family was only carrying the lightest of suitcases into exile, hopeful of a speedy return. But I knew it would not be as soon as they fondly imagined, because the same thing would happen to them as happens to me on my travels. For on every trip I suddenly see that Iraq, which I left two days before, has become an inferno in my absence. That is what the media show me. So I deem it wiser to stay safe by staying out of the country a little longer. 'Why are you in such a hurry to get back to hell?' I ask myself.

I savour the sense of security as I stroll peacefully past the Hussein Mosque in Cairo, even if I can smell the urinals and am dazzled by all the harsh strip lights. I stay out all night in the cafes of Schmeisani district of Amman, enjoying the *nargila* pipe and the shouts of people playing backgammon. Each night I decide: 'I'll postpone my trip tomorrow morning. Maybe things will get clearer.'

But then the next morning I wake up in the hotel and I look at my suitcases and they talk to me as if they were alive: 'Get dressed and get going. Things will not get clearer, not today or tomorrow or even after a month.' And that's how I find myself in 'lounge 6' at Amman airport, the salon for passengers on their way to Baghdad, amid a throng of passengers living the same tension as me. Every single person is numb, saying to themselves: 'Where are you going, you fool? Why are you in such a hurry to go to hell?' In spite of that, we're waiting for the plane to land, to resolve our indecision, to confirm that we are going because that hell is our home and our destiny.

The plane arrives from Iraq and we see, from behind the glass separating pane, the arrivals walk past us, free, relaxed, the worry gone from their faces because they have escaped the car bombs and mortars and death by ID card, and reached the land of safety. An unspoken dialogue passes between us and them through the glass. 'You've made it!' we say to them, a little envious. 'Where are you going? Are you mad?' they say, as they look askance at us.

The plane takes us. Before we have snapped out of our worry, the plane circles on its approach path, Baghdad is laid out beneath us like a fantasy, calm, splayed out on either side of the river. Nobody knows at this moment which street a plume of black smoke rises from, the latest car bomb, or on what street a functionary has just been abducted on his way to work. We will leave the airport and discover that, as on every day, there are cars in the street and people on their way to work and others shopping in the markets. Life goes on, and all we imagined was an illusion. But then this bustle, in turn, can be misleading. At any moment that pickup truck groaning with crates of vegetables could explode – or the car behind us, or the one parked along the street. Maybe those young men who are laughing will leap out of their BMW and abduct us away to certain death. What is real, what is illusion? The hell on earth we saw when we were out of the country, or this normal life that engulfs us when we return?

The violence escalated and spread like some mythical beast which feeds off its own flesh and spawns even more ferocious offspring who devour their mothers instead of feeding at their breasts. It spreads like a stain to embrace regions where even a few days previously locals had looked at Baghdad in astonishment and said: 'What is it with those Baghdadis killing themselves?'

The monster escaped the clutches of the politicians who had unleashed it. The militias too slipped out of the grasp of their leaders. They were privatised and were fuelled by their own dynamic, splitting the country into zones of influence. The most ferocious group imposes itself on the others. Wallowing in violence becomes a way to impose authority. I both understand and don't understand the Shia who kills a Sunni just because he is Sunni, to avenge the death of a Shia. But that he would kill him then cut off his head, open his stomach, and put the head on the stomach – that is not political violence, that is violence for the sake of it.

The degree of violence and its endlessness astonished and disgusted people. When al-Qaeda took control of Ameriya district, it was not only the Shia who fled. Original Sunni residents also fled.

Those who were government employees wanted to continue working, something which was not possible under al-Qaeda. So they left the district, like the Shia, under cover of darkness.

Everyday life always contained a few moments of respite, when the two sides would meet and discover the humanity in the other, and that the Beast was gnawing at both of them with its jaws. Our neighbourhood was mixed Sunni and Shia, and fear belonged to both of them. Young men from both groups went into the street and put up barricades with tree trunks and stones, laid out with great method and engineering so that they would impede entrance but not exit. The bare street was a theatre for these young men and boys where they became knights defending the neighbourhood from outsiders. The younger kids played the role of look-out. They would whistle to warn the young men gathered at the doors of their houses, whereupon they would take out their guns which had been stashed behind the doors, and prepare for the possibility of battle. They stared at any strangers, more aggressive than scared.

A young woman, the daughter of one of our Sunni neighbours, came to tell us about the retired general's concerns.

'He has left the house and gone travelling. That's what you say if anyone asks,' she said.

'He has left the house and gone travelling,' my sister taught her children. 'Left the house and gone travelling.'

Our family, which was mixed Sunni and Shia, was thrown into confusion by this war. It did not affect our relationships, we drank *araq* together every night, and our children played together outside without even being aware of the differences. It was more a kind of astonishment: how did things get like this? Where did this violence come from?

Previously, the state had held a monopoly on violence, and the militarisation of society. I remember being on my way to a cafe in the 70s, clutching my books, when a procession of the Ba'ath vanguard had held me up. A long line of children, between twelve and fifteen years old, wearing military uniforms and marching in step, chanting in time: 'Vanguard, Ba'ath, sacrifice.' The marching erased their individuality, gave them identity as small parts in the big machine. The bloom of youth was still on their cheeks, but they swaggered with a fake gravitas, imagining they were grown up. They were trying to grow moustaches.

As I watched them, I felt deep despair at the uselessness of the books I was carrying, of all the debates we had in the cafe. These teenagers who shook the ground beneath me with the stamping of their feet, and the air around me with their chanting – 'Vanguard, Ba'ath, sacrifice' – were more real than us. The dust kicked up by their marching landed on me and my books. I felt superseded, bypassed, outside life.

This long line was the lowest rank of a chain of organisations that began in youth and went past the age of fifty. It began with the Vanguard and ended with organisations such as Saddam's Private Guard and the Republican Guard, passing onto the Popular Army, and the regular army. For the Ba'ath, militarisation was a goal in its own right, to subject society to the discipline of the party, and of the barracks.

The culture of violence went with being at war. Whole generations of Iraqis grew up with life in the trenches, and learned the culture of violence and militarisation in three external, and a series of internal, wars. Their slang belonged to the trenches. Their reactions were quick and decisive. No struggle was solved except by force. The weapon was their favourite toy.

When the single party fell, Iraq experienced what Eastern Europe had. Societies which had been nominally united under one party fragmented after it fell, and reverted to first allegiances – ethnic, religious, tribal, sectarian. In Iraq, weapons also found their way to all these parties and factions, as well as the gangs of criminals who had been released after the war in 2003.

A weapon is not a silent thing. It calls like a woman: 'Try me!' It is a call which weighs more to a young man without work, without culture and without love. The weapon gripped in the hand brings out that confused force which has found no way to discharge. Like masturbation, the weapon can take the load of the young man who grew up in the trenches, or with the violence of the street. This man, marginalised, thrown away, will find in his weapon a tool to achieve power over a society which has abased him.

I was shocked one day when I found an army of youngsters dressed in black, the same age as the Ba'athi vanguard I had seen twenty-five years previously: the Mahdi Army youth wing, soldiering now for their religion. They ruled the street, shouting in people's faces to get out of their way as they marched down it, their fingers on the triggers of machine guns, at the ready for any enemy, declared or not.

The atmosphere of freedom had paved the way for freedom of expression with not just words, but also with suppressed violence. Authority was scattered among many individuals, who forged their own authority by force of will, and the weapons which supported that will.

So we looked at our own relationships and our children and we did not want to believe that it had just gone like this on its own. We looked for the hidden hand, the agent provocateur. Sometimes it was al-Qaeda, sometimes it was the Americans. We would always find something in hidden interests which justified our suspicions. Al-Qaeda's support had dwindled and they wanted widespread disturbance to infiltrate new regions. The Americans had been shaken; they would prefer their adversaries on both sides to be busy fighting each other instead of both concentrating on killing

US soldiers. When the two fought each other, the occupier would be in demand.

I have a Sunni relative who refused to recognise any difference between al-Qaeda and the Americans. 'The Americans built al-Qaeda. They were the ones who trained them in Afghanistan and allowed them into Iraq. You've seen the famous picture,' he said, 'which shows that George Bush Sr and the Bin Ladens were friends and business partners.'

Nobody wanted to admit that the sense of national values which had connected us was now in retreat. The ruling party, and then the charismatic leader, had played this role for thirty-five years and now they were gone, parties with national platforms receded and those with sectarian agendas came forward. People went back to what they owned by birthright, the primitive reference points of sect and tribe. In the absence of any unifying symbols, sectarianism became entrenched from above by instigating fear of the 'other' and from below by transforming that fear into action.

I had never before felt that I belonged to a religious sect. I was secular, born to secular parents. But I too entered this sectarian divide, and began to see the 'other' as frightening. He secretly meant me harm.

In the days when killing by ID card had started, I went out looking for a barber. I hailed a cab in an abandoned street. The driver and I remained silent for a few moments, each uncertain of the other. I tried to make out his name on his licence certificate hung in the front, and listened carefully to his speech in the few words we exchanged in the disturbing silence. I wanted to know if he was Sunni or Shia before I initiated conversation.

'It's like a city of the dead,' I said.

'Like?' replied the driver. 'It is a city of the dead. How would living people put up with all this?'

We were stopped at a police checkpoint. They were mostly from the Mahdi Army or sympathetic to them. They looked at my ID card – 'Zuhair Ali al-Jezairy', a classically Shia name – and handed it back with deference. 'Please go ahead, sir'.

The origin of this respect was not that I am a well-known writer, or editor of a newspaper. The ID cards do not reveal these details. It could have been because my name resembles a minister's, or that they imagined I came from one of the big families of Basra. We passed through the checkpoint and that feeling of security, of being on my own side, suffused me.

The same taxi driver took me to Ma'mouns, a Christian hairdresser in Karada district where his son always went to get his hair cut. I was placed in front of the mirror, between a picture of Jesus and another of Mary. On my left a bleeding, pale Jesus hanging from the cross, his face radiantly gentle and forgiving to his persecutors. The Madonna on the right leaning into her baby, stroking his head: 'You will suffer much, my child.'

I offered the Christian barber my throat, unafraid.

Because of the fear, I could fear sectarianism rising in me, the secularist. I countered it by harsh criticism of my own sect. I would watch state TV, the Shia call to prayer, the pictures of the Shia shrines, the tone of the political commentary, and turn myself into a Sunni viewer.

'With all this sectarian obscurantism, how can we persuade the Sunnis that this TV channel is his TV channel, and the state which takes charge of him is his state?'

Riyad Qasem and I took to criticising the Shia leadership as we saw the situation deteriorating. They were ruling the country but had not managed to escape their identity as leaders of a sect, of one party within a sect in fact. Once on a road trip we continued these discussions, forgetting our Sunni colleague the back of the car.

'Brother, is this fair?' he asked. 'Half the parliament is turbans, Shia clerics.'

'You're a Sunni, you can't criticise our sect,' we told him. 'Leave that to us, we'll do it more than you. You just sit there and shut up.'

He laughed and said: 'Suheil' – a Sunni friend – 'will come and we'll do the same as long as you shut up too'.

My working analysis of the situation kept changing, getting worse. In the beginning, I would reassure myself and anyone listening with the idea that this was simply the reaction of those deprived of freedom, and the state would soon come with the consent of all: order!

When internal fighting started I called on the Kurdish experience, saying that this internecine strife would eat itself up and be replaced by a political process. Then the killing by ID card started, and the analogy changed ... to Lebanon.

We Have to Act

Out of despair arose the idea that we should do something. Perhaps we could not change anything but we should try. The same group of secularists as had gathered in the beginning met. We had the vague feeling that we could convert people's disgust at sectarianism into some kind of action.

We no longer had the burning conviction of the first days. We did not think we could fill a void left by the collapse of authority. Other authorities had filled it. We could not form an alternate force. The appropriation of political space by sectarian parties was an established fact and we did not even know to what extent. We oscillated between setting up a lobby group and research centre, and between cultural activism. For most of us, the word was our only tool so we thought of setting up a newspaper to represent people like us, the educated secular middle class: Iraq's progressives.

Jamal al-Maashta was at one of the gatherings. But he no longer believed in the power of the word and was harbouring other plans which he told me about later.

'I have come to believe that speech and the media cannot change anything. I am preparing instead to go into politics. I have been offered a political job, so I will probably not be with you if you launch a new publication,' he said.

The job was as advisor to the president. I described to him what it entailed from my vivid imagination: 'You will write reports for the president that he will never have time to read. Is that what you want?'

'I will be of more use in that position,' he replied. And so one of Iraq's greatest journalistic talents disappeared into the corridors of the presidency.

We would come out of our meetings onto streets that were deserted apart from the militias – whether they were wearing police uniforms or their own. We knew that we could be killed at any time for the things we had written and said about both sides in the newspapers and on satellite TV.

Every time we left a meeting, my nephew Yasser would look in the mirror while driving away to check for other cars following us. When we had left the danger zone, he would ask me: 'Uncle, is all this really worth it?'

'What do you mean "worth it"?' I asked.

'I mean will you get a big government job to make all this danger worthwhile?' he asked.

'Where have you been, Yasser? That's not what we're talking about,' I said.

'Don't tell me it's a newspaper or some writing thing?'

'Pretty much,' I answered.

'Just. What. Planet. Are. You. Living. On?' he said, picking out each word for special emphasis. 'All your lot who came back from abroad, they are all ministers, or heads of department stashing away piles of cash. Because they can see the country collapsing with their own eyes.'

I looked out of the window in silence. Three armoured cars with gunmen dressed in black on the back were overtaking us, on their way to heaven knows where. We slowed down and pulled over to let them pass.

Yasser gestured towards them: 'As long as they are ruling the streets, and the people, what good are your articles and your writing?'

I was convinced people's alarm at sectarianism would find some expression. What we write could prick people's conscience; plant something which maybe could be transformed into action. I was aware that people had learned how to yield to force. But in the past, that force had extended itself into some form of authority which gave them a little bit of security and some basic guarantees. This violence does not even give them the semblance of security, and so subservience would not give them the security they crave. Beyond the sectarian fear, people were groping for some symbol of peace and beauty.

One such symbol came on 31 March 2007, when Shatha Hassoun, a young Iraqi woman, won first prize in the Star Academy programme run by the Lebanese TV channel LBC. Nine million Iraqis paid millions of dollars to the telephone companies to vote for a young woman who wore the latest fashion, in complete contradiction to the Islamic dress that the militias wanted to impose by force. I was discussing the meaning of this with a young journalist friend over the phone, and asked him: 'How can we explain the lack of a *fatwa* by any religious authority against a young woman in tight jeans draping herself with a flag which carries the words "God is Great"? Or a *fatwa* forbidding either side to vote for her?'

He was silent so I continued: 'This was a protest vote against the 'Talibanisation' that the armed militias on either side would like to establish.' My friend considered it was a vote for the idea of Iraq, not for Shatha Hassoun.

'How has this Iraq which voted for her taken form in a young woman who sings and dances in public? How is it that no one has asked if Shatha Hassoun is Shia or Sunni, or if those who voted for her are Shia, Sunni or Kurds?'

I felt this was a vote for secularism, beauty and progress. And yet I also had the contradictory feeling that the sectarians had the power to channel this same kind of emotion into alarm, and fear of the 'other'. The Iraqi people always surprise me for both good and ill. On the one hand, the overwhelming participation in the elections, our first democratic experiment; on the other, an overwhelming acceptance of violence, and the perfection of its techniques. On the one hand voting for Shatha Hassoun, on the other voting for sectarian warlords. This contradiction which Ali al-Wardi complained of in the Iraqi persona is not a struggle between primitivism and civilisation. The ninth-century scholar Abu Othman al-Jaahez understood the Iraqi personality fault. From his *Book of Eloquence and Demonstration*:

> The defect of the people of Iraq is that they oppose their rulers because they have strong opinions and are permanently contentious. But along with that go investigation and curiosity, and with that also go contestation and calumny. Iraq can be described as un-law-abiding, and fractious.

I am putting all my money on that contestation, which will come sooner or later.

My work as a writer has made me the object of people's need to know. Although I am as confused as they are, people direct their tough questions at me. They want to know what's going on. On the roof of the house, while we are installing the satellite receiver, the workman, a supporter of the Mahdi Army, asked me as he handed a screwdriver to his apprentice: 'you are a journalist and you know what's going on. Where are we headed?'

I summoned the optimist argument, saying we are not the first people to pass through something like this. Many other states had survived civil wars to become more homogenous. The violence could not continue forever but would consume itself. A time would come when the politicians would stand up, the bodies piled high, and reach a point of reason where they would realise that neither side can reduce the other one to zero. And that is where politics and negotiation kick in.

Before I could finish, a violent explosion shook us, cutting my thread of optimism. A column of black smoke appeared.

'A car bomb,' the apprentice said, stating the obvious.

Our practical skills kicked in to define the location – obviously very close, by the sound it made, and the shaking of glass in the windows and scattering of the birds on the street.

'On Palestine Street.' Our neighbour who had come up onto the roof gave more precision. 'Just by the street cafes where the police go to eat.'

The workman stood next to me as we watched the plume of smoke settle in the sky like a tree, swirls of birds circling it, alarmed off the roofs and frightened to return to the ground.

'You really think these disasters can end one day?'

'We need time. There is always a madman, who would like in one moment to transcend his miserable life to a more giving existence,' I said.

How Long, How Long?

The Journey

The airport road made me more afraid. The worst things can happen in those last moments before escape. The resistance fighters had chosen this road to lay their explosives, waiting for that moment of relaxation when the American takes a deep breath, relaxes, smiles: 'I've made it.'

On this road, just a few metres away from the concrete barriers that define the extent of safety, a car had exploded on a passing American convoy a few moments before we passed. I saw a car burning. Beside it, the booby-trapped car, also burning, killer and victim fused together in an embrace across the fire. The American in the burning car had just started to look forward to seeing his family again, to visualise that gasp when his children run towards him, his wife following. He was thinking of the taste of his wife's kiss as she whispered, 'You've got sunburn.'

The suicide bomber had interrupted his reveries, burned him with the explosion. His wife will wait for a now impossible reunion.

The American patrol which had come to the rescue of the victims blocked our way. Panicked soldiers ordered us to turn around, pointing their rifles straight at our chests. We were as afraid as they were.

At the entrance to the airport, Fijian dogs sniffed us. Us and our bags. Then South African dogs sniffed us, and our cars. They sniffed my groin and my behind and then went back to their air-conditioned rooms. On the tarmac, a few metres away from the plane, it was American dogs that sniffed us this time. They sniffed our intentions, our inner thoughts, before the plane took off.

Multinational dogs smelling out suspicious Iraqis. The occupation reached amazing levels of humiliation at the hands of these foreigners to the country. But, in fact, we were more foreign.

From Baghdad to Beirut

I'm flying from Amman to Beirut. I left Amman thirty-two years ago at the start of the fighting in September 1970. I left the people in the refugee camps as they came under artillery fire and the tanks of the Jordanian army bore down on the entrances to the camps. From there I had gone to Beirut, where later I had left as Israeli tanks bore down on the city from the surrounding mountains. Two cities I had left when they were under siege, to return in a time of oblivion.

Delving into them is like delving into my memories.

From Amman, our path takes us up the Lebanese coast. Clouds carpet the sky but shafts of light beam up through the cracks from the sea below, like some kind of silver fountain. There are tufts of white cloud above, less formed grey clouds beneath them. And in-between, Lebanon beneath us, drenched by the rain. I know what rain does to the city. I have come down mountain roads towards the city, following an off-flow dragging all the debris which humans leave wherever they are. I will come down with the rain into the city, which has been cleansed for me.

Here is Beirut, laid out like a long tongue projecting into the sea, in rebellion against land and sea alike. There is the outcrop that

Ibrahim Zayir tried to commit suicide from, returning deflated: 'The water is deeper than I thought.'

Here is where I saw the sea for the first time, when I was twenty-one. I remember being split between the tiny details of the waves, and its sheer infinity.

Right beneath me are the outlines that the water has etched on the rocks. Outlines which can make you dizzy, but which can be absorbed.

I raise my head a little and lose the shoreline. I try to see, and feel, where sea and sky meet on the horizon. This is the expanse where the creation was born, when the Sumerian god Analil separated the upper from the lower waters. I am caught between two beauties. One which enjoins me to possess it. And the other which loses me in its vastness.

The plane turns in the air to face Beirut. A long line of white buildings extends. I wonder where the 'Green Line' is. Back in 1975, at the height of the Lebanese civil war, we had landed at Beirut airport and Nazar Mrowe pointed out a row of buildings blackened by fire. 'That's it,' he had said.

Decades later, I return to Beirut, this time from a country where another civil war has started.

I demand healing, or despair, for my country from Lebanon.

One of the makers of the Lebanese Civil War, my friend the artist Fawaz al-Trabulsi, asked me when I came from Baghdad to Cairo: 'How can you go through another war after you got out of Lebanon alive?'

I said: 'I've got used to it. Just like we did in Lebanon.'

He said that war should be forgotten: 'I can't even stand the sound of a bullet.'

Throughout these long years of hell in Iraq, I have cheered myself up and endured it by recalling my Lebanese experience. I have said to myself and to others: 'There will come a time of despair, from which reason is born. A moment of danger, in which both sides realise at the same time that no one can bring the other side down to zero, or force him to accept death. At that time, all belief systems, all allegiances, will seem meaningless. From this time of despair, politics will begin and the word will supplant the bullet.'

In the early morning, I leave the hotel to find Hamra Street and Sabra refugee camp. I fix place, abolish time, and picture myself as that same Zuhair who came down from Talat Abu Shakir's place, alongside the dirt soccer pitch, in the same square where I saw my first corpse killed by war. A mortar fell and ripped apart a young militiaman. I had seen him just a short time before in the street, casually smoking a cigarette.

There was no trace of the mortar now. Nor of the blood that was spilt that super bright, sunny noon.

And here was the building we had hidden under when the Israeli planes flew over Fakhani district. But the doorman had no recollection of me. He looked straight through me, unimpressed by the fact I was still alive.

When the Israeli planes started to bomb, the young men reacted with an agility I will never forget. The young men of the district were pricked out of their sloth, and quickly brought the women and old men into the bomb shelters.

I went to get a haircut at a barber's the same age as those young men. He had opened a shop in the same place the young men used to lounge around in. I thought I could ask some questions as I was being done.

Grey fell from my beard. I watched a face in the mirror trying to find his real self in another time and place. Neither seemed right. It was neither me, sat in the chair with the white overall around my chest. Nor that young man who would say hello to the guards, joke with them, then go up to the magazine on the second floor.

'Who lives on the second floor of the building?' I asked.

The young barber did not know why I was asking. Quite possibly no one had told him the story of the young men, his age, killed in this alleyway where white towels were now blowing on the washing lines.

The buildings changed. A new building had arisen from the rubble, and new people. All of them were fixed in time and place. I was the only one lost, searching for the war and its effects on these walls.

And then ... as though I had found, at last, a sign that it had all really happened. Bullet marks on the walls of the building which had served as the headquarters of the popular struggle front. In this street ignorant of its own history I was the only one who remembered the battle which had left the marks on the wall. But even I did not remember the reason for the battle. And maybe there was no reason. Maybe it was just weapon seeking weapon.

I wander in the streets of Fakhani district, here in Beirut, bringing all my people to see the severest of battles. I am the guide of a people still mesmerised by weapons and violence. A tourist guide:

> This is where I saw my first war corpse ... This spot where the greengrocer has opened his shop, exactly on this corner Adil Wasfi was killed by three bullets from a silencer. The three bullets of the Ba'athi slogan: *U*-nity, *Fra*-ternity, *So*-cialism. But his picture was no longer on the walls ... This is the building where the magazine *Palestine Revolution* saw multilateral bombing ... Phalangist, Israeli, Syrian, American ... Now, there was a hostel for female university students and an estate agency. Now I am looking, and my people with me, for the posters of the martyrs on the walls. My people are still fascinated by martyrs and martyrdom ... Their pictures used

to change every day. The new martyrs would be pasted over the old ones, smiling, looking straight at you: 'You're next!' My wife used to look at all the pictures, and then at my thick beard, and say: 'You look just like them.'

The walls had been cleansed now of the pictures of martyrs. Everyone wanted to forget them. Instead, there were adverts for Nokia, Coca Cola, LM Cigarettes, Total. There were models, Heyfa and Hiba, who stretched their legs towards us out of the poster.

The martyrs' disaster begins when the guns stop firing and peace begins, and the enemy leaders sit down and smile at each other, amazed: 'How come all this carnage?' That is when the martyrs become the biggest losers. They have gone for no reason.

I went to the same cafe that we had gathered in with our gypsy songs, and Gaulloises and Gitanes cigarettes, a clutch of people from the revolutionary press with us: *Working Man's Banner*, *The Revolutionary*, *Palestine Revolution*, *Popular Struggle*, *Voice of the Guerrilla*. In this cafe, we had determined by debate the fall of the Arab bourgeoisie, its betrayal and passing over into the status of enemy. Then the debate was around the petite bourgeoisie – could it really be an ally of the revolution?

I mounted the few small steps to the cafe, and prepared myself for the clouds of smoke, the old comrades. None of them were there. There was nobody sitting in the middle of the cafe. In a corner, a group of young veiled women ducked their heads, taking precautions against the arrival of a stranger just as they were discussing the innermost details of their love lives.

I asked the barman if he could switch TV channels to *al-Jazeera*, which just then was broadcasting the details of Saddam Hussein's trial.

He smiled apologetically: 'I'm sorry. My customers don't like the news, or politics. They only like songs and music'.

Car Bombs

I trudge all that way to get to my real object: the Sateetiya Building. I look for the hole in the ground the explosion made. There used to be a huge hole, the remains of the building which was blown up from its foundations during a meeting of one of the Palestinian factions who used one of the apartments. Ordinary families used the other apartments, families who were blown into space in the midnight explosion.

I stopped on a terrace opposite and tried to imagine those moments of innocent attention just before the explosion: the newly married couple just at the point of climax when they were hurled naked into the air along with their bed, or the family watching a romantic film. Perhaps the villa swimming pool was the last thing they saw. Everything flipped just as the leading lady dove into it. She remained frozen in mid-air, arched in a dive, and the family were scattered into the air like a handful of seed thrown by a farmer. The boy asleep after a kiss from his mother dreaming of a horse he once leaped onto, thrown high into the air, never to return to the ground.

I tease out the stories of the people that the bomb took by surprise, drinking coffee on the terrace, gazing at the hollow the bomb made, and the plants now grown over debris from the ceiling of the building.

But the hole has disappeared beneath a new building, and with it the rubble and bodies that were buried with it.

Those moments just before the explosion preoccupied me for a long time. I had a hard time forgetting the ticking of the clock in the seconds before. They exhausted me afterwards. They would neither stop, nor explode.

The car bomb later evolved from an event into mere routine. As both sides despaired of making progress or winning, car bombs became a daily occurrence in this small city Beirut in the early 80s.

The engineer also preoccupied me. The evil intelligence who took advantage of our daily heedlessness to plant the box of explosives in a car, attach the trigger and set the timer, then leave, looking both ways as he went to check that none of the people who were about to be blown up had noticed. Who is he? What does he think about as he sets the trigger? Does he think about us? Does he justify it to himself? Does he *know* the scale of the slaughter, or is he tripping on drugs, or dissociated from it like he's playing some video game?

So many questions. And no one to answer them except more car bombs.

The sheer number of car combs led the Lebanese playwright Ziad al-Rahbani to create a character, a madman running in the streets. He runs away from one car because he believes it is booby trapped, only to realise as he is running that maybe the car he is running towards is also booby trapped. This is exactly the message the terrorist wants to convey to the ordinary citizen: your known, safe world can explode at any moment.

One of these bombs exploded the building where I lived.

I had put down my papers and pen on the small table on the veranda to go into the kitchen and make some coffee. I was thinking of that crucial first sentence which, in the end, never came. Instead, the coffee pot and I were thrown against the ceiling. I dropped what was in my hands. I lost control of my movements. For an instant, I seemed to be on the ceiling looking down at the floor. Everything started swimming and I lost consciousness for a few moments. Then I opened my eyes to hell. Screaming from every window, bodies scattered on the street below, splinters of glass falling from above me – weird snapshots of a world on fire.

I struggled to my feet, trying to breathe through the smoke and dust. Grey clouds of dust were obscuring the view down to the street, and I could smell fire. The storefront of the elegant women's clothes shop, the boxes of fruit which were scattered on the ground among the severed limbs and bodies, the front of a flower shop, Abu Ali's *kanafa* shop, Um Nabil's restaurant. Fire swept along like the wind, jumping from one car to another down the street, exploding their petrol tanks.

In some place the satanic engineer who had pressed the button was watching this carnage. Maybe he had already sent the good news: 'We have delivered the message!'

I looked for the engineer. I tried to sense him among the onlookers. Who was he? He waits for us to be distracted. He waits for daily routine to overcome caution again, and comes to place his booby-trapped bomb with its timer, and goes to some nearby cafe to watch, calmly smoking a cigarette. Then he presses the button.

It took a long time before I was cured of the tick-tock, tick-tock of that moment of explosion. Those moments cut through my life.

After some twenty years in exile, here I am living again among car bombs in Baghdad.

We had invited our colleague Mowaffaq Rifai, editor of *al-Manara* newspaper, to lunch in Mansour. Mowaffaq, who had come from Basra, at that time a haven of security by comparison with the hell of Baghdad, was not convinced it was a good idea to go out to eat. What he had seen in the media made him think that there was no real space for normal life between all the car bombs. Those living in Baghdad became used to the idea that life is what happens in-between bombs.

I tried to reassure him. 'Can you believe it? This is my third year in Baghdad and I have not seen a car bomb.'

'Me neither,' said Hussain Ajeel.

'I've just seen the smoke from afar,' I added.

While we talked we saw a black plume of smoke rising at an angle across the sky. One of my correspondents phoned by mobile to tell us there had been an explosion at the entrance to Muthanna airport – which we would have been passing some ten minutes later. Up to that point, the main targets of the bombs were Americans or Iraqi national forces, not civilians. Civilian casualties were just collateral damage, even if we calculated that up to forty Iraqis were dying for every American.

We changed route to get to the restaurant by a back route which our driver knew, an expert in Baghdad street geography. As we ate at the restaurant and compared security in Baghdad and Basra, we heard the muffled crump of a mortar. We didn't want to upset our guests. 'It's far off,' we said.

And we stayed at the table eating until another explosion, which was closer. We looked around and saw spoons suspended in space, as they are after an explosion. A third explosion was closer still, as though they were approaching us. But the restaurant owner reassured everyone. 'Don't be afraid! That's the sound of a door closing on the upper floor.'

We laughed, a little embarrassed, and recovered a little of our bravado. On the way back, we passed through four American checkpoints. 'No, no, no. Impossible,' said Mowaffaq. But no sooner had he spoken than another cloud of black smoke blocked off our route back to the office. The security correspondent of the news agency called us a few minutes later to warn us: 'Where are you now?'

'On Republic Bridge.'

'Don't go towards Palestine Street. There's been a car bomb at the entrance to the Interior Ministry,' he said.

This was a fine spring day, the day after six car bombs had gone off in Sadr City.

Between all the car bombs and covering them in the news, I have got to know the bomber a little. I almost saw him, for the first time in my life, when a boy who had escaped a bomb in one of the new parts of Baghdad described him to me.

'Dark skinned and thin, a bit like an Egyptian. First he was driving slowly, muttering something to himself, I don't know what. He was bent forward over the steering wheel. He turned for a second to see the crowd of boys gathered around the American soldier. Then he turned the car, and stepped on the gas. He took out two of my friends who stood between him and the crowd, and then everything exploded.'

I have begun to understand what kind of drug it is that eggs a man on to kill himself and others. Blind faith leading to death. A faith that demands frightening enemies. A faith that the *takfiri* can hang all his own evils on so that in the end killing the enemy becomes a religious obligation.

They call the Shi'a 'rejectionists', the Sunnis 'the people of heedlessness', the Christians 'crusaders'. Sectarian labels cancel the other's humanity, and in the process the humanity of the perpetrator himself as the thought is built: 'I do not distinguish between civilians and military.' This is what Abu Musa al-Zarqawi said to Ayman al-Zawahri. 'I divide them into Muslims and infidels.'

By these labels, they give themselves the right to evoke *fatwas* to kill Muslims as they pray, or make religious chants. The suicide bomber is told that the gates of heaven are open to him. He is drugged with promises and illusions, then he straps on the explosives and goes to spread death, blind of vision, conscience, humanity and emotions. He sees nothing in front of him but death and blood. The identity of his victims, their religion, does not interest him. He does not care that they are Muslims in a Muslim country. The more he focuses on his own impending death, the more a sense of normal life ebbs away from him, leaving only blood and death in front of his eyes. The idea of another world, fuller and richer than ours, both exalts life and debases it. The suicide bomber need only shout *Allahu Akbar* to enter this other world and, within a few seconds, to be sitting beside the Prophet. He is armed with both dynamite and religious pieties. When he is asked about the fault of the innocent, he replies: 'Heaven is the allotted fate of the child who has not yet eaten of the apple of guilt.'

With this belief, which allows no exceptions, no review, all evils are allowed.

We were filming in the district of Nu'airiya after a bomb had killed thirty children. We wanted to remember the children and register this event for history because Iraq's overall history of tragedy has unfolded by a process of amnesia. Each new tragedy effaces the memory of the last one, like the stampede on the bridge at Kazimiya.

It was the place that first struck me. A street with no name – wide and straight, dusty, exposed to the fierce sun. There is nothing to distinguish it from other streets of poor neighbourhoods of Baghdad. It encompasses modern Iraq: Muslims, Christians, Arabs, Kurds, all neighbours to each other. The contrast with the other streets was just that it was empty of people and, stranger, of children. At the spot where American soldiers had been handing out sweets to the children, the relatives had erected a small monument made of cement. We took one of the children to draw a picture there on the memorial, our idea being to follow the growth of the picture during the shooting of the documentary.

There was hardly a house without a black banner of mourning and the legend: 'Child Martyr'. All of the victims were boys between the ages of ten and fourteen. When the suicide bomber drove out from a side street to where the crowd was thickest, many of them were playing soccer, others watching.

Our guide, a child called Muhammad Hashem, stopped in the middle of the street, holding his hand over his brow to shield from the sun.

'There used to be five teams who played here every day. But no one plays now,' he said.

'Why?' I asked. 'Fear? Mourning?'

'There aren't enough players,' he replied.

Muhammad lost his twin brother in the explosion and was no longer himself. The child within him had died at twelve. His mind constantly wandered, he didn't want to go to school because he could not concentrate. We took him with us to the Arab Eagle School, which he had not returned to since the bomb. He sat still on his bench for a few moments, not wishing to look at the empty places. He did not utter the name of his brother, who had sat with him on the same bench, as if the name was a sign of life, which disappeared when he disappeared.

The headmaster and teachers were in mourning. They handed out exam results with so many of the successful students no longer there to receive them, their lives torn apart by steel fragments. The stories the survivors told poisoned my spirit as I gathered the details. I will never forget the divorced mother who made clothes to save money for her only son so he could become a doctor and look after her in her old age, make her heart glad before he left for work. As she talked of him, she folded her hands across her stomach, as though he might still be inside it, waiting to be born. She could not believe she had lost him.

The Real Jihad,
Fighting for Truth

The Eyes of Iraq

For the first time in my life I find myself master of my own work, both director and employee. In a small office in Karada district, I run a small TV documentary production house under the name 'The Eye of Iraq'. The idea behind this project is that present-day Iraq is just a succession of scattered moments. Each new event erases the previous one and consigns it to oblivion. One day we will wake up and find ourselves trying to tell stories to our children without pictures, just as the history of Iraq has always been. Our idea is to record the present, to record what doesn't interest the satellite TV stations. Specifically, the ordinary life of the Iraqis, far removed from car bombs and ruling council meetings, and statements by leaders. My partner is new to the profession and the goals of the project, but is persuaded that it will yield a modest profit and is better than leaving his money under the mattress.

My travels and contacts have given me a wealth of subjects that would take the rest of my life, and that of my son, to film. Iraq was full of strange sights. The families taking over prisons and living in them. The slightly simple man with a bunch of military medals pinned to his chest, who shouts: 'Five for a dollar.' The boys who bought toy American guns and put on sunglasses and pretended they belonged to the security details. The donkey carrying boxes full of Sony electronic goods in the marketplace in Sadr City.

Baghdad offers arresting views if you take a boat on the Tigris. Here, the river curls around to receive the sun's ball of fire at dusk. There, the old Baghdad houses lean over towards the river. Beneath them skinny boys await the coming of the camera to leap into the water, creating ripples. The camera hardly knows where to turn. In our eagerness to record, we seized each passing moment and ignored the constant and repetitive in everyday life, thinking we could come back to it later. We were unaware that everything would change, and that soon the camera would be unable to move except within narrow confines, and for short and dangerous periods of time.

This work gave me the chance to hear many people's stories, and to hear their views on what was going on around them. I discovered the gap between words and reality. When the camera was on, the average Iraqi would summon some long political speech, replete with national and religious references, seeking the transcendent above personal and tribal interests. When it moved away, people went back to their normal narrow concerns.

Once, filming in Najaf, we were interviewing shopkeepers just next to the shrine whose businesses had been badly damaged by the fighting between the Mahdi Army and the Americans. We asked them what they would do if the shrine precinct was enlarged and their shops destroyed, as had been mooted in a reconstruction plan. One of the traders, a short, fat man, jumped in front of the camera. 'Where do they want to exile us to? For us, it is enough to see the Commander of the Faithful every day, and the glint of sunlight on his shrine.'

As he was in full cry, someone tapped me on the shoulder and said: 'Don't let this noisy display of tears deceive you. He's got three other shops like this one, and two hotels. Believe me, if the Commander of the Faithful arose from his tomb, he would kill him and put him back in the tomb so he could carry on selling his image.'

Thirty-five years of oppression had taught people to say things they didn't believe in public. A friend told me: 'We were always worried about our children just before term started, that they might retell the whispered conversations in our house during the holidays. So about a week before school started, we would change our discourse in the house and train our children to say different things, very far from our own convictions. We taught them how to lie, because this was our escape from a regime which made our children their ears inside our houses. This culture has left an abiding mark in a natural dissociation by the speaker from what he says.'

The directness of our producer Hadi al-Rawi helped us to push these lies away and get people to tell stories instead of deliver political invective. 'We want information, not slogans,' Hadi would interrupt the interviewee to say.

These reporting trips taught us people's preoccupations, the contradictions and fears. It also taught us the stifling bureaucracy involved in getting permission to film. We always got the same question: 'For which channel?'

Which channel would tell them what the purpose of the mission was – for there were friendly channels and hostile channels. When we said we were not shooting for a channel but for posterity, the procrastination and doubting began. No one at that time was interested in posterity. State institutions still suffered from the lack of transparency of the former regime. The camera could expose corruption and so must be kept at bay. Faced with this, we tried all the tricks we could think of, including forging official permissions.

As the violence mounted, the camera came to be regarded as a bad omen by ordinary people, the sign of a killing or bomb, or some serious incident of the sort to appear on television. So ordinary people became hostile to the camera as this bad omen, when in fact the bad stars were present in any case and the camera is only a tool which carries the message.

Our work was different from that of the news teams. They have to finish their work in minutes, and the camera will never stop to consider the best angles, but just shoot as quickly as possible and then leave. The longer you stayed, the more dangerous it was. By contrast, shooting documentaries required study beforehand, attention to the detail of the general context and location in which interviews will take place.

The enemies of the camera grew over time. Masked gunmen either wanted it to be their propaganda tool or suspected it as a form of espionage. Looters would find the lone cameraman easy prey. Kidnappers would find TV crews to be a rich and lucrative source of spoils, or publicity.

After a looter shot at us, and a fellow TV crew was taken hostage, we stopped work. We put the cameras back in their cases and let the dust accumulate on our equipment, and closed the doors of the office.

The Voices of Iraq

After I left *al-Mada* newspaper, I received many offers of work: advisor to a minister, head of a satellite TV bureau, secretary for the national branch of the International Federation of Journalists, a journalism trainer, a news editor. Among them was the directorship of a new news agency called *Aswat al-Iraq* – Voices of Iraq. I had sat on its board as editor of *al-Mada*. I have always thought the name more suitable for a new collection of poetry than an independent news agency.

I accepted the post for a number of reasons. First among them was people's need for news to provide them with information that affected their lives. News here in turbulent Iraq does not only touch politicians and those who follow politics, nor is it a hobby like other pastimes. I have seen even inside my own family how impatiently parents wait for the news bulletin. They abruptly hop from the entertainment programme their children have been watching to hear the latest news. They don't listen to the news as those it was someone else's, the politicians in the Green Zone or the policy wonks, they plunge into it heart and soul, hungry for more detail. What happened, where and how? They exchange news heatedly with relatives, friends and neighbours. This exchange of news is not an idle interest. It is their news first and foremost, the knowledge it brings offers ways to avoid death. In the absence of the state, it is down to them to protect themselves and their children. So they listen to it with anxiety. Their lives could depend on it.

Nor does the news just pass like that. Every item provokes a fierce debate, because it demands an opinion and a decision; and after the decision, action. Should we move neighbourhood, go shopping, send the children to school, or leave home? It all depends on the news. The future, long awaited through the years of sacrifice, also depends on the news.

The profession has completely changed. The training programme we have put in place will educate an entire generation of journalists to a culture of news and objective information. For decades, news had lost its meaning in the Iraqi press. Events were presented in a biased and sanitised way. Reality was kept from the citizen by stage-managed media.

There is a secret history to the country that its people do not know and do not want to know as long as the price of knowing is so high, perhaps as high as their lives. In this secret world Iraqis, including journalists, don't know the most important things, despite the fact that these things play a crucial role in their lives.

For example, they do not know that 5 percent of Iraqi oil revenues belonging to the magnate Calouste Gulbenkian were placed in a secret account when the oil industry was nationalised in 1969 and put at the disposal of the Ba'ath Party; or the size of the defence and internal security budgets, or indeed the amount of oil revenues and how they are spent; they do not know the truth of what happened on 17 July 1979 when a third of the Revolutionary Command Council and a quarter of the Regional Assembly of the Ba'ath Party were executed on a single day, as Saddam rose to power, sweeping away former president Ahmed Hassan al-Bakr; or the death toll from the war with Iran, or even from the second Gulf War; the terms of the Algiers agreement, which renounced Iraqi sovereignty over regional waterways in return for Iran stopping support for the Kurds; the border security agreement which allows Turkish forces to enter Iraqi soil to up to 20 kilometres to pursue rebel Turkish Kurds; the terms of the Safwan agreement which then defence minister Sultan Hashem signed in 1991 to end the first Gulf War, giving international organisations evaluation rights over plans for development, imports and industrialisation, something which rendered any talk of Iraqi sovereignty after that point mere idle chatter; Iraqis do not know the extent of extravagant spending by the elites surrounding Saddam and members of his family under sanctions, when the country was starving; the enormous bribes that the regime handed out through the oil coupon mechanism to politicians, parliamentarians and publishers around the world for their support of Iraq's official position; even the weather forecast during the Iran-Iraq war was considered a state secret.

Journalists themselves did not know any of these realities, nor did they investigate stories they would not be able to publish or even talk about. They knew by bitter experience that the censor was never punished for excessive zeal, but rather if he let slip the slightest detail that the authorities on high considered to break the taboos. So the lowly censor would himself increase the realm of the forbidden, and the journalist would do the same thing again. He would rather move the censor inside himself and double it after seeing colleagues taken away from their workplaces, never to be seen again, or coming back broken.

One example I cannot forget is that of my colleague, the photographer Boulos al-Sunati. He was held responsible for the publication of a photo of president al-Bakr in which Bakr's hand, waving to the crowd, was partially cut. The regime did not understand, and did not want to understand, how this could happen through a technical fault. The conspiratorial mind sees foul play in everything. Boulos al-Sunati was strung up by his hands from the ceiling in the torture room for days at a time. When he got out of prison he was broken. His nerves and ligaments were shattered and he could no longer control his own body functions. He died at the age of thirty-five.

Fearful of meeting the same fate as Boulos and others, the journalist would prefer to wait for the official version of any event to come from the official news agency. There was no place for the journalist to find his own information. He had simply to wait for what the regime said, as it was the only source, and the only voice. The people, including journalists, were mere listeners and receivers.

My colleague Jabbar Tarad was operations manager at the newspaper of the ruling party, al-Thawra. He told me how he went into the newspaper on the morning of 9 April 2003, the day the Americans entered Baghdad, but found that according to the official media, nothing had happened. The editor-in-chief pale and confused: 'What distribution are you talking about? Baghdad has fallen and the regime has escaped with their lives.'

At the Aswat al-Iraq news agency, we cultivated the opposite. We familiarised journalists with the practice of looking for information outside the official formulations. I would always ask journalists before they set out from their homes to cover a news event: 'Did you listen to the morning news? Have you read the main items in *al-Sabah* newspaper? Do you have in your head some item you are intending to clarify, or amplify?' I was seeking with these questions to push them beyond being mere receivers of news, to finding information for themselves.

Our options in seeking to hire and enrich the news agency were limited by the small number of professional journalists. The giant leap required by the press on the fall of Saddam happened at a time when there was a scarcity of professionals, and an infrastructure which was destroyed.

The last decades had seen a series of emigrations of journalists. The flight of the 70s was caused by the Ba'athification of the media following a resolution at the eighth regional conference of the ruling party. The flight of the 80s was caused by the mobilisation of journalism and journalists in service of the war with Iran. The flight of the 90s was because of sanctions and the impoverishment of the middle classes, including journalists. And the flight of the new era is because of the threats and dangers that journalists face in carrying out their work.

And any journalists we could access who were professional only used pen and paper and had no experience of computers. At *al-Mada* I had urged my colleagues to leave pen and paper and just once to try sitting in front of a computer, to try and get familiar with the new writing tool. Salwa Zako avoided this appointment with the computer: 'Leave me with my pen. I love it and it is as much a part of me as my own handwriting.' Abdul Zohra did not approach computers except for the briefest moment, and Suheil copyedited by hand.

Writing on the screen appears divorced from the writer, the product of the machine, unlike on paper, where it is tangible. How could the fingers get used to the place of the letters on the keyboard? The letters as we were used to them were stored in our heads with the words and the thoughts. The new machine seemed to interpose itself between the thought in the head and the paper on the table.

The younger generation, in contrast to their elders who suffered from what Salwa called 'technophobia', used computers and the Internet capably. But they lacked the basics in journalism, or even the general knowledge needed for journalism. They knew politics only through the prism of the Ba'ath Party, and did not know any other party. While the older generation had entered journalism from the door of literature and culture, the younger one entered it as a profession. Their basic material was the simple story, devoid of any political background. They also lacked such basic technical skills as how to build a sentence, or structure a news story or feature.

We had to work with this new generation. News agencies need to carry the news quickly. They cannot support the leisure of the pen and tomorrow's edition. Despite its poor training, it was down to this generation to build an agency which was young, fast, and free of domination by the state or political parties.

In Iraq I was to bear a number of names which did not suit me. In the street young men would call me 'pilgrim', or 'uncle', general terms of respect for older men. At work, the young journalists would refer to me as 'doctor' or 'teacher'. And, being over sixty, it is true that I loved being the teacher of these young journalists. I was as anxious to make sure they got more training as I was to ensure that they produced more stories for the agency.

The first thing we tried to teach them was credibility. The hardest thing was neutrality. Neutrality is not just a word that is said. Holding onto it in a country polarised to death is like grasping a hot coal. My correspondents were not from the secular generation spared the pull of sectarian allegiance. They had their own doctrinal, regional and religious affiliations. One of them, for example, from a Shia heartland would not mention the leading Shia ayatollah Ali Sistani in a news item without adding religious titles, such as 'His Grace', and 'May God Protect his shadow'. I constantly brought him to task, shouting: 'We are not in the seminary. This is an independent news agency. You should use only his formal title "ayatollah".'

He insisted he had to use the whole panoply of religious titles to exonerate himself before God and the holy law, saying I could then take out what I liked. But I insisted he had to do it himself. He agreed to separate his religious beliefs from his professional duty in the end, but only after he had officially obtained permission from Sistani's representative.

In areas where religious militias dominate, the correspondent often had to yield some of his neutrality to keep the militias happy, by restricting himself to quoting only them, for example, or not running stories which would adversely affect their reputations. Knowing this, we had to be very careful with sourcing, and seek balance from elsewhere.

Neutrality made us a target on all sides. Supporters of armed groups launched an attack on us from Egypt, accusing us of collaboration with the occupier because we used the term 'armed groups' rather than 'resistance'. Meanwhile, government supporters would demand we prove our *'Iraqiness'* which they defined as using the word 'terrorism' in open copy, not in quotation marks or attributed to a source, as well as referring to dead from the state security forces as 'martyrs'.

Not only were we neutral, we tried to find the common ground that bound Iraqis in the middle of their polarisation. We carried the views not just of the combatants but also ordinary citizens who had no interests in the conflict, the views of victims and refugees from both camps.

The journalist in this atmosphere was both in demand and 'wanted'. Violence in its most barbarous forms is a media act, seeking to pass a message to others that this is what will happen to you if you are not with us. The picture and story amplify the effect of the violence, from the physical victim of the violence to all the others it violates emotionally, with fear. Media and the journalist carry this message.

But the journalist also becomes 'wanted' – proscribed – if his work defies one or both of the warring parties. Assassination of journalists has taken the place of censorship. The official censorship of the state withered and vanished after the ministry of culture was dissolved. But the censors have increased in number, and are to be found everywhere. Now there is censorship by religious authorities, by society at large, and, most dangerous of all, by armed militias and unknown killers. All of these censorships, and what goes with it in terms of anonymous death threats, form an enormous burden on the journalist. His fears are only increased by the invisible censorship in a society where the true balance of power is not yet clear, nor the boundaries between public and private interests. When the censor is hidden, and taboos are undeclared, writing becomes like walking through a minefield. You never know which story will kill you.

When we opened our office in Baghdad, the first warning came from our guards, who noticed strangers taking pictures of our gates in Waziriyya district. The second came from one of our correspondents, when young men at the end of the street stopped her car and warned her against frequenting the building.

Somewhere in-between assurance and terrorisation, the security advisor gave us advice on how to protect ourselves. Change the time you leave home for work and the route you take to get there. Make sure no one is following you. Be wary of fake checkpoints. Change residence by staying with relatives if you can. But my own experience in Beirut was that it is all Fate in the end. This presentiment, and my own absent-mindedness, taught me that all these security measures, which the killer knew as well as the victim, were really no use. The only difference was the killer could pick his time whereas the victim was hostage to it.

In Beirut I knew I had become the prey of assassins, and I knew the sole reason for it was that I was an oppositionist whose pen had achieved a certain fame inveighing against a dictator whose 'arm is long', as he himself liked to say. Now 'the reasons are many but death is one'. The fact I was hostile to the former regime and a fierce critic of the current one, or that I edited a critical newspaper, or carried a British passport and walked in the street without protection. Last but not least, the fact I am a citizen, and Shia by birth.

Every day I read the news, with that cold hardness created by habit and repetition. The police have found the bodies of people hanged with their own belts ... beheaded corpses ... bodies in the rubbish bins ... bodies, bodies, bodies. And the killer and the victim are always unknown. In fact, I have not got used to the news, despite the repetition. That unknown body is mine.

Sometimes in Baghdad I would go out driving with one of my relatives, a Sunni and a former Ba'athist. I always remind him that really, we shouldn't be in the same car, because we are doubling our chances of assassination. If the death squads want to get him, I will be killed alongside him. If the Ba'athists want to kill me, he will be killed beside me.

But still we went out together.

Assassination is not just a theoretical possibility. I was talking to some relatives in our front garden when four bullets whistled past my face. At first I did not believe it. But then I found the marks and crushed heads of the bullets, one of which was supposed to lodge in my body. I reassured myself, as always: 'I wasn't the target.'

I have started to distinguish between different kinds of death, choosing for myself one which is quick and relatively painless. When I see on TV the scenes of carnage with knives and swords, I get alarmed. 'I don't want to die like that, at the contemptuous hands of Holy Warriors.'

I have begun to imagine my death. The way they will kill me. Sometimes I play dumb, the role of the unsuspecting victim. Then I quickly flick my eyes left and right when I leave the house, to catch the car that could be waiting for me at the end of the street, or in one of the side streets, or the man who will give the signal to the killers.

This fear sits with me until the car enters a crowded street. The crowd gives me the illusion of safety, just being in the thick of ordinary people. My fears fade when I reach the newspaper. Despite its feeble guard system and flimsy walls, I say: 'I'm safe!'

The security advisor told us about all the possible risks. 'You are among the first targets. And you,' he said, pointing at me, 'are the first of the first.'

This man, despite all his knowledge of the dangers and how to avoid them, was himself killed. His killers chose the one moment where he let his guard down, taking his daughter to school.

We at the agency left Baghdad and the spectre of death which had started to become our main preoccupation to begin a training period in Cairo. We hoped things would start to get clearer.

I followed events in Iraq moment to moment. Our work became more tinged by calculation and illusion, at this distance, for although the events were happening over there, I was editing them here. There is a bomb blast at Tayran Square with fifteen dead and thirty wounded in the heart of Baghdad, two bombs within seven minutes of each other. I am following it from the building of the Journalists Syndicate in Cairo on Abdel-Khalik Sarwat Street. I do not hear the blast and I do not see the bits of bodies mingled with the debris. Some demonstrators from the opposition '*Enough!*' movement are standing at the entrance to the journalists building, surrounded by a cordon of police with shields and body armour. They want to prevent the demonstrators from crossing the threshold of the building – such are the limits of democracy given to the opposition.

There is a big gap of time and place between the theatre of events there, and the editing room in Cairo. It is the gap between a country which is exploding, and this one, Egypt, which is lulled by security. As time passed the few months we had been separated from the flow of events seemed as though they were decades. Our job as editors to relay the truth is muddied by the feeling that we abandoned our positions and came to a safer place.

When I edit stories I feel like I am dealing only with words. Words are my profession and in theory you don't need to live what you edit; that is the role of the correspondent. Nevertheless, I would press my reporters for more details, seeking to get to the heart of the subject. I railed at my correspondent who was sitting in the courtroom in Baghdad where Saddam Hussein was being tried.

'Don't just say "he entered the court". How did he enter exactly? Was he between guards with his hands in chains? Did he carry a Qur'an? Was his hair combed or dishevelled? Had he dyed it again? Was he wearing a suit, or a *dishdasha*? These are the details which tell us if he is being drawn into the process of the trial despite himself, or sticking to his resolve to ignore it,' I said. 'Did he wave his hand threateningly at the judge?'

'Don't forget you are talking about the president of Iraq,' she replied.

In our work with Egyptian colleagues, we learned professionalism and precision in details. Assem Abdel-Mohsin, one of the veterans of the Reuters Arabic service, dealt with the team like a stern father, reminding them of how to build a news story. They gleaned from us the context behind the news, who the new political leaders were, and a little of the Iraqi dialect.

We differed a lot in our points of view, and in the fact that most of us Iraqis were secularists while they were very religious. Prayer times would find us in separate places. Politically, they were mostly Nasserites while we were leftists shading into liberals. Despite that we managed to work well together.

But in Cairo I was surrounded by bad faith. Ba'athists there, and those who had profited from the 'Oil for Food' scheme, were not pleased by the presence of an institution like *Aswat al-Iraq* news agency in the heart of the Egyptian capital.

As the date approached for elections to the Journalists Syndicate, the arguments grew fiercer. We were part of the fuel of the debate. An orchestrated campaign targeted me specifically with lies. They said I had escaped from the Lebanese civil war to Israel and lived there for three years and got Israeli citizenship. They said I had re-entered Iraq with the American tanks. My friend Farida al-Niqash described those who conducted the campaign as 'professional besmirchers'. They divided the public into two camps: those who believe everything they hear, and those who are sceptical. They ignore the second category and concentrate on those who will believe rumours through ignorance, or because they want to believe them.

I found in this campaign something of the Ba'athist revolutionary psychology which enters any adventure relying on striking the first blow. Ba'athist arrogance does not care about the reasonableness of the accusation, or if it is ethical or legal. It follows the technique of the bully who fells his opponent with the first blow. The hardest blow possible that takes away all initiative from the opponent and leaves him little room for response. Then they follow with a quick succession of blows to make him give ground.

I was amazed at how newspapers with a legacy could publish stories like this without any verification, and how the profession of journalism had deteriorated in many Egyptian newspapers. But the head of the Egyptian syndicate told me, with the dispassion of someone used to it: 'This kind of thing has become normal before elections. We are the real target here, you are just the means.'

My Palestinian and Egyptian friends pressured the newspapers which ran the campaign to retreat. Nevertheless the campaign poisoned my time in Cairo and created a gulf between me and the city that could not be closed.

Our raw material in the news agency was information, but obtaining information became more and more difficult as the crisis of government in Iraq deepened. Leaders find the media an easy scapegoat for any crisis, saying: 'Well, things were not that bad until the media got hold of it.' The restrictions on the media became more stifling. The press office near parliament was closed, and press coverage of parliamentary sessions banned, veiling the debates from citizens who were the ones affected by what their representatives said. Saddam Hussein's trial was closed. Only portions of it were broadcast and only after the session ended. Press passes from the prime minister's office were limited, and a large number given to presenters from official channels that were better at concealing information than explaining it, and who in the end said nothing.

This closure was returning us to the secret world we had lived in for the last thirty-five years. It allowed the authorities to control information flows, to say what they want to say and convert the journalist into simply a channel for their own good news.

But all of that was trivial compared with the dangers journalists now faced.

Wherever I went in Cairo and whoever I met, I would get the same question: 'What is happening in Iraq?'

From my knowledge of people's preconceptions, and from the sheer number of times I had had this conversation, I came to hate this question and answering it, and the ensuing debate which would bring no answers. I hated the pious invocations that God would heal the country and return it to the peace it had known before.

I had in my notebook a long list of Egyptian friends I had lived with in Lebanon or elsewhere. But I was hesitant to call them. Iraq, complex, defeated and slaughtered, stood between me and them. Everyone was talking about Iraq but the question would never be asked in its own right. They would ask me: 'What's happening over there?' But I knew that no one would wait for any description. No one would wait to hear how it really was. Everyone was waiting for the judgement. So I would just say a few sentences and allow the others to fill in their own judgments, as if they were talking about another country than the one I had been in.

I would go out on mild nights to walk along the corniche beside the Nile. I would try to relax, stuffing my hands in my trouser pockets, slowing my pace to a stroll, looking over to the Nile, that great river passing through time and generations of people, watching the reflections from the lights of the cafes on the other riverbank and the ripples of the felucca boats, and listening to a voice singing in the distance: 'I listen to the pipes playing, but there are nails in my heart. The world has forsaken me, though I am a young prince.' And something inside me gave me a start: 'You are not here,' it said.

I lose myself in the crowds of shoppers on Tala't Harb Street. I want to be among those dazzled by the shop window displays. But all of a sudden I have this piercing feeling that I am lost between two places, neither here nor there, in my homeland or in exile.

When I get to the office and follow the work produced by correspondents in the danger spots, I get this painful feeling that here am I in Cairo, far from danger, and far from the correspondents that I have left there. I kept telling them: 'There is no story so interesting that it is worth risking your life for.'

I bury myself in work and then go straight home. I sit in front of a whisky bottle: 'Should I drink, or not?' I go to bed early, still listening to the clamour of the street.

Iraq pursues me wherever I go. The corniche along the Nile does not give me any peace. I find myself walking fast again, as though in flight from something just about to happen. There is no calm, basically, except before the storm. When I entered the apartment building on Taha Hussein Street, I jumped at my own reflection in the lift mirror, mistaking it for someone waiting for me inside the lift. I felt as though I could sense my killer on the long corridor on the fourth floor of the building. Every time I put my chair and coffee out on the balcony and sat down to stretch out and relax, the image would come of a man, his leg gone, stretching out his hand after an explosion and begging for help. I have to get up and go looking for something, although I'm not sure what.

I wanted to get away from work and the news from Iraq which was killing itself without mercy. So I went to stay in a hotel in Alexandria overlooking the sea. I could see the horizon out of my window and beneath me were people out strolling all through the night. The bustle of people and cafes and refreshing night air all called me to go down. But I stretched out on the bed and listened to the sea, prey to chaotic thoughts of truncated Iraqi stories. Between my thoughts and the sea, I dozed off and dreamed that I was flying through the air from a nearby explosion.

I turned on the TV as soon as I woke up in the early morning, like an addict. What's happening while I'm away? Another voice inside me says, angrily: 'What do you expect except tragedies?' Car bombs. Headless corpses.

I left the TV to go out onto the balcony and look at the sea. I can't get rid of the images of violence. I try to take control, telling myself: 'Forget that country and live in the moment. Smell the wet, salty sea breeze. Draw the scene into yourself.'

It is a deep blue sky, white clouds scattered across it waiting for a wind to move them on. There is a mist on the sea, and in the distance the water is blue-grey. The waves come from the distance, surging towards me with their foam to break on the rocks and scatter in groaning sprays. The waves have it to themselves, no swimmers. Suddenly, a fisherman appears and climbs a rock planted in the middle of the sea. He stands up and casts out his rod, waiting. A long time passes; the fisherman alone, his attention divided between the sea in its vastness, and the expected tugging on the line.

I thank nature, and her son the fisherman, who both cured me by their respective beauty and patience and made me forget the mayhem happening in my country. I whisper to Mother Nature: 'How beautiful you are.' I say to myself: 'Put away your fears, and take this beauty in!'

I am watching the next wave when I hear an *al-Jazeera* report from the country which is slaughtering itself – a car bomb in a crowded part of southern Baghdad.

Which one?

I go down to the hotel salon, with its semi-circular window looking onto the sea. Between me and the sea is another big TV screen, like a window into a void, blocking the view. Mother Nature and the world of the image, vying with each other. The sea offers its blue, the white foam and the waves that crash against the rock at the feet of the fisherman. The TV offers a video of Hefa and Heba gyrating among a crowd of men, dressed to kill. What to look at? The sea, before me at my feet, or the TV with its silver window? Hefa relapses into outstretched hands singing: 'I want to live. Every second of my life.'

'Learn from her,' I tell myself. 'Forget that country.'

But the scenes on the TV slice through the real world like a knife: fire, smoke, and a man with a broken leg screaming for help.

'I know that man!'